THE GENIUS OF PAUL

by Samuel Sandmel

PHILO'S PLACE IN JUDAISM
A Study of Conceptions of Abraham in Jewish Literature

A JEWISH UNDERSTANDING OF THE NEW TESTAMENT

THE HEBREW SCRIPTURES
An Introduction to Their Literature and Religious Ideas

WE JEWS AND JESUS

WE JEWS AND YOU CHRISTIANS

HEROD, PROFILE OF A TYRANT

THE FIRST CHRISTIAN CENTURY IN JUDAISM AND CHRISTIANITY
Certainties and Uncertainties

OLD TESTAMENT ISSUES

THE GENIUS OF PAUL

A Study in History

SAMUEL SANDMEL

With a New Introduction by the Author

SCHOCKEN BOOKS · NEW YORK

To Erwin R. Goodenough

First SCHOCKEN EDITION 1970

Library of Congress Catalog Card No. 76-111287
Manufactured in the United States of America

Contents

Introduction to the 1970 Edition vii

I *Paul the Man* 3

II *Paul the Jew* 36

III *Paul the Convert* 61

IV *Paul the Apostle* 99

V *Paul and the Acts of the Apostles* 120

VI *Paul and Other New Testament Writings* 163

VII *Paul's Stature* 209

To the New Testament Scholar 221

Acknowledgments 228

Index to Subjects and Names 229

Index to Scriptural Passages 235

". . . A scholar, as my most intimate critics tell me, is a cross between a detective and a puzzle addict."

Henry J. Cadbury, *The Book of Acts in History.*

Introduction to the 1970 Edition

In the Foreword to the hardcover edition of this book, published in 1958, I wrote that the audience for whom it was intended was that of the "intelligent layman," and added that "no honest presentation of Paul's thought can be simple."

Perhaps I was not aware then, as I think I am now, of the elusive character of any blend of a supposedly clear and readable account, on the one hand, and, on the other, of material which is admittedly the opposite of simple. Perhaps a solution of the implied contradiction is to distinguish between a "popular" book and a "nontechnical" one, as I have had occasion to do in other contexts. A "popular" book tends to avoid the genuine issues and the problems, and is necessarily thin or glib; a "nontechnical" book deliberately seeks out the issues and problems, but attempts to present them in such a way that people other than academic specialists can follow the presentation, if only they are interested in doing so. A nontechnical book, for example, would avoid the use of foreign languages; it would also not bog itself down in every item, including those which by common consent could be regarded as at best secondary.

This book, then, is a nontechnical one. Whether or not it is clear and readable is not for me to determine; certainly I have tried to make it so. Yet there has been a related elusive factor which also merits some comment and which shapes this present Introduction. Accordingly, if it is granted that one is justified in preparing for the intelligent layman a book that must trespass into complexities, then the question arises of gauging the amount of antecedent information the layman possesses. I think that, in first preparing this book, I perhaps overestimated not the intelligence of the general reader, but the quantity of information in the realm of religion which is the current possession even of intelligent and educated persons. I have thought, accordingly, that the opportunity provided in this paperback edition could be one in which to set forth at this point certain elementary data which can perhaps be helpful to the person whose background knowledge is not too full. Some of this data will be encountered later in the book, but some of the most elementary of it will not be.

To begin with, it may be well to say a bit about the Epistles (that is, "letters") of Paul which are found in the New Testament. They are there arranged on the basis of their length, the longest first and the shortest last. These Epistles were "business letters"; they were dictated to a scribe, rather than written. They were intended for, and addressed to, immediate situations, and not to or for eternity; indeed, their author believed that the end of the world was soon to come. The Epistles are named traditionally for the addressee, either for the city in which a church was located (such as Romans) or for an individual person (such as Philemon). They are:

To the Romans
To the Corinthians (there are two of these, known as I Corinthians and II Corinthians)
To the Galatians

To the Ephesians
To the Philippians
To the Colossians
To the Thessalonians
(two Epistles, I Thessalonians and II Thessalonians)
To Timothy
(two Epistles, I Timothy and II Timothy)
To Titus
To Philemon

In addition, a writing, The Epistle to the Hebrews, begins in a form that is not like that of any letter and does not, at its beginning, purport to be an Epistle; it ends, though, as if it were an Epistle, but is unsigned. (Epistles, in those days, like letters in ours, had the convention of beginning with an ancient equivalent of "Dear Sir," and ending with "Yours truly"; Hebrews lack the "Dear Sir," but has the "Yours truly"—without a signature.) Hebrews is traditionally attributed to Paul.

Modern scholarship has been concerned, for over a century and a half, with the question, did Paul really write all the letters which carry his name or are attributed to him? By our time the concensus among Christian scholars has been that Paul did not write Hebrews or Ephesians. As to I and II Timothy and Titus, scholars two generations ago ordinarily denied that they were by Paul. Today some scholars suppose that they are letters expanded a century after Paul's time from genuinely Pauline letters; they would thereby contain both "authentic" Pauline material and also later added material. About Colossians there has been an on-going debate, some scholars denying Pauline authorship, others affirming it; such is the case, too, with II Thessalonians (but not with I Thessalonians). The "unchallenged" Epistles, then, are Romans, Galatians, Philippians, I Thessalonians, Philemon, and I and II Corinthians; II Corinthians, though, is often believed to be a union of portions surviving from as many as three separate letters to the church in Corinth.

In the world of New Testament scholarship, this frequent,

almost universal division of the writings attributed to Paul into the genuine and the inauthentic is a reality, however one may regret the fact. This issue naturally complicates any quest to understand Paul. But there are even further complications. Chief among these complications is that Paul figures very prominently in the Acts of the Apostles. This work is almost universally held to be a sequel to the Gospel According to Luke, and, indeed, to be its second volume. The Acts of the Apostles (alluded to simply as Acts) is a patterned survey of the history of the very early church, encompassing the period from the Ascension of the Risen Jesus to heaven, that is, from the time after Jesus' death, about A.D. 29 or A.D. 30, through the arrival of Paul in Rome, possibly around A.D. 55. That is to say, Acts deals with the history of the church after Jesus' time, and that period is often called the "Age of the Apostles" or the "Apostolic Age." In Acts, Paul is first mentioned in 8.58, that is, about a third of the way through Acts; thereafter in Acts the focus turns more and more to Paul, rather than to other, and earlier, apostles. After Acts 15.36, the focus is almost completely on Paul, and remains so through the last chapter, 28. The reader could well at this point read Acts of the Apostles; at least, he could turn ahead to pages 129–41 where I give a brief summary of Acts—in a chapter which deals in detail with some relevant questions.

Those questions arise because contradiction and direct conflict exist in the data provided by Acts and by Paul's Epistles. The consequence is that the two, Acts and the Epistles, rather than supplementing each other readily, clash not only in details, but even more importantly in tone. The Epistles are written in an austere manner; Acts is rather "folksy" in tone, and it abounds in frequent miracles and miraculous healings.

Now, respecting one array of mildly disputed matters, Paul's precise missionary journeys, these have not seemed to me germane to the present task. From the sources it does not seem fully clear whether Paul made two missionary journeys or three. Again, a good many problems of detail cluster about the route that Paul followed, especially across the area in Asia Minor known as Galatia. I have regarded this kind of legitimate problem to be outside the orbit of what I have wanted to present here.

A late second-century writing, The Acts of Paul and Thekla, not only gives us a description of Paul, but is a clue to the fact that Paul was among those early Christians about whom the unfolding tradition wove an increasing amount of legends. We can wonder, if it is indeed true that some Epistles which bear his name are not really by him, why it is his particular name that these Epistles came to bear.

There is, in sum, a genuine problem in isolating the Paul of history from the Paul of legend.

But still another complexity needs our attention, a particular matter which for some students is a constant impediment to comprehension. It is this: that the Gospels, all four of them found in the New Testament, were, by common consent among scholars, written *after* the time when Paul's Epistles were written. Accordingly, the writings, dealing with the earliest days of Christian history, were written after the Epistles of Paul, reflecting a period somewhat later than the very earliest period. The question has been asked innumerable times, and answered in diverse ways, as to whether or not the Gospels, the product of a period later than Paul, may or may not reflect the relatively late period in which they were written. If we are to understand Paul and especially his influence, we must necessarily inquire into this delicate matter. There is, in addition, one more item of some complexity which I defer for the moment. But already, in the light of the foregoing, the difficulties in presenting a portrait of Paul emerge as considerable.

I am now persuaded, as I was not when I first wrote the book, that some preliminary review of Paul's historical setting can be useful to the beginner or to the stranger to early Christian history. We should begin with the latter part of the century previous to the one in which Christianity was born within Judaism. Palestine (that is, Judea, Galilee, and the northern trans-Jordan area) was willed by Herod the Great on his death in 4 B.C. to three of his sons, and the Romans, who had conquered Palestine in 63 B.C., gave the approval necessary to this arrangement. Just as in the days of Herod's reign (37–4 B.C.), there had been frequent uprisings against the Romans and against Herod, especially in Galilee, so disorders of a similar nature continued throughout the next decades.

In A.D. 6, Herod's son Archelaus, who had reigned from 4 B.C., was removed by the Romans as the ruler of Judea on the complaint of Judeans, and he was banished. Judea was governed from 6 to around 38 by a succession of Romans called "procurators," an office like that of a governor. Agrippa I, Herod's grandson, reigned in lieu of the procurators from 38 to 44, when he suddenly died. Galilee had been assigned in 4 B.C. to Antipas (known in the Gospels as Herod, the "fox"), and was a "tetrarchy" (we might say "dukedom"). Antipas, like Archelaus, was removed by the Romans and banished, this around 39; Galilee then fell to Agrippa I. But after the death of Agrippa I in 44, Roman procurators ruled again. Agrippa II was named the king of Judea, under the Romans, in 66. About that time the recurrent internal disorders mounted into a full-scale rebellion against Rome. It was put down by the Romans in 70; they destroyed the Temple in Jerusalem; the Arch of Titus in Rome depicts that general's victory and his capture of some of the sacred vessels of the Temple. The rebellion came to its tragic end with the fall of the fortress of Masada in 73.

The movement, inaugurated by Jesus, or else woven around his person, came into being some time during the first period of the Roman procurators. It was the Roman procurator Pontius Pilate (whose term ran from 26 to 36) before whom Jesus was tried and at whose verdict he was executed; the date is unknown but often given as 29 or 30. Among the followers of Jesus, the conviction arose that he had been granted a special resurrection. With the birth of this belief in the resurrection of Jesus, the movement gained a new impetus. It sustained itself in Jerusalem and Judea, and spread beyond the Judean borders—even far away from Judea. This spread of Jews is called the Dispersion, or the Diaspora (the latter word is Greek, the former is derived from Latin; both mean the same). There were many Dispersions, for Jews were to be found east, north, south, and west of Judea.

Most of the attention of modern Jewish and Christian historians of Judaism and Christianity has been on events and movements within Judea. This one-sided attention has the result that the Dispersion, especially that in the Grecian lands, is too much ignored. Indeed, the misconception exists that the Dispersion awaited the events of 70, and was a consequence of the crushing of the rebellion against Rome. Actually, however, the Dispersion in the west, that is, in Grecian lands, began no later than the time of Alexander the Great, who died in 323 B.C. Some three-quarters of a century after Alexander's death there were already very sizable Jewish communities in the Mediterranean areas; around 250 B.C., Greek-speaking Jews were numerous enough, and sufficiently estranged from Judea, that they found it useful, even necessary, to translate the Five Books of Moses into the Greek language, for they no longer knew Hebrew. In due course the remainder of the Hebrew Bible was translated; moreover, Jews began to produce Jewish writings in the Greek language. Some cities, such as Alexandria in Egypt, had extremely large Jewish communities. Inevitably, facets of the Greek world entered into the ken of Greek Jews, whether this was the knowledge of Plato and other philosophers, or else echoes of Greek culture or even of Greek religion. This was the case even though such Greek Jews were in their own terms quite loyal to Judaism.

The arrangement existed in the Western Dispersion whereby the Roman overlords accorded the Jews certain rights of self-government, and also certain exemptions from the Roman laws obligatory on the other peoples they had conquered. Accordingly, there continued in the Greek world a corporate Jewish life. Worship went on in synagogues; there were Jewish courts to administer Jewish laws; there were schools to teach Jewish youngsters the ancestral faith. Paul was a Greek Jew. In his Epistles there

Paul must be seen against the background of the Diaspora.

are echoes of synagogue worship, of his punishment by Jewish authorities for disorders he occasioned, and of his education in Judaism.

But now, to our immediate purposes. The Christian movement, we have said, had progressed to a certain stage before Paul came into it. It was originally a Judean movement, carried on in Aramaic and Hebrew; now the Greek Jew Paul entered it. On his entering it, he affected it most profoundly. This effect was much more in the area of his religious ideas than in any series of incidents, though there were certain decisive events in his lifetime. The Epistles allude to these events (his "conversion," his relationship with the leaders of the founding church at Jerusalem, his travels, his quarrels), but they abstain from any connected account of them. It is in Acts that the connected account is found. Even if there did not exist the problems, hinted at above, about events as between Acts and the Epistles, there would nevertheless still remain the most basic of problems, namely, just what was the distinctive teaching of Paul, and just what was his distinctive contribution to the developing Christianity. In Acts, his doctrine purports not to be the least bit iconoclastic, but only an unimportant partisanship on the issue which divided the Pharisees and the Sadducees from each other, the issue of resurrection. Because of this strange element in Acts, Acts falls short of providing us with the materials whereby we could acquire a rounded appreciation of the man.

It is the latter which this book attempts to provide. It tries to tell what kind of a man Paul was, and specifically what his contribution to early Christianity consisted in. The book falls into two parts: the first, an exposition of the information about Paul as found in his Epistles, and here put into the broader Jewish and Dispersion setting of his time and situation. The second—and this is the final complexity referred to above—since Paul appears in the first part of the book as a unique man who had a tremendous and abiding influence on the Christianity after his time, the book, in its latter part, seeks to show how pervasive that influence was. It tries to accomplish this by noting how the influence of Paul appears in the literature of the New Testament, all of it composed after his Epistles. Such a presentation of material is tolerably difficult; perhaps this introduction can eliminate or reduce the difficulties.

I give in the text a nontechnical exposition of Paul's doctrine. But again a few introductory comments here may be useful: Before Paul had entered the young movement, the view had already arisen among the direct followers of Jesus that, since Jesus had been granted a special, unique resurrection, he was surely more than a man, that he had been in at least some sense divine. Insofar as the special explanations of that divinity are concerned, our sources respecting the views of the predecessors of Paul do not enable us to inherit much more than mere clues. With Paul the case is exactly the opposite; he gives specific explanations of that divinity. His view, however, is not so much that Jesus was himself this divine being, but rather that a divine entity came to earth and took on the form of Jesus. Inasmuch as the tradition before Paul spoke of a human career on the part of Jesus (that is, Jesus was born, he lived, he died), Paul was concerned to explain the significance of the human career of that divine being, known in Paul as "the Christ."

Paul's "doctrine" may be said to be his theological exposition of what it meant that the Christ was for a while the human Jesus, and then returned to heaven, this after undergoing death through crucifixion. Paul provides us with some clear and precise expositions—at least by implication—such as, for example, what the death of Jesus meant, and what, in Paul's view, the old Jewish word "messiah" (Christ) now meant. He tells, too, that he had had a vision of the risen, that is, the resurrected Jesus. He believed that at some moment in the near future the divine Christ would come to earth for a second time, and this second coming would bring an end to this world. In his theological explanations of these matters, Paul discloses the brilliant, intuitive character of his mind and heart.

Moreover, Paul, like the human Jesus, was a Jew. Paul's ideas are never separated from his Jewish moorings. Since Paul, like his fellow Jews, inherited the Bible, his views necessarily had some relationship to the Bible in general. Of great significance is the fact that the nub of Paul's inherited Judaism was the laws of Moses, the biblical commandments and prohibitions by which Jews were expected to live. Therefore the centrality in Judaism of these laws was of great consequence to Paul, and this centrality elicited from him an astonishing set of conclusions.

These conclusions involve religious ideas that are carried in the vocabulary of religion; sin, atonement, righteousness, grace, and the like. In our time these terms are often fuzzy in their meanings; moreover, modern people are not always prepared to accept as their norms those which antiquity has bequeathed. It is therefore hard for a modern person to grasp sympathetically what an ancient mind was thinking. For some moderns, the mere effort is not worth while.

I, of course, feel otherwise. It is very worth while to try to grasp how ancient minds grappled with the human predicament. In the case of Paul, there are indeed obstacles to overcome, but these are not insurmountable. We need only to bear in mind the following: He was a Greek Jew; he was a most loyal Jew, yet the Greek environment had worked on him intensely. He came into the young movement, as we have been saying, after it had spread from Judea into the Dispersion. He received some data from his predecessors; some of what he received he drastically reinterpreted. In addition, his creative mind brought new facets of religious intuition to bear on the young, unfolding tradition. He was a tireless worker, a tireless traveler on behalf of the new movement.

Above all, he was a unique man, one of the most unique in the history of the human race. By some circumstances we do not know enough about, and therefore do not fully understand, his eloquent Epistles came to survive, and these enable us to penetrate into his remarkable mind.

Our chore is not to seek religious guidance from Paul; indeed, many of us will find his views uncongenial. Our task is only that of trying to comprehend him and, whether agreeing with him or not, of confronting his great stature.

THE GENIUS OF PAUL

I

Paul the Man

Paul was a religious genius. In that eminence his position is secure from the assaults of his detractors and from the misguided plaudits of some of his partisans. His detractors have either opposed him directly or have attacked him obliquely and unintentionally. Some opponents wanted to discredit the man, but others sought to distort not Paul but his teaching. While Paul's message was distinctive and bold, his writings nevertheless became easy to distort by those who used his prestige in order to proclaim a diluted doctrine.

We are first concerned, not with his distinctive teaching or with its fine details. Paul the man is our interest. Yet the important and abiding considerations are not, Who was this man? but rather, What did this man do and what legacy did he leave? It is the authentic Paul of history that interests us, not his figure as embroidered in the fanciful legends which arose after his time.

For our purpose we assume that reliable history about Paul lies only within the New Testament literature. Within this material, it is only in his Epistles that there is incontestable authenticity. Three Epistles attributed to him, First and Second Timothy and Titus, are not really from his hand; these pseudonymous ("falsely titled") writings came from a century after his time. Moreover, tradition incorrectly ascribes to his pen the Epistle to the Hebrews; neither the New Testament nor modern scholarship participates in this unreliable and impossible attribution. Three additional Epistles, Second Thessalonians, Colossians, and Ephesians, are possibly not from his hand.

The biographical details recoverable from the remaining Epistles do not enable us to know about Paul's birth, education, or death. While we do know that he was a single man when he wrote his Epistles, we do not know whether he was a bachelor or a widower.

His Epistles alone do not yield the kind of information about the milestones in Paul's life out of which a journalistic human interest story could be fashioned. Moreover, his writings contain so relatively little personal information that from them alone we would never suspect even the existence of such well-known but uncertain data as his "Jewish" name Saul. Furthermore, the full chronological order in which his Epistles were written is unknown. Therefore the pleasant though fruitless task (which has appealed to some writers) of tracing a supposed development of his thought cannot be embarked upon.

The Paul who emerges prior to scholarly inquiry is less a figure of authentic history than a blend of much legend and little history. Perhaps the best device for understanding Paul is to forget almost all the data of the pious biographies. We shall in time try to discover what there was about him that made him a legendary figure and why those legends assumed a particular shape and form. How little we know about him in matters of specific history is underlined by the circumstance that his Epistles include but one reference by which a real date can be fixed.

Paul speaks in II Corinthians 11.32-33 of his escape from a "governor of Damascus under a King Aretas." While this reference is by no means entirely clear, its chronological aspect provides us with our one single bit of knowledge. Outside scholarly information, though justly controversial, fixes this date as roughly 35 A.D. No other reference in Paul's Epistles alludes to a securely known date or datable event. Even if it is correct that in 35 Paul escaped from Aretas' governor, we do not know what his age was at that time. A reasonable date for his Epistles is somewhere between 50 and 55.

In the area of geography, we have fuller though not abundant data. Paul's Epistles not only do not give us information as to when he was born but as to where. Tarsus as his birthplace is not given in his Epistles, though we find it in another New Testament writing. A fourth century work describes him as a Galilean by birth, but this description is legendary. What is important is that his place of birth was undoubtedly somewhere in the Greek world and not in Palestine.

We do know the geographical orbit of Paul's work. He became a convert to Christianity outside of Palestine. Thereafter he visited Palestine at least twice, the first visit lasting fifteen days. He made another visit, of greater significance, fourteen years later,* but we do not know its duration. Again, he tells in Romans 15.25 that he is about to go—for a third time?—to Jerusalem; but his preserved Epistles do not report the accomplishment of this journey.

In his Epistles, Paul alludes to places where he has been and where he plans to go. He unquestionably was in Antioch, Syria, in Galatia, elsewhere in Asia Minor, and especially in what is today Greece. The orbit of Paul's travels then was in Grecian lands, whether in Greece proper or in the Near East. His Epistles, written in Greek, confirm this geographical datum; Greek was his native tongue and it was in Greek lands to Greek-

* Some scholars want to amend the fourteen to four, but this is a highly subjective tampering with texts.

speaking people that Paul addressed himself. That his activity centered in Grecian lands does not of itself exclude the possibility of his having been born or at least bred in Palestine; it only makes it less likely. But his Epistles emphasize the infrequency and the tenuousness of his contacts with Aramaic-speaking Palestine, and we would not, from the Epistles alone, ever feel the need to raise the questions about him and his relationship to Palestine which are prompted by other New Testament writings about him, though not by him. These questions we too shall need to raise in their appropriate place.

The chronological datum and the geographical orbit combine to form the basis for a conclusion of tremendous significance. Jesus and his immediate followers were Palestinian Jews, whose native tongue was Aramaic, a Semitic near relative of the Hebrew language. Assuming, as most do,—though it is assumption, not certainty—that the date of the crucifixion of Jesus was 29 or 30 A.D., then within half a decade after that event, there emerged a Grecian Jew who had not known Jesus but who believed he had witnessed a resurrection appearance of him. Thereafter this Greek Jew traveled about Greek lands proclaiming the significance of the appearance of the resurrected Christ Jesus. It cannot be claimed for Paul that he was the *first* "Christian" to travel and preach in the Greek world; rather, in the perspective of history, he is the most eminent. But Paul distinguished himself from other missionaries to Greek lands. The latter either achieved small impact or were mere middle-men, transmitting that "Christianity" which they received. Paul was not a mere transmitter; rather, he transmuted "Christianity."

Paul's personality is known to us in only a limited extent. I do not find him combative. Some interpreters have seen him as a man who was always in conflict; they have noted that of the authentic Epistles it is only Philemon which has no mention of an opponent or opponents. In the Corinthian Epistles, Paul alludes to parties which we cannot identify—the parties of Paul, Cephas, Apollos and Christ. The Corinthian correspondence is the history of a quarrel. His Epistles do reveal Paul to us in his combats. We might conclude that Paul was apparently perpetually embroiled. Certainly he could, and did, lose his temper, as reflected in Galatians. But it is more prudent to say that while we have inherited the record of Paul in combat, we have received little information about the moments of serenity which he no doubt experienced.

His Epistles were dictated to a stenographer. Many passages attest that his mind worked faster than his stenographer's pen. His mental agility, indicative of a quick and inventive mind, has its negative side, for all too often Paul gave ingenious and clever responses rather than straightforward ones. In using Old Testament passages, he tends to quote out of context, or give them farfetched meanings. When he presents a consecutive argument, he often brilliantly links biblical verses whose connection is not one of pure logic but of associated phrases or words. In such passages, Paul manages to make a telling point not so much through the quotations but in spite of them; such a chain of quotations has a momentum which transmits facets of thought, but not clear and readily communicable ideas. Indeed, there is a deficit in this ability of Paul's to quote the Bible (Old Testament) so effortlessly, for in paragraph after paragraph he is only glib or superficial. Although mentally alert, Paul is neither unremittingly deep nor invariably perceptive. He gives no evidence of formal education or academic knowledge and, accordingly, those who evaluate him as a profound thinker have been extravagant in their exaggeration.

Paul did possess another kind of profundity—that of feeling rather than of philosophical perception. No just assessment can overlook Paul's emotional depth, for he searched his heart and soul as few men in history have done. But it must be understood that his was an undisciplined mind and that his perceptions were the products of human experience and intuition, and not of any philosophical acumen. He was, we may say, a lyric poet like Keats or Shelley; he was no Aquinas or John Dewey.

The key date, 35 A.D., is significant in its own right. In the short half-decade that the movement (later to be known as Christianity) was in existence, a "mother church" had already been established in Jerusalem. Although Paul came into Christianity quite early, he was to those who had preceded him a late-comer. Paul was never willing to accept such a secondary status on this account. Opponents tried to relegate him to it, and even to deny the authenticity of his credentials as a leader. Overtones seem unmistakably present in Galatians and in Corinthians that Paul was determined to transform the liability of his late-entrance into an asset. As we shall see, his inventive mind found a plausible explanation.

On several occasions, he alludes to his having persecuted the "Church" prior to joining it. Here again, Paul transformed a liability into an asset. He believes that his confession of having been a persecutor—in his Epistles this "persecution" is only alluded to, never described—is a demonstration of his integrity. His record of persecution even became an aspect of his credentials, paradoxically attesting to his worthiness. That Paul turned from persecution to espousal is wholly consistent with his character as an extremist.

For inchoate, formless Christianity, the acquisition of this Hellenistic Jew at this moment in its history had tremendous significance. It meant that a Jew born and bred in the Grecian world had entered a Palestinian movement just at the moment when that movement was entering the Grecian world. Once this happened the movement could no longer remain a sect within Judaism which had merely added to its inherited Jewish tradition views about Jesus and his imminent return. It was no longer a Palestinian movement for Jews alone; it was, through Paul, a world movement for all humanity.

Paul's Hellenistic Jewish background was important insofar as it was his frame of reference. A Jew of Babylonia or of Ethiopia could not have expressed himself or have acted as Paul did. But the background alone cannot account for the great metamorphosis which came to Christianity through Paul. Environment never totally explains a man; it only explains about him. True, Paul was a Hellenistic Jew, but above all, Paul was Paul. We may say that to the extent that Paul's environment shaped him, it shaped his transmutation of Christianity. In a word, Christianity was significantly affected by Paul the man, as well as by Paul the product of Hellenistic Judaism.

In brief, Paul gave early Christianity a new direction which resulted in its detachment from Judaism. Paul could well have done so had he been a Palestinian Jew or an Ethiopian Jew or a Roman Jew. The particular form of this significant change and the circumstances under which it took place are the results of a particular person's having been placed in a given set of circumstances. But there were other Greek Jews who became Christians, and the Greek environment exerted influences on them, too. That a common environment produced these Greek Jews can explain their language, the political and social forces of the time, and the like. But Paul stands out not because he was a Hellenistic Jew but because he was Paul.

Since we have emphasized for the reader, however, the importance of recognizing that Paul was a Greek Jew, it is proper now to set forth the great, yet limited significance of that emphasis. It is twofold. In the first place, one must understand what was involved in the adjustments and the blendings which took place when Jews moved in numbers from Palestine into the Greek lands and became fully acclimated there. Secondly, the need to emphasize the Greek origin of Paul's personality and thought derives from explicit statements directly to the contrary in the New Testament (outside Paul's Epistles); the reader, therefore, is entitled to know at the start something of the basis on which one sets aside direct and explicit statements.

As to the first, the merger of Judaism and of Hellenism was in many respects the blending of antitheses. The Greeks had bequeathed views on the nature of man which were different from those bequeathed by the Jews. While the vocabulary of virtually all religions contains common terms such as sin, righteousness, faith, and the like, these words had meanings and overtones quite different to Greeks from what they had (and have) to Jews. That Paul was both a Greek and also a Jew raises the question of the sense in which he uses these terms. Was it an exclusively Greek sense, or an exclusively Jewish sense? Or was it something conceivably in between the two, some Graeco-Jewish harmonization that by Paul's time was fairly well standard?

It comes as a startling fact to many that in Paul's time there were more Jews living in the Greek world than there were in Palestine. Scholars all agree on this conclusion. It is only on the question of the ratio of the Grecian Jews to the Palestinian that they differ. Some reckon that the ratio was five to one; others reckon that it was ten to one. We know that by Paul's time Jews had lived in Grecian lands for a few centuries. The Bible had already been translated into Greek; indeed, the Five Books of Moses were rendered into Greek at least two hundred and fifty years before Paul's time. Not only was there, by Paul's time, the Jewish Scripture in Greek, but even more significantly Paul's age inherited a tradition of interpretation of that Scripture.

By Paul's time, then, there was already a Graeco-Jewish tradition. It overlapped with Palestinian Judaism in many ways, yet it had also come to have facets of its own. It had been made adaptable to the Greek world.

The phase in which the primary overlapping of the heritage was to be found was in the common possession of the Bible. For Palestinians, the original Hebrew was Scripture; Greek Jews, though, possessed a translation which is called the Septuagint ("seventy"), so termed because of a romantic and unreliable legend that seventy (two) men had translated it with unreserved skill and accuracy. The import of the legend was to assert that the Greek translation was fully as reliable (and as sacred) as the Hebrew original. We can scarcely expect the Greek Jews to have derogated the version of the Bible which they were using.

In any religious tradition interpretation is the lubricant that transforms the rigidity of a Scripture into a pliable mass. The interpreter, living long after the Scripture has come into being, invariably reads into it that which he wishes were there, or feels ought to be there. He does so unconsciously, for he believes firmly that he is reading out of the Scripture what he is in reality reading *into* it.

In Paul's time the Stoic philosophers had already been manipulating Homer so that the great epic poems were no longer merely the narrative of a long and costly war occasioned by a man's abducting another man's wife; by "allegory" they made Homer mean something noticeably different. The earthy myths about the Olympian deities of oral folk-lore or in written anthologies, similarly "allegorized," lost both their literalness and their piquancy. Characters—whether deities or only heroes—were interpreted by "allegorizers" as mirroring characteristics of human nature, such as the mind, the senses, the passions, and the like. Moreover, the Stoics understood the narratives about these characters as depicting the spiritual dilemmas faced by every human being in his transition from infancy to adolescence to maturity and to old age.

Greek Jews had adopted this Stoic type of interpretation, and in their hands the Greek Bible, especially the Pentateuch, was handled wondrously, even if to our minds artificially. Adam was the symbol or allegory for any mind, Abraham the symbol for the good mind, Abimelech, the king of the Philistines in Genesis 20, was the foolish mind; the Pharaoh who abducted Sarah was the hypocrite, while Sarah was virtue. Allegory, then, was the method of Biblical interpretation which appealed to those Jews who could not resist the Grecian scheme of things.

But beyond the mere question of allegory as a method, we must consider the purpose involved in such capricious interpretation. To speak of virtue, or of minds, good, bad, or foolish, supposes that these terms have some kind of meaning. What were these meanings, and where did they come from? Invariably, what the Graeco-Jewish allegorizers did was to invest the Jewish Scripture with meanings derived or directly borrowed from Greek philosophy. So thoroughly did this process of adaptation take place that Jews were confronted by this occasional embarrassment, that their reading Plato or Aristotle into Scripture meant in effect that Scripture and the Greek philosophers were saying the same thing. Greek Jews (and Christians later) never denied the similarity of content, and they never repudiated the Greek philosophers as being wrong or perverse. Rather, they accounted for these similarities by the conceit that Plato and Aristotle were expressing verities because they had plagiarized their ideas from Moses.

But the "why" of this method is the preeminently important thing. There was a significant purpose and result in this process of borrowing, assimilating, and then staking out a claim to prior and full possession of Greek ideas and Greek explanations. In so doing, Greek Jews were able simultaneously to retain undiminished their loyalty to their Jewish Scripture and their Jewish ancestral practices, and yet feel perfectly at home in Greek conceptions and modes of thought. In quoting and using Scripture, they understood its words in the Greek sense. By Paul's time, to repeat, this Graeco-Jewish approach was well established, as I shall point out when we speak of Paul the Jew.

The basis of our scepticism about New Testament statements which link the Hellenistic Paul closely to Palestine is this, that Paul's Epistles, written in Greek and redolent of the Greek atmosphere, point unmistakably to his being a Greek Jew; but the Acts of the Apostles contains a portrait of Paul which is at variance with this, for Acts states and then underlines Paul's supposedly intimate contacts with Palestinian Judaism, his saturation in it, and his dependency on and obedience to the early Jewish-Christian "church" in Jerusalem.

It is one of the hoary problems in Biblical scholarship that in many places the Acts of the Apostles is in direct contradiction with specific information furnished by Paul's Epistles. To select one single item, Paul tells us in Galatians 1.15-22 that after his conversion he first went to Arabia and then returned to Damascus, and that as yet he had not been in Jerusalem. He did go there, he tells us, after three years; at that time he had visited Cephas and had seen no other apostle except James the brother of Jesus. Yet Acts 7.58 and 8.1-3 portrays Paul as already present in Jerusalem at the execution of Stephen and as making havoc of the church at Jerusalem. In Acts 9.1 Paul, still in Jerusalem, receives permission from the high priest to go to Damascus to extradite any Christians who may be found there; Acts 22.3 describes Paul as having been brought up in Jerusalem at the feet of Gamaliel under whom he studied; but Galatians 1.22, on the other hand, contains Paul's assertion that he was unknown to the church in Jerusalem prior to his conversion.

Conservative scholars of our day, like all traditional interpreters, Jewish, Christian, or Mohammedan, are able to square and harmonize direct contradictions. In Chapter V, I discuss the portrait of Paul in the Acts of the Apostles in detail. Accordingly, there is only this that needs to be said here, that the straightforward student of Paul must make a choice between the evidence of Paul's Epistles and the evidence of Acts. Since Chapter V considers this discrepancy between Acts and Paul's writings more fully and deeply than the sample contained in the previous paragraph, I have no hesitation in choosing Paul's own evidence as preferable, more reliable, and more authentic than that of Acts. I conclude that Paul, a Hellenistic Jew, had never been in Palestine until after he had joined the new movement.

One passage in particular is frequently cited as an argument against a separation of Paul from Palestinian Judaism. In Philippians 3.4-6, Paul asserts that he is fully as Jewish as some of his opponents, and he says of himself that he was "circumcised on the eighth day, of the tribe of Benjamin, a Hebrew born of Hebrews; as to the law a Pharisee." (The Pharisees are known to us from the Gospels, from Josephus, and from rabbinic literature as one of the Jewish sects in Palestine in Jesus' day.) The argument contends that since Paul by his own statement identifies himself as a Pharisee, manifestly his views and dispositions were exactly the same as those we know elsewhere as characteristic of the Pharisees, and hence Paul was not different from them.

There are two difficulties in this argument. In the first place, it assumes that all Pharisees had ideas and opinions so thoroughly shared in common that difference of judgment did not exist among them. The literature which Pharisees of later times produced exhibits some marked inner divergencies of opinions and ideas, though within a framework sufficiently common to mark the Pharisees off from their opponents, the Sadducees. The divergency plainly present makes it difficult, almost impossible, to characterize one single person's ideas, such as Paul's, by using a label pertaining to unlimited thousands. John Doe is a Democrat. Does that tell us whether he is a states-righter or a New Dealer? Is he an exponent of southern agrarianism or is he an active worker in a ward consisting largely of naturalized immigrants in an eastern metropolis?

Even more acute is a second difficulty. The literary materials out of which and through which we identify the Pharisees are a product of times much later than Paul, and we need to reckon with the changes that took place in Pharisaism immediately after Paul's time, especially when the Pharisees came into the ascendancy. In sum, the laconic label by which Paul describes himself falls far short of a sufficient characterization. That he believed in resurrection would certainly keep him out of the category of the Sadducees; but this negative statement does not tell us affirmatively what Paul is and was even as a Pharisee.

Paul's use of the word Pharisee is the earliest literary record of the term, though the movement was in existence long before his time. Did the movement spread into the dispersion? We do not know for sure. We know all too little about Pharisaism in

Paul's time.* Although Paul called himself a Pharisee, one cannot say that he was closely identified with Palestinian Judaism before his conversion.

To come to a conclusion, though by-passing here some of the relevant steps in between, the issue about the phrase in Paul can be put this way: Shall we try to explain Paul on the basis of a single labelling phrase which in the Greek runs only three words? Or shall we look at his religious ideas, opinions and dispositions, and understand the label only after we have seen the fuller thought of the man?

We must realize clearly that to delineate Paul as a Hellenistic Jew does not asperse Paul's loyalty and allegiance to Judaism. In these he remains as firm as any Palestinian Jew would have been. It means simply that the content of his Judaism, like that of other Greek Jews, had undergone a subtle, but radical shift. Not only did he give the terms which he employed meanings different from those of Palestinian Jews, but even beyond such elementary things there was a change in the fabric of religious suppositions and in the goal of the religious quest.

Analogies are dangerous, yet some light on what is meant by Paul's being a Hellenistic Jew can come from discerning the problems in the religious thinking of Jews of our own time. Before the Revolutionary War, Jews had lived on American shores in limited numbers. Beginning with the 1830's, they began to come in larger numbers; after the 1880's their numbers increased even more rapidly. The more recent emigration of Jews, two generations ago, was from the ghettos of Eastern Europe. There they lived in relative isolation from the general community, separated in their language (a German dialect known as Yid-

* Those scholars who are inclined to believe that Paul's Epistles underwent interpolation after Paul's time occasionally incline to view the phrase as a later addition. I see no need to come to such a conclusion. I would rather retain the phrase and understand it in the light of Paul's broader thought; I would certainly not try to understand Paul's broader thought in the light of this brief phrase.

dish), their garb, their economic structure, and their religion. They moved to free America and begot children who spoke English as a native tongue, who dissolved the economic pattern of petty-trading and peddling, who wore clothes and who engaged in foibles indistinguishable from those of the general population, and who faced the need to adjust their ancestral religion to the new scene. The Paul of Acts is to the Paul of the Epistles as the Jew of the East European ghetto is to the American-born Jew. There is a sharp environmental difference in each situation, and the result is beyond being overlooked. The American Jew attends the public schools, plays the games, reads the books, and breathes the atmosphere of his homeland. He still sees values in his inherited Judaism, but quite unconsciously he equates these values with matters inherent in the American scene. He may be superficial when he describes Passover as the Jewish Easter, or suggests that he has Hanukka while the Christian has Christmas, but the process of such identification is well nigh inescapable. He will add to his Judaism from his environment elements which he feels are already implicit within it, and he may tend to slough off elements which seem ill-suited to it, but such adoptions and subtractions are almost never the result of deliberate selection, but of unconscious accretion on the one hand, or of disuse on the other.

To call Paul a Hellenistic Jew is not to put a value judgment on the nature of his Jewish fidelity, but is only to state a fact.

The Hellenistic world into which Paul was born, we know now, was one of many religious expressions and of earnest philosophical disputations. It was not, as is often mistakenly thought, a world barren of religious impulses. Quite to the contrary, cults were numerous, exerted strong influences, and their contentions attracted even a kind of intellectual justification, mostly in allegorical terms. Many of the cults had entered the Greek world from the East; similarly, Judaism was from the Greek stand-point one more cult which had been transplanted into the hospitable Hellenistic world.

The Jewish heritage of Paul was primarily the Old Testament. There is no reason to be sceptical of his statement that in his study of Judaism he had surpassed his fellow students of his own age. Nor should we doubt that he had achieved a skillful knowledge of Judaism. His statement that he had learned the traditions of his fathers is to be accepted—but the content of those Graeco-Jewish "traditions" is not to be confused with that which later centuries recorded as the product of the Jewish schools in Palestine and Babylonia.

Paul, as we have suggested, inherited both a Scripture and also a tradition of interpreting Scripture. In this regard, we know a great deal, for a Graeco-Jewish contemporary, Philo of Alexandria (20 B.C.-40 A.D.), has left us a large library of his writings. These are primarily interpretations of Scripture. Again and again Philo tells us that some of the key interpretations which he is giving are not his own, but are traditional.*

As the legatee of both Scripture and of its interpretation, we need not be surprised at the centrality of Biblical phrases, ideas, and motifs in Paul's own writings and his own thought. The motif from Scripture which is the most clearly discernible in Paul is that which we call the "apocalyptic." By this term we allude to scattered writings in the various prophets which are "revelations" of what is to take place at the end of time. Indeed, we usually distinguish the "apocalyptic" from the "prophetic" in the Old Testament in this way: prophecy, an earlier manifestation, dealt with immediate or proximate situations; apocalypse, a later form of prophecy, dealt with the events to come in the remote time.

The apocalyptic message was often couched in colorful, and thereby obscure language. Since it was frequently a product of times of oppression, its content was that of reassurance, for it promised that the grievances of the moment would be redressed at some future time. Whether individuals or nations, the wicked

* For an ample discussion of Philo as an interpreter of Scripture see my *Philo's Place in Judaism*, Cincinnati, 1956.

who at present prosper will be judged and punished at some crucial future moment, while the suffering righteous will be compensated for what they have undergone.

Apocalypticism was most vivid when the bearer of the message was persuaded that the climactic moment was no longer delayed to the far distant future, but was now on the threshold of realization. Mythical language recounted that the evils of this world were the result of dominance by Satan. How had Satan come to rule this world? He had rebelled against God. But when the right time arrived, the power of Satan would be destroyed and then the dominion of God would be established; indeed, God's kingdom was very near at hand. Such, in brief, was the typical Palestinian apocalyptic message. An agent of God, the Messiah, was in some way connected with the climax. The apocalypticists do not bequeath us a pattern always the same. In some apocalyptic thought, the Messiah might appear before the redeeming event or directly after the event; in others, the judgment of the world might come just before the event, or just after.

In Christian thought, Jesus—whoever and whatever he was—was considered to have been this agent and to have been in some sense divine. Whereas in the typical Jewish apocalypse, the divine agent was conceived of as appearing but one single time, in Christian thinking the pattern was altered into a two-part career. The initial coming of Jesus, in the recent past, had been only preparatory, and Jesus, after his resurrection, had ascended to heaven. His return (parousia) would bring the expected climax to realization, and at this Second Coming the judgment of the world would take place.

In regard to these matters, Paul was an apocalypticist. He claims that he has direct revelation about what will happen at the future climactic moment; he asserts this belief while anticipating the nearness of the End of the world. But being also a Hellenistic Jew, he understands and explains this inherited Jewish message partly in Hellenistic terms. Indeed, there is a marked difference between Paul and a Palestinian apocalypticist.

On the one hand, the Palestinian Jew, oppressed by the Roman occupying force, conceived of his liberation in terms of the destruction of the alien power; he would gain his personal liberty in his country's national liberty. For him, Messianic activity would necessarily be centered in Israel.

For Paul, as for Philo, national issues were not involved in the misery each faced as an individual. While the economic and political situation of these Jews of the Dispersion may have been slightly different from that of Gentiles, Rome dominated Jew and Gentile alike. Grievances were for them not apt to be matters related to national integrity or pride, but rather those difficulties inherent in the situation of every human being; in a word, they were universal. The improvement in affairs which one like Paul would seek would be little different from what a pagan neighbor would seek. The Messianic activity for one like Paul would be "cosmic," rather than national.

The Hebrew word "Messiah" when rendered into Greek became "Christ"; along with the translation of the term there was a transition of great moment in the expected function of the office. To anticipate, it may be summarized that Palestinian Jews saw in the Messiah the divine agent who would help the collective people out of their national predicament, while Paul saw in him the means of the salvation of individuals out of the human predicament.

Paul came into the new movement as a result of a problem which was to him personal and individual. In turn, he interpreted the movement to be applicable universally to each and every individual. In this shift from national Judaism to individual and universal emphasis, Paul was neither first nor unique. Before him, and in his own time, other Greek Jews were making the natural shift, and doing so unthinkingly. While a sense of solidarity with fellow believers yielded a group feeling among Greek Jews, this sentiment was broad and "ethnic" rather than limitedly national-political. Once the political element was subordinated and eliminated, the threshold from "nationalism" to universalism was crossed.

Universalistic thought holds that one's concern must be all humanity, not just one's special group. This universalism stands in contrast with particularism, which holds a solicitude exclusively for one's own group (and sometimes an unconcern, or even antagonism, for humanity).

In the early history of the Jewish people, there is evidence by which we conclude that at one stage men believed that there were many gods, each people having its own. Later, though, Jews came to believe that there was only one God and it followed then that He was the God of all humanity. A question is raised in several parts of the Bible: if God is indeed the God of mankind, does He have some special relation to the Jewish people? If He does, is it a relation so special as to contradict His being the God of humanity? And conversely, if He is the God of humanity, can He have a relationship to the Jewish people without contradicting His universality?

A characteristic Jewish answer blended universalism and particularism: True, there was only one God and only one humanity. The Jewish people were the particular vehicle through whom God's way could and would become the order for all humanity.

But no one can be wholeheartedly universalistic without in theory liquidating his own particularism. Pure universalism of such kind did not exist in Jewish thought, not even in the heights of the universalism of the Exilic period in the 6th pre-Christian century.

Paul was in some ways a universalist, and in a marked degree; but his Jewish particularism never disappeared completely. He wanted all individuals who heard him to be persuaded by him, and then to come into a specific and corporate group; in other words, in spite of the universalism and the individualism in his message, Paul advocated a particularism, "Christianity." Paul did not use that term; for us to use it in connection with Paul is anachronistic.*

The name is anachronistic, not only because it arose after Paul's time, but also because Paul had no sense of his being something other than a Jew. He was fully aware that convictions separated him from his erstwhile coreligionists, but he had no sense that he was abandoning Judaism. Rather, from his standpoint, his fellow-Jews had failed to come along with him on the final step which he felt that they, as true Jews, should have taken. When Paul, as in Romans 2, discusses the question as to who is in the correct religious line, he does not discuss who is the true "Christian," but still, who is the true Jew. We today call Paul a Christian; he would have denied it and would have asserted: "I am a Jew and what I am preaching is the purest and truest version of Judaism."

Paul felt that his version of Judaism was for all humanity, yet Paul was no thorough-going universalist. His universalism did lead him to deny any difference between Jew and Greek, so long as both are *in Christ;* but he bequeathed his inherited particularism by assigning a favored spot to Jews in the scheme of things even when he disparaged them. He did not depart from particularism; and his "church" was but a new particularism for him.

Or, to put matters more precisely, Paul never abandons particularism, for "Israel" is still his particular concern. In his understanding, however, Israel is no longer the Jewish people; instead Israel is now the "Church." So much for the particularism of Paul.

To insist that Paul was by no means a thorough-going universalist, must not blind us to the large measure of universalism in his approach. Paul shared with both Graeco-Jews and with pagans a similar attitude and approach towards what we can call the "human predicament." Thereby Paul seems to be more univer-

* Professor James H. Cobb suggested to me in a letter that "Pauline Neo-Judaism" is a term which avoids the anachronism.

salistic than he really is, for in reality Paul did not believe that all men would escape from the human predicament. He believed, though, that all men were in it.

Notwithstanding his Jewish loyalties, the attitudes and approaches of Paul to the human predicament were inherently Hellenistic. The Palestinian Jews saw the universe as good, man as God's noblest creation, and life as eminently worth living. To the Greeks, the world was a place of sorrows, man was an unhappy mixture of the soul, which was spirit and good, and of the body, which was material and evil; and life was a burden. The goal of Greek religion, indeed, its leitmotif, was that of escape: escape from the inevitable end, death, escape from bondage to the body.

This bondage involved the struggle within the individual by which his enlightened mind succumbed to his sensual desires. The passions and the senses could and would drive him into irrational action. The lust for power, for food, or for sexual satisfaction as well as anger or hilarity—all these could make man act unreasonably and impetuously. The bodily nature of man bound him to these unseen masters; he could escape from their toils only if he could change his nature.

Such a transformation might occur by man's holding his passions and appetites in good restraint. But such a task required a sturdiness of mind which was beyond most men's capabilities; to be more precise, most men, on their own, could not accomplish such a change. Some external device was needed; and such a device was available in the mystery religions.

The mysteries brought the initiates into communion with deity. When the devotee of the Dionysiac mysteries ate a piece of the sacred bull, something divine came into him in the eating—he became "enthused"—God (*theos*) came in (*en*) into him. Thereby man's "nature" became changed; he underwent "rebirth," and he was no longer "bodily," but had now become spiritual. The rites he had undergone, plus the secret knowledge transmitted to him, were symbolic of the change in his nature. Buttressed by this change, man was now equipped to ignore or to withstand the perils of this world. Man was now able to escape from the bondage to the body, he was able to escape death.

This motif, I have said, was characteristic of the pagan cults. We must understand that this same motif was adopted most wholeheartedly by Philo and by his associates. In Philo's hands his Judaism became the means by which the individual escaped from this world and became "spiritual"; the Torah (the Five Books of Moses) was the symbolic vehicle through which the domination of the soul or mind by the lusts and passions was thrown off; the rites of Judaism symbolized various facets of the process wherein the mind attained supremacy. Thus, circumcision symbolically prunes passion from the body; Passover represents the "passing" over of the soul from the body.

While Philo did not perceptibly alter the external requirements of Judaism, he did alter the appraisal and the significance of these externals. Philo did not change the ritual and the regimen; rather, he viewed it primarily as to its utility.

Moreover, while Philo (and other Greek Jews) had come to consider the Bible as the true source and repository of Greek philosophy, what we must not fail to recognize is that the character of the Bible as a religious book was never lost. The abundance of Greek philosophy which its pages were made to yield was never other than a servant of a more fundamental function, religious conviction.

When one speaks of Philo as a Hellenistic Jew, it is exceedingly superficial to regard the epithet as denoting no more than that Philo was born in the Greek world, knew Greek, and used the Greek Bible. The true import of the term is that the purpose, perplexities, quests, and sense of achievement of Greek religion were accepted, harmonized, and assimilated. Similarly, when we speak of Paul as a Hellenistic Jew, it is to invite attention to his pre-occupation with the same kind of religious problem that any pagan had—the individual predicament.

Philo and Paul have in common that each sees in his Judaism the answer for which all Greeks, pagans and Jews, were universally searching. Both are offering to their auditors a recognizable, even familiar satisfaction for religious yearnings. What they are offering is indeed familiar; otherwise Paul's and Philo's messages would have fallen on deaf ears. They are saying to those who listen to them, "What you are looking for (and not finding) is here and available. It exists in only one true and pure vehicle, my Judaism. The other vehicles—the worship of Isis, Orphism, Epicureanism—are totally wrong. If you really want the ultimate which you think they are offering, the only true form in which that exists is in what I can provide for you through my Judaism."

Immersed as Paul was in his concern with the universal predicament of man, the apocalyptic motif, so crucial in his thought, combined with his Hellenistic orientation to bring him to a heightened plane of metaphysical intuition and purpose. The apocalyptic side of him, which derives from his Jewish orientation, persuaded him that the end of the world was very, very near. The Hellenistic side, absorbed unconsciously from his environment, prompted him to urge his hearers both to escape ("salvation") from the present predicament of the individual and also to prepare for the climactic event still to come. The "Christian" side of Paul disclosed to him what he thought was a newer and better vehicle for salvation than the cumbersome Law of Moses. The two stages of salvation, the preparatory initial appearance of Jesus in the past, and the climactic parousia destined for the near future, fitted most congruently with each other.

While Paul's Judaism and his Hellenistic conditioning were significant, the most crucial aspect of Paul is his conversion to Christianity. Unhappily for us, Paul does not himself tell us what specific event or events directly prompted him to become a convert. We can be certain, however, that his conversion provided for him the solution to the human predicament. When Paul became a "Christian," he came into a movement of course, but he also brought his distinctive self into it. However much Paul might have wanted to submerge himself completely into the new movement, it was impossible for him simply to dissolve himself. The meaning of the movement for him specifically was what brought him into it, and therefore we need to understand not only the movement, but also the man.

A complex set of factors constituted his special personality. These factors made him first the persecutor and then the convert. Though he came to some conclusions which were general, he began with a problem which was individual.

What is most important in this respect is that which troubled Paul about the Law of Moses (*not the Bible itself but only the legal enactments found in it, primarily from Exodus through Deuteronomy*). He found in the legal code a highly personal and intense problem. While he believed his solution to be universally applicable, the problem as such was quite unique to him; it was not an abstract or theoretical problem to Paul but rather an immediate and vivid personal one.

To understand this individual aspect of Paul's thought—to the extent to which it can be understood—we have to begin with an assumption that Paul was always entirely earnest. We must take him at his face value, though penetrating beyond some of the surface manifestations. To understand his earnestness means to accept along with it some unfortunate by-products of his quickness of mind and of the nature of the Epistles which have come down to us.

While translations into English smooth out and conceal the true character of Paul's style, certain aspects of his dictated Epistles must not be overlooked. For example, Paul's quickness of mind occasions frequent unclarity, as he begins on one subject and allows himself to be diverted in the middle of it; sometimes he reverts to what he has begun, but more often he does not. Yet I see no evidence of contradictions in Paul which can be considered basic, his inconsistencies being minor and surface, or the result of a going off briefly on tangents. Again, when

That is what he says. He experiences no trouble, no problems, no qualms of conscience, no feelings of shortcomings.

he uses Scripture to prove his points, he employs a caprice and lack of restraint that is typical of all interpreters who unconsciously use Scripture to reinforce predetermined conclusions. If Paul is no less restrained than the rabbis of the Talmud, or Philo, or the Church Fathers, he is, on the other hand, no more so. There is no mistaking the agility and dexterity of Paul's mind, nor its lack of self-discipline.

The consequence of these characteristics is this: the statements in his Epistles by which we can understand him are ready responses to immediate practical problems rather than an artificial system of well-thought-out solutions for theological problems. Only in Romans does Paul attempt to offer some tolerably thoroughgoing exposition of his thought; yet Romans is recognizably derivative from Galatians, and is therefore only a calmer statement. Romans represents the effort of Paul to find himself on a map after he has already embarked on a journey; Romans is not the course plotted out before the journey has begun. Accordingly, Paul's statements in Romans are not calculated, but rather a mixture of responsiveness and of impulse.

That this is so is in no sense a derogation of them, but instead an enhancement of their significance. They are ruggedly honest thoughts, unblemished by the gloss of fine writing, or the evasions possible in it. Paul tells us what he thinks, not what he believes it is incumbent upon him to think.

However much allowance need be made—it is little—for the possible partisanship present in the reports of his controversies, his reports can be accepted for what they are. Respecting substance, his humorless zeal was a deterrent to deliberate distortion; respecting form, his quickness of mind prompted the ingeniousness and therefore the honesty of what he tells us. This is what I had in mind in speaking of his earnestness. In the same regard, some seek to besmirch Paul's integrity by accusing him of hypocrisy. For example, a passage is often cited out of context, in an effort by some interpreters to demonstrate such hypocrisy on Paul's part. In I Corinthians 9.20 it is true that Paul says that "To the Jews I became as a Jew that I might win the Jews: to those under the law I became as one under the law . . . that I might win those under the law." Again, two verses later, he says, "I have become all things to all men that I might save some of them." In Paul's context he is not discussing the function of the Law of Moses, but only his tactics in his missionary work. His full intent in the passage is discernible a chapter later (10.23): "All things are lawful to me but all things are not expedient."

The issue here for Paul is scarcely that of definite hypocrisy. A doctor who refrains from volunteering distressing information is different from one who, being asked, withholds it or lies about it. A liberal minister or rabbi, who has personal reservations or doubts about facets of his tradition, is scarcely under the compulsion to volunteer his reservations at all times, especially in the presence of the pious who would be needlessly distressed; but if the minister is asked directly about such matters and then withholds or prevaricates, that would indeed be sheer hypocrisy.

That is to say, if tact, delicacy, and matters of expediency are tangential to hypocrisy, then in this sense we can convict Paul (and ourselves too). But when the discussion focuses on fundamentals, I have found neither evasion nor shilly-shallying in Paul. That in his missionary activities he became all things to all men is a description of the relentless drive which impelled him to travel and to preach; it is not a clue to some supposed dissimulation in his approach to basic matters.

We can take as a further example of Paul's genuine integrity his description in Romans 7 of his difficulties with the Law of Moses. Paul's major argument here is that the Law of Moses was not permanently binding, but only on a term basis, and that the Law is now passé for the "Christian." As an example of such temporary restraint, he suggests the freedom from obligation to a husband owed to a husband by a woman when she becomes a widow. As by the death of the husband the woman is free and may marry another without thereby being an adulteress, so the "Christian" is freed from the Law of Moses by its "death," its departed validity, and the "Christian" can now "belong to Christ."

Were Paul merely playing with words, he might have stopped at this point. But having been reared a loyal Jew, and having been deeply attached to the Law, it has penetrated his being so completely that he cannot bring himself simply to cast it aside. His hearers, he feels, must not misunderstand him; they must not suppose that in abrogating the Law, he is deliberately derogating it. He goes on to ask, Was this Law, before its demise, sin? By no means, says Paul. "Yet if it had not been for the Law, I should not have known sin. I should not have known what it is to covet if the Law had not said, 'You shall not covet.' But sin, finding opportunity in the commandment, wrought in me all kinds of covetousness . . . I do not understand my own actions. For I do not do what I want, but I do the very thing I hate . . . I can will what is right, but I cannot do it. For I do not do the good I want, but the evil I do not want is what I do . . . I delight in the law of God, in my inmost self, but I see in my members another law at war with the law of my mind . . ."

Paul here is being autobiographical, and not theoretical. His inability to live up to the Law is assuredly a reflection of the previous unrest in him which later led to his conversion. I have read the commentators who disagree with this judgment and who believe that Paul found the Law difficult only after he became a Christian. My reading of Paul leads me in the opposite direction, and into the conclusion that Paul's difficulties with the Law antedate his conversion, rather than follow it. It is not his Christian convictions which raise the Law as a problem for him, but rather it is his problem with the Law that brings him ultimately to his Christian convictions.

Moreover, as I have said, Paul's account of his difficulties with the Law need to be understood as honest and basic for him. In the interpretative literature, we quite frequently encounter the view that his nullification of the Law of Moses (*but not the Bible*) was the concession which he made in order to gain converts among the pagans; to re-phrase this vulgarly, Paul was offering a reduced rate to entice customers. This view I regard as nonsense. Similarly, the judgment is sometimes offered that the lack of success which Paul met in his dealings with Jews prompted him to abrogate the legal requirements and then turn to Gentiles. In my judgment, this is a turned about point of view. Rather, I suggest, it was Paul's attitude towards the Law which cost him success with Jews. The error in both of the above-rejected views is that they fail to recognize the authenticity of the personal, subjective difficulty which the Law occasioned for Paul. By treating Paul's attitude toward the Law as one of mere expediency, these interpretations rob him of his stature at exactly that point where his stature is the greatest.

When Paul relates his difficulties with the Law in the Bible, he does nothing less than tell us of his struggle with fundamentals. He had been searching for that which was the ultimate for man in the quest for salvation. Reluctantly, Paul concluded that the Law of Moses was not this ultimate. In light of his Jewish conditioning, this conviction brought him into direct conflict with the most precious part of his Jewish heritage. Paul was confronting himself not with a side issue, but rather with the most nearly central religious dilemma conceivable.

While we recognize the earnestness and the basic integrity of Paul's difficulties with the Law, it should not escape our notice that after Paul came to his Christian convictions, he, like many a "convert" long after that day, could not resist derogating his "pre-convert" stage. Accordingly, Paul says things about the Law, and about Jews, that scarcely reflect credit on his sense of fairness. The sympathy which his genuine difficulties with the Law might arouse in a modern Jewish reader is quickly dissipated when such a reader encounters in the Epistles statements about Judaism and Jews which are grotesque and vicious. Indeed, several statements are quite out of keeping with what in our day would represent a standard of good taste.* A Jewish reader must inevitably conclude from such passages that Paul lacks for those who disagree with him that love which he described in I Corinthians 13: "If I speak in the tongues of men and of angels, but have not love . . ."

Thus, the harsh judgment which Paul expresses in certain passages on the Law reflects the apostate's disdain and partisanship for that which he has abandoned. Such judgments are on record both in the case of Protestants who have become Catholics and of Catholics who have become Protestants. They exist also in the case of individuals in Christendom who, though remaining with the tradition, feel that they have experienced God, and therefore are constrained to cast aspersions on their co-religionists. Such criticisms are partisan affairs. They reflect less the truth than the all too human qualities of men who have been sure they have been divinely illuminated. In Paul's case, his harshness is a lamentable off-shoot of his negative judgment about the Law. Yet the negative judgment itself is the product of a firm conviction, arising out of a profound wrestling with ultimates.

To put it in another way, Paul would not have become "converted" had he not begun with religious problems, the nature of which was largely individual, a reflection of his personality. But they also had a wider overtone. That is to say, we know from reading Philo that Jews in the Greek dispersion had had issues raised for them abstractly on the question of the value, relevancy, and claim to eminence of the Law of Moses. Quite a segment of Judeo-Greek writings is an apologetics designed to buttress by logic or by other means the Jewish contentions about

* See Romans 2.21-24 and 8-9 for examples of Paul's partisanship and unfairness; and for his questionable taste, see Gal. 5.12, which is to be translated "I wish that those who unsettle you (about circumcision) would castrate themselves." See also Philippians 3.2, where Paul, in speaking of circumcision, says: "Look out for the dogs, look out for the evil-workers, look out for those who mutilate the flesh."

the abiding validity of the Law. Such writings would not have been needed had not the Law been, as it were, a "problem"—even to those Jews who did not abandon it. To turn to the modern scene again for an analogy, every rabbi who deals with products of the American soil has been challenged by someone in his congregation to defend the value of the Torah as compared with, let us say, the Magna Charta, the Declaration of Independence, and the Constitution with its Bill of Rights. Frequently I have heard the question, In what way is the Torah better, or even the equal of the historic landmarks of human culture?

The response to such challenges is quite explicit in Philo, and it is implied elsewhere in Judeo-Greek literature. The answer not only pursued the line that the Jewish contributions were better, but also included the assertion, as we have intimated, that Judaism was the source from which such admired pagans as Plato and Aristotle plagiarized. It is the type of answer which could satisfy only those already satisfied.

The concession that the Greek heritage contained so much that was good and tenable would lead to the next questions: What is there in the Jewish heritage which is found exclusively in that heritage, and not contained in the Greek? If Plato is in the Bible, then isn't the Bible automatically in Plato? Is the sole issue of the respective merits of Plato and the Bible that of which came first? Is chronological priority the sole eminence of the Bible? And to this last, the questing student would be apt to comment, Let's forget this business of which came first and instead let's get down to fundamentals.

Greek Jews were called upon, probably by inquiring minds within the community, to defend the validity and the value of the Law of Moses in a context in which pagan Greeks had not only compiled law codes of their own, but had also tried to justify the essential philosophical validity of their own Greek law. Questions of the "written law" versus the "law of nature" were a commonplace among pagan philosophers. The Platonic dream of the philosopher king was in the train of a speculation which had come down from earlier times and abided into later times. Such speculation wished to discern what it was about the laws that made them truly legal and who was it who could promulgate "law," in contradistinction to tyranny on the one hand, or anarchy on the other hand.

We shall see that Paul and Philo have in common the feature that for neither of them is the Law of Moses primary. They diverge, of course, on whether or not the Law, being secondary, required continued obedience. Philo asserted its eternal validity and felt no personal difficulty in observing it.

Where other Greek Jews found the Law an intellectual, and therefore a remote or theoretical problem, Paul found a deep personal difficulty, not *about* the Law, but in his own observance of it. Had Paul not found this personal difficulty, he would not have been led to a virtual abrogation of the Law.

The honesty of Paul stands out no more clearly than in his description of his difficulties with the Law. A dissembler would probably have omitted his personal attestation, and would have been content to argue dialectically that the Law was a secondary matter, not the primary. With Paul it is otherwise, for he tells us, in great anguish, what the Law means to him. He gives the unabashed personal attestation: "What I will to do I cannot, what I will not do, I do . . . Wretched man that I am" (Rom. 7.15-24).

The phenomenon of the inability of a person to do what he knows he should do is well attested in modern psychological and psychoanalytical studies. Among disturbed people it is quite a frequent occurrence for them to say, I cannot bring myself to do that. Counsellors who fail to recognize the emotional involvements and blocks among those who come to see them often issue gratuitous and useless advice: "Don't get angry"; "don't let that upset you"; and the like. But the disturbance in the person is precisely that the specific thing does upset him, and that his becoming angry is outside his volition and control. The counsellee may understand intellectually that his reaction is out of proportion, or oblique, to the stimulus; but were he undisturbed, he would not respond as he does, indeed he would not need to come to seek counsel.

What Paul is telling us in Romans 7 is that he knew intellectually what he ought to do under the Law and what he ought to abstain from. It was not his understanding, but his actual observance which was impossible to him.

What modern psychoanalysis attempts to do is to help the patient understand the genesis of his disturbance, so that out of the recognition of the origin the disturbance will either disappear or else abate. The successful psychoanalyst does not cure the patient, but steers the patient into curing himself. Modern psychoanalysis rests on the premise that self-cure, in the sense of the preceding sentence, is possible.

Paul confesses to his inability by himself to find the cure for his disturbance. The Law did not bring him serenity; instead, the requirements of the Law even increased his disturbance. The serenity which Paul sought did eventually come to him but it was through what to him was an outside source, the atoning death of Christ. Just what this meant to Paul we shall see later. At this point it suffices to say that the Christ, in dying, did for Paul what Paul was unable to accomplish alone, and certainly was not able to accomplish merely through the Law.

His own individual predicament rather than the general plight of man, then, was a decisive factor in Paul's decision about the Law. It was not that a friend or relative of Paul was unable to observe the Law; for to him, Paul might well have said, at least in his pre-conversion days: "Just control yourself and try harder." The situation for Paul was that the issue was pre-eminently his own; initially, it was his very own salvation which he was seeking.

But Paul went on from the personal and the particular to the universal. A difficulty which subsequent generations have had with Paul's thought is that Paul assumed that his predicament, since it is shared by *some*, or many other people, was therefore necessarily fully universal. His idiosyncratic involvement became expanded into a kind of universal and philosophic approach, and

Paul also assumes that to understand him and his position one would have to understand his experience of Christ which in this explanation is hardly even mentioned!

when his Epistles became canonized into Scripture, that philosophical matrix came to be considered by orthodox Christians as revelation itself. But not everyone is built as Paul was.

Not only in relatively modern times, particularly in most of the nineteenth and part of the twentieth centuries, have serious minds had difficulties with Pauline thought. Whereas men such as Augustine and Calvin built upon it and extended it, there have likewise been Pelagius (flourished about 410) and Arminius (16th century) who expressed their disagreements.

Indeed, much of Christian thought in the nineteenth century and until the last two or three decades was scarcely Pauline. Until recently, liberal Protestantism tended to ignore Paul, or else not to take him seriously.

American secular thought supposed that man was just around the corner from working out his own salvation along political, economic, and social lines. Paul's insistence on man's "inability"—though he was talking about salvation in a different sense—was uncongenial to liberals. That Paul went into a kind of eclipse is not surprising. It became a cliché in the technical scholarship that Paul was an epileptic—for which there is not one shred of real evidence; and none of us would continue to retain as a personal physician a doctor who would presume to diagnose from scanty and vague details seen from a distance of six thousand miles and almost two thousand years. To call Paul an epileptic was to dismiss him as inconsequential.

Protestant neo-orthodoxy of our own time is little other than a return to Paulinism. This constitutes a return not to Paul himself, but to doctrines derived from him, departed in from him, but still ascribed to him. This neo-orthodoxy would seem to have already captured the minds of most professional Protestant theologians, or else to have nearly done so. It has made in-roads into New Testament scholarship, and threatens to make a shambles of what was once an intellectually honest endeavor to find the truth.

In the mood of optimism of the nineteenth century, Paul was

out of favor, for his personal predicament did not seem universal. In the pessimism of our time, Paul has regained an erstwhile eminence.

It is mood rather than dialectic which makes some person either the optimist or the pessimist. The mood of Paul was a determinant of his convictions; to the extent that those who read and study him share totally, partly, or not at all overtones of the same mood, they will read with full, partial, or negative identification and empathy. This lack of uniformity in the response to Paul is the product of his high individuality. Once one encounters him, one is never neutral about him. One who is predisposed towards him shares his dismay, his bewilderment, his finding of himself, and his triumph. One who is not so predisposed can have difficulty in the bare task of understanding him.

One need not be his disciple as a prelude to understanding him. Indeed, there is a fascination about him for any reader who is challenged by a vigorous, original, and creative mind. Paul is fascinating rather than lovable. He is exciting, rather than winning. He is, indeed, both an attraction and, at the same time, its opposite. On many matters he was wrong. But he was never puny.

In sum, a few short years after the movement later known as Christianity came into being, it spread into the Greek world. A certain Greek Jew named Paul first opposed this version of Judaism and then joined the movement.

He opposed the movement because it differed from his view of Judaism. When he joined it, he was convinced, rather, that it was the true version of Judaism.

When Paul joined the movement, it received no ordinary man, but a highly individualistic genius. Almost half of the writings in the New Testament come from his hand. Even when we subtract the Epistles attributed to him, which are now not regarded as from his hand, his writings are more numerous in the New Testament than those of any one else.

II

Paul the Jew

On the one hand, Paul had the clearest sense of preaching something startling, something novel, and something original; on the other hand, he had no sense that he was preaching anything other than the surest and truest version of Judaism. The significant events in the career of Jesus—and for Paul these are primarily the Crucifixion and only secondarily the Resurrection—are from his standpoint only the newest and last rung of the same Jewish ladder which he was raised to climb. To the history of Jewish revelation, begun with Abraham, stabilized by Moses, and carried further by the prophets, the revelation of God in Christ is the climactic and logical conclusion. For Paul there is no semblance of a break between the revelation of the remote past and that reaching into the present. In his mind it is a continuous and unbroken course. Any idea of rupture occurs only in the minds of his contemporary Jews who have failed to discern that to the revelation of old there has been added a new revelation. Paul in his own heart and mind has not deviated from Judaism; it is these opaque Jews who do not share his conviction who have deviated and gone astray.

A key problem in Paul is: what was it that prompted him to regard the new and continuous revelation as implying a modification of the old, rather than an addition to it? And more specifically, what was there about Paul or his environment which questioned the continued validity, indeed the eternity of the Law of Moses? What was there in the religious climate beyond the confession of a Paul of his inability to observe the Law? How did Paul move from personal attitude into a more or less reasonable justification of it? Beyond telling us what he himself could or could not do, what relevant dialectic, or religious, or philosophical arguments lay at hand for him to advance?

The Epistle to the Galatians provides us not only with the substance of the problem of the Law of Moses for Paul, but also with the series of incidents that raised the question of the Law to the height of a focal controversy. To comprehend the problem in its setting is an excellent beginning to understand its nature.

Paul had founded the church in Galatia—a region in Asia Minor settled in by Gauls of Europe—and then he had moved on. When he had founded the church he had not laid upon it the obligation of observing the regimen of Jewish law. He later received a report which angered him. It stated—we do not know whether orally or in writing—that certain people were attempting to require the Galatians to observe the law and that the Galatians were complying.

Here are some of Paul's words from his Epistle to the Galatians: ". . . I am astonished that you are so quickly deserting him who called you in the grace of Christ and turning to a different gospel—not that there is another gospel, but there are some who trouble you and want to pervert the gospel of Christ . . . As we have said before, so now I say again, If anyone is preaching to you a gospel contrary to that which you received, let him be accursed . . . I went up again to Jerusalem with Barnabas, taking Titus along with me. I went up by revelation; and I laid before them (but privately before those who were of repute) the gospel which I preach among the Gentiles. . . . But because of false brethren secretly brought in, who slipped in to spy out our freedom which we have in Christ Jesus—to them we did not yield submission even for a moment . . . When they (the Pillars) saw that I had been entrusted with the gospel to the uncircumcised . . . and when they perceived the grace that was given to me, James and Cephas and John . . . gave me and Barnabas the right hand of fellowship, that we should go to the Gentiles and they to the circumcised. . . . But when Cephas came to Antioch I opposed him to his face because he stood condemned. For before certain men came from James, he ate with the Gentiles; but when they came he drew back and separated himself, fearing the circumcision party. And with him the rest of the Jews acted insincerely, so that even Barnabas was carried away by their insincerity. But when I saw that they were not straightforward about the truth of the gospel, I said to Cephas before them all, 'If you, though a Jew, live like a Gentile and not like a Jew, how can you compel the Gentiles to live like Jews?' . . . O foolish Galatians! . . . Let me ask you this: Did you receive the Spirit by works of the law, or hearing with faith? . . . Does he who supplies the Spirit to you do so by works of the law, or by hearing with faith? . . . For freedom Christ has set us free; stand fast therefore, and do not submit again to the yoke of slavery . . ."

The question is this: why was it that in Paul's career there arose the issue of whether or not a Gentile, in order to become a Christian, had to become a Jew first? Why was it that in Paul's career the validity of the requirements of Judaism was first questioned?

It is true that in the Gospels (Mark 7.1-19 and its parallels, Matthew 15.11 and Luke 11.39-41) there is reported a controversy in which Jesus is depicted as participating. It begins with the question of whether or not the hands must be washed before eating; it ends by stating that Jesus had made all foods "clean," that is, acceptable. The scholars are divided on whether or not this Gospel item authentically reflects the view and reports the words of Jesus. Some suggest that it is not authentic, but is an effort to invoke the authority of Jesus for a church practice which was current long after his time, and after Paul's too. Others, however, accepting it as an authentic report of Jesus, need to concede that Paul had no knowledge of it, for in the controversy as recorded in Galatians, Paul abstained from quoting what could and would have been the decisive word of Jesus. The controversy recorded in Galatians seems unmistakably to be over an issue which was not only still unsettled, but had not even been adequately raised before Paul's time. When viewed in the context of Galatians, the minor issue of table fellowship is only the rock on which the split occurs; the weighty issue is no less than the Law of Moses as a totality. Indeed, if the food laws were no longer valid, would other parts of the Law remain valid?

If the Law of Moses was thus a new issue, one would need to conclude that previously "Christianity" was a Jewish movement which differed from other Jewish sectaries not on the Law, but on the convictions about Jesus, convictions which were simply added to the Law, and which were not in any sense in conflict with it. Unless this was the case, the controversy in Galatians is quite meaningless.

It was, then, in Paul's career that this focal issue was raised. The manner in which the Law was questioned is revealed in Paul's defense against Cephas. Paul contended that he had been set apart as the apostle to the Gentiles, while Cephas, his opponent, was designated for the Jews. This contention rests on the recognition by Paul that there was a difference in the terms and the practices of the missionary activity of the two. Paul, in some passages, appears passively content for Cephas to preach something different from his own message, provided that the Christ Jesus constitutes the center of the preachment; but when Paul is pressed by opponents, he will not hesitate to move from a toleration of Cephas' way into a direct denunciation of it. Paul's defense of his own approach is nothing other than a defense of his "antinomianism" * as being the inherently right way and therefore basically the only true way. Paul finds the need to defend his way because it is different from that of the other missionaries. The manner of Paul's defense amounts to the virtual abrogation of the Law.

The movement from the individual matter, table fellowship, to the Law of Moses as a totality constitutes the logical progression from a single instance to a general rule, from a specific detail into a general principle. I have already mentioned that I regard as absurd those interpretations which suggest that Paul took this momentous step out of mere expediency or strategy. There is a frequently cited "explanation" which I believe is likewise unfounded. It is contended that Paul is drawing on a passage to be found in the rabbinic literature which supposedly declares that in Messianic times the Law will be abrogated. No such passage is to be found, though Sanhedrin 97a is distorted to yield this view.† There are a number of obstacles to accepting this dubious rabbinic item as explaining Paul's individual, specific attitude towards the Law, even if the passage had said clearly what it really does not say at all. In the first place, were

* Christians usually wish to protect Paul from the term "antinomianism" ("against the Law"), for it appears to them as an uncomplimentary adjective. Various types of word-juggling have appeared about the term antinomian. Catholics who want to avoid it for Paul denounced it among sixteenth century reformers. In short, Catholics define antinomianism as "the heretical doctrine that Christians are exempt from the moral law" (*Catholic Encyclopedia,* "Antinomianism," I, 564-567). Jews define it as "the opposition of certain Christian sects to the Law; that is, to the revelation of the Old Testament" (*Jewish Encyclopedia,* "Antinomianism," I, 630-632). If it is conceded that Paul's ethics and morals were undeviatingly Jewish, then my use of the word for the want of a better one is without any implication; it is, as I use it, merely descriptive.

† See Baeck, "The Faith of Paul," in *The Journal of Jewish Studies,* III (1952), p. 106. All that Sanhedrin 97a says is this: "The world is 6,000 years. Two thousand are confusion (Hebrew *tohu*), two thousand Torah, two thousand days of the Messiah." Those inducted into the Talmud may consult Rashi to the passage. A reliable view on the Jewish belief in the perpetuity of the Torah is to be found in Moore, *Judaism,* I, 263-280, especially p. 271.

this rabbinic dictum already known to the participants in the controversy recorded in Galatians, then surely the partisan who might have won his case by citing it would have done so. That is to say, Paul might have quoted the dictum to Cephas, who should really not have needed to have a wide-spread dictum quoted to him! The item, though, does not appear at all in Galatians (any more than it does in the Talmud).

Secondly, this type of explanation makes meaningless not only Paul's controversy, but also his attitude towards the Law, and indeed those sections of the Epistles in which he discusses the Law. For if the abrogation of the Law is only a detail, only a byproduct of the arrival of the Messianic age, then it is not simultaneously the central factor in the question: How can I achieve my individual salvation? This explanation which we are examining suggests the sequence that first the Messiah comes and thereby, among other benefits, the Law is abrogated. But there is no mistaking Paul's view. To him the sequence is just the opposite. The climactic moment has as yet not arrived but still awaits the future Second Coming of the Christ. Paul's question is: Can observing the Law prepare you adequately for that climax? His answer is: No! The far-fetched explanation, which needs to be rejected, fails to give rounded consideration to these implications.*

I have gone to such length to refute this frequent explanation, for it is typical of an abundance of them which have the double opaqueness: the failure to discern Paul's high individuality and thereby his true genius, and the failure to recognize the local, Greek setting which is part of the atmosphere which Paul breathes.

To resume with our thread, it is in Paul that the issue of the Law came to the forefront; his answer constituted a personal attestation to his experience. But the Hellenistic Jewish atmosphere

* It is a piece of the misbegotten and inaccurate exegesis which assumes that the Hellenistic Jew Paul can be explained by remotely tangential passages from the rabbinical literature.

made the Law a general problem for all Jews who came into more than surface contact with the Greek spirit. In part, though only in part, Paul reflects this general problem.

The Law of Moses was a problem to Hellenistic Jews from both an internal or practical consideration and also from an external or theoretical one.

Internally, the state of affairs presupposed and explicitly set forth in the Law was this: The Temple in Jerusalem was central and focal. From the standpoint of the Pentateuch, it and it alone was the only legitimate Temple.* There only could animal sacrifices be offered. No less than three passages of the Pentateuch (Exodus 23.17 and 34.23, and Deut. 16.6) enjoin that each male must appear three times a year at the Temple. It is likely that this requirement, especially in its context in Deuteronomy, presupposed that distances were small and that Jews, living in relative proximity to Jerusalem, could fulfill it.

The Temple, moreover, was the scene of sacrifices every day, and of more elaborate ones on the holy days. We do not know how much of the ritual consisted of spoken or sung prayer, but manifestly the distinctive character of the Temple was its animal sacrifice.

The Temple was presided over by hereditary priests who, according to a romantic fiction found in the Pentateuch, were the direct descendants of Aaron, the brother of Moses. A man was a priest only by birth; he could become a priest neither by study nor by consecration. The priests did the work of offering the animal sacrifices, and they received emoluments for their labors. Moreover, Jews the world over paid an annual tax to maintain the Temple.

But what happened with those Jews who dwelled in places too remote from Jerusalem to make the expensive pilgrimage? Ob-

* Jews overwhelmingly rejected as invalid and perverse a temple at Gerizim created by the Samaritans, and a less well known temple at Leontopolis in Egypt, built by the defeated partisan in an ugly rivalry among two claimants for the high priesthood.

viously, they could not go there each and every time they were required to. While their sentimental attachment to the Temple was not diminished, it is likely that most Jews in remote places made only a limited, scattered number of pilgrimages, or else none at all.

Indeed, this problem becomes more vivid when we consider a later development. After Paul's life-time, the Temple in Jerusalem was destroyed by the Romans. This took place in the year 70 A.D. Jews, even in Palestine, were thereupon faced with the dilemma that Scripture obligated them to visit and sacrifice at a Temple which no longer existed. Thus, what was, before 70, a problem for those Jews remote from Jerusalem became, after 70, a universal Jewish problem, encompassing even those Jews living in Palestine.

After 70, the character of Palestinian Judaism changed almost completely. Animal sacrifice was impossible, yet Scripture demanded it. A resolution was accomplished in this manner: prayer in the synagogue came to be a completely adequate substitute. Along with this transition from Temple sacrifice to synagogue prayer, there was after 70 an accompanying change in religious leadership. The priesthood as a reality was gone. Now there emerged the rabbi.

NB

The rabbi was a religious personality in a broad sense; he was not, as today, a functionary. The rabbi was a layman whose eminence and prestige depended on his scholarship in the Bible and his attendant ability to decide uncertain cases which touched on Biblical law but which were not explicitly mentioned in it. When the Temple was destroyed in 70, the institutions of the rabbinate and the synagogue were sufficiently advanced and entrenched so that the transition, in spite of its momentous character, was not a difficult one. After 70, necessity spurred the rabbinate and the synagogue to an importance they had previously not obtained. Yet both were in existence before 70.

Thus, the Judaism we term rabbinic Judaism was in existence in Paul's day, though its name and its recorded literature come onto the scene much later. The synagogue, as we have said, was well known in the Greek dispersion of Paul's time. There is, however, no trace of the title rabbi in Graeco-Jewish writings of Paul's day, or in Paul's Epistles. The title rabbi came into use only thereafter.

Just as there was development in the rabbinate and in the synagogue from what they were in Paul's time, so too there was a development in Pharisaism. Paul speaks of himself as a Pharisee. What Pharisaism became after 70 is clear to the modern student, yet exactly what it means in Paul's time, and in the Greek dispersion, is not clear at all. Of the major items of dispute between the Sadducees and the Pharisees, Paul is clearly with the Pharisees in his affirmation of resurrection (which the Sadducees denied); and if we are to interpret the Sadducees' opposition to the so-called "oral law" as being equivalent to scriptural literalism, again Paul is with the Pharisees, for he is not a literalist. What we must beware of is equating a dispersion Pharisee of the years 35-55 with a Palestinian Pharisee of 200 or 300. Pharisaism was able to flourish after 70 when there was no Temple in existence. Could a Pharisee of the Dispersion, remote from the Temple when it stood, flourish in indifference to it? What do we know of Paul's attitude towards the Temple in Jerusalem?

Although Paul speaks of the "mother church" in Jerusalem, and although he visited there, his Epistles contain not one mention of his personal relationship to the Temple in Jerusalem. To make a gross inference from this silence is dangerous, for we do not possess all the epistles that Paul wrote, and quite conceivably all that he wrote was much less than all that was in his mind. The fact is, however, that he mentions the Temple in Jerusalem only once, in Second Thessalonians 2.4; moreover, this Epistle is considered by many scholars not to be by Paul. Yet even if we accept a Pauline authorship, all that the passage tells us is that the "son of perdition . . . takes his seat in the

Temple of God, proclaiming himself to be God." * There is, however, one other mention of the Temple of God in Paul's writings, but here he alludes not to the building in Jerusalem, but to "believers": "Do you not know that you are God's temple and that God's spirit dwells in you?" (I Cor. 3.16; see also in the same Epistle 6.19 and II Cor. 6.16).

If we are justified in concluding that Paul was indifferent to the Temple at Jerusalem, then we can understand all the better that it was his native synagogue which was the center and scene of his Jewish education and expression. His Judaism is explicit in his every paragraph. As to his Jewish education he tells us in Galatians 1.14, "I advanced in Judaism beyond many of my own age among my people, so extremely zealous was I for the traditions of my fathers." Paul's effortless citation of Scripture confirms his claim to some good measure.

As one raised in a Dispersion synagogue, and advanced in Judaism, Paul inevitably faced the contradiction that he studied and read in the synagogue scriptural legislation which he and other Jews were not fulfilling, for the simple reason that for them this legislation had fallen into disuse. In our day we read from time to time of some one arrested for violation of a law he did not know was on the statute books. Laws do fall into disuse, and it is not a far step to jump from disuse to a conclusion of inapplicability and invalidity.

As we have seen, Paul lived at a time before rabbinic Judaism had come to such maturity that it was able to supplant fully Biblical Judaism and thus to provide for Jews some sense of completely fulfilling scriptural requirements. Consequently, Paul encountered, as did other Greek Jews, both the irrelevance of some aspects of Biblical legislation and their inoperativeness.

* The passage is an explanation of the need for certain scheduled events to take place prior to the Second Coming of Jesus. "The rebellion comes first . . . the man of sin is revealed, the son of perdition who opposes and exalts himself against every so-called god or object of worship, so that he takes his seat in the temple of God, proclaiming himself to be God."

Of this we can be certain, although the confirming evidence is not supplied in Paul's Epistles.

The living Judaism of Paul and his contemporaries was scarcely identified with Biblical religion, especially with the sacrificial requirements of the Pentateuch. For those to whom religion is more than mechanical, some thought and questioning are inevitable. That Paul was a person who thought and questioned seems clear on every page. We do not always have his questions; but we can be sure that he was a questioner. We know from Philo's writings that questioners, presumably such as Paul, existed. For example, Philo has a long section justifying Abraham's willingness to sacrifice Isaac, narrated in Gen. 22. After Philo has vindicated Abraham, he urges the questioners to put "a barrier on their unbridled and evil-speaking mouths!" *

The internal challenge came inevitably. Sometimes its basis was the ideas involved, whether they were acceptable or unreasonable. At other times its basis was the observable discrepancy between the Torah which envisaged a temple and promulgated a Law, and a synagogal Jewish life devoid of temple and sacrifices, and with the Law consequently neither observable nor fully observed.

This latter was a challenge on a practical level, as though the question was, "Are we Jews who are not doing all that the Law demands really doing what we should be doing?"

The external or theoretical challenge, however, was even deeper. It would be phrased, "What is the justification for us Jews to be asked to do these specific Jewish things? Is our Jewish way better than that of our Gentile neighbors? In short, what is the merit of our Jewish Law compared with Gentile Law?"

There is, in the last question, a peculiar turn of key importance. Namely, Greek Jews focused their attention on Judaism as though it was both in essence and as a totality *law* and nothing but *law*.

For modern Judaism, the Hebrew word Torah is a broad

* *De Abrahamo,* XXXV.

term. For Hellenistic Judaism, the casualness with which the Hebrew word Torah was translated by the Greek word *nomos,* "law," is apparent on every page of the surviving literature. Greek Jews nowhere raised the question of whether Torah really means *nomos,* law! And whenever they defended their Jewish convictions, it was always on the premise, startling to modern Jewish students, that *nomos* did adequately translate *Torah.* To Palestinian Jews, and their spiritual descendants, the word Torah never had so restricted a connotation; they equated *Torah* with our word "revelation." While they would have conceded that the Torah was a revelation which *included* "law," they would properly have denied that revelation and "law" were interchangeable. It is true, the legal portion of the Torah uses such terms as judgment, statute, commandment, and (especially in Priestly writings) *torah,* with a small t, to describe an individual requirement. But the Torah, with a capital T, also included exhortation (as in the pre-exilic prophets), prayer (as in the Psalter), prudential wisdom (as in Proverbs), and the like. Indeed, Torah, with a capital T, was not "law" but revelation.

The whole cast of mind of Greek Jews, especially as evidenced by Philo, is shaped by the unquestioning acceptance of the premise that Torah meant Law. Philo even undertakes to defend the proposition that Genesis, with its relatively few laws and its narratives about the Patriarchs, is nevertheless basically a book of law.*

Philo's acceptance of Torah as *nomos* is paralleled, though not precisely, by Paul. At times, as in Romans 2.17-18, Paul seems to regard the entire Pentateuch as Law, though his emphasis on legal matters would seem to indicate that by Law he refers only to the legalistic section which begins, as is usually considered, in Exodus 12. Paul gives no clarification of a view of the narrative materials in Genesis, and their sequel in Exodus

* The content of his treatise, called *De Abrahamo,* is largely devoted to the defense of this proposition.

1-11 and their possible relation to Law. Nevertheless, it needs to be clear, even at the cost of a dozen repetitions, that it is not the Pentateuch as a totality, or indeed the Bible, which Paul turns his back on, but only those legal requirements in Scripture which came from or through Moses. It might, perhaps, be put in this way: in Graeco-Jewish terms Paul considers outmoded not the Law but the laws.

The Graeco-Jewish equation of Torah and law was picked up and propagated by church fathers; this dubious identification appears in some of the scholarship of our own day. Out of the misunderstanding of what Torah meant to rabbinic Jews, there emerged two reactions among Protestants, in particular since the 1870's: (1) the identification of Judaism with "legalism" and (2) a supercilious and condescending attitude both to Judaism and to legalism itself. Out of some of this Protestant literature one would infer something which no Jew has ever experienced: that the Torah was a burden. These expositors do not seem to stop to think that if the dilemma which Paul had with the Law was only its burdensomeness, then he is automatically barred from confronting the Law on the deeper basis of principle. One might gather from such writings that Paul was a Jew who lived remote from kosher butcher shops, needed to pay a little extra for this type of food, needed to maintain two sets of dishes, and the like, and that rather than struggle with such inconvenience he developed a rationalization which only touched on principle. In short, Paul, it would seem, abrogated kosher requirements because they were burdensome. This sort of explanation, I am persuaded, is wrong in details and wrong in spirit. Rather than conclude that Paul found the Law difficult and then found a principle on which to turn away from it, I am persuaded that Paul turned away from the Law on what was to him entirely principle; and if Paul found it "difficult," it was never in the sense of inconvenient.

The question of the Law as principle agitated Greek Jews besides Paul. To notice the defense which Philo makes of the

Law will illustrate some typical Hellenistic Jewish involvements and will strengthen our contention that it is principle not burden which prompts Paul. Not everything which is in Philo is reflected in Paul; but some basic items are common to the two. Also, from Philo we have a rather full exposition; from Paul only random statements. But some coincidences are striking, especially when one remembers that Philo remained a Jew while Paul became a "Christian." So relatively close to each other are they on facets of the significance of the Law that we need not be surprised that the fourth century church historian Eusebius could blend together items from the two of them.

Philo sets out to defend the proposition that the Law of Moses is valid law and that it is as law superior to any law which the Greeks have created. This defense he will rest on considerations of dialectic and also on arguments taken directly out of the Greek tradition; for Philo does not become apodictic nor does he simply appeal to authority. Rather, he will prove the case.

His frames of reference are these: He accepts from the Greek tradition the assumption that there are two levels of law—the "written law" and the "law of nature." Here on earth, on the mundane level, law is something which is promulgated by someone in authority; it is "written" and enshrined in a code. It is always a list of details, the application to specific legal situations of some fundamental which is higher. The "written law," to adopt Philo's term, is at the mercy of a king who succeeds his father, or overthrows his predecessor; the new king may abolish or alter the older law, or he may add to it. The characteristic of "written law" is that it is not eternal; it is, on the contrary, subject to time. Moreover, if one moves from Athens to Sparta, or from Antioch to Alexandria, he will find that specific laws change; the Greek "written" laws, then, are subject to place. They are valid neither everywhere nor eternally. Thereby they differ from the "written law" of the Jews, says Philo, for it is everywhere the same, and is not to be added to or subtracted from or altered.

That is to say, the written law of the Jews is of the same *kind* as that of the Greeks, but it is better. Its admitted deficiency is that like that of the Greeks it is "written"; its superiority, Philo argues, lies in that the law of the Jews alone is in conformity with what he calls the law of nature.

By the law of nature Philo alludes to those general principles which belong, shall we say, in Plato's ideal realm. Whereas the written law is subject to error in its wording, or lack of clarity and/or to misunderstanding, the law of nature is unwritten, pure and clear, and without error. The relationship of written law to the law of nature is that the written law is a substitute for the unwritten; or, to use another figure, it is an imitation of it; or again, the written law is to the unwritten as a specific table (which may have one leg too short or can be destroyed by burning) is to Plato's "idea" of a table.

Accordingly, Philo makes the contention that the Law of Moses is the very best possible imitation of the law of nature, and fully consistent with it. Where in the Bible does Philo find reflected the law of nature? To answer simply, the laws which Moses promulgated in Exodus and the succeeding books are the written law; but for the unwritten law one must understand the true import of Genesis.

Is Genesis with its narratives and its lack of statutes, judgments and requirements a book of law? Philo answers this question with a resounding yes. Genesis is the book of the law of nature.

In his effort to prove this contention, Philo utilizes a phrase to convey his idea out of Stoic and other conceptions of proper kingship. True kingship, in the Platonic tradition, was the province of the philosopher who could distinguish between those things which were mere sensual perceptions and those which were mental conceptions. Unless the king were such a philosopher, he would not tend towards justice; if he was selfish, he inclined towards tyranny, or if weak, towards anarchy. But the true king was the person who was able to rise above material existence into the ideal realm of the law of nature, and then bring down to the material realm a reflection of that which he had discerned in the immaterial realm. In possessing this capacity to transform the ideal into the practical, the king was in effect an "embodiment of the law"; and "law," being by definition the midpoint between tyranny and anarchy, was "legal" only if the promulgator of it was of the philosophical stature to legislate in harmony with the law of nature. Philo's term for a man who embodied the law is the same as used among Stoics: *Nomos empsychos kai logikos:* the law embodied and made vocal.

Perhaps it is helpful, in understanding the notion of "law embodied in a man," to recollect that a recent New Jersey politician was known by the nickname "I-am-the-Law," and in *Iolanthe* the Lord Chancellor sings:

> *"The Law is the true embodiment*
> *Of everything that is excellent.*
> *It has no kind of fault or flaw,*
> *And I, my Lords, embody the Law."*

An "embodied law," then, was an outstanding individual. This individual promulgated written, specific laws for others, but he himself lived by the unwritten law of nature. Abraham, Isaac, and Jacob, Philo tells us, were laws embodied in men. All of them preceded Moses in time. The patriarchs lived by the law of nature; the laws of Moses are the result of translating into a specific, written code that which the patriarchs were and did.

For Abraham did not live by the Law of Moses, which he preceded in time, but by immaterial law. His righteousness (Genesis 15.6 reads: "He believed in the Lord and He reckoned it to him as righteousness") stemmed from his faith in God, and not from any performance of specific requirements.*

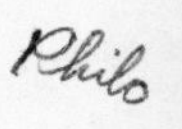

To buttress his contention that the Law of Moses is consistent

* It is at such points that Philo is at sharp variance with the rabbis; they make Abraham an observer of the Law of Moses, and its rabbinic expansions, even before the Law came into being.

with nature and is its best possible substitute, Philo ultimately embarks upon an allegorization of the laws the net effect of which is to transform each of the specific requirements into a symbol of a deeper principle: Circumcision symbolized pruning passion from the body; Passover symbolized the passing of the soul out of its domination by the body; pork is abstained from, in spite of its pre-eminence as the sweetest of meats, so Philo says, as a means of practicing self-control.

The difficulty with reducing Law to symbol is that it is a common human tendency for one, when confronted with certain symbols, to declare he knows already what the symbol represents and that he no longer requires the symbol. There is all the difference in the world between declaring that one must abstain from pork because God commanded it, and declaring that abstention is merely a symbol. There is all the difference in the world between believing that the Christ is truly present at the eating of the wafer and the drinking of the wine, and regarding the ceremony only as a memorial symbol. By and large people will do, and gladly, what they earnestly believe God has commanded. But by and large people will quarrel about the necessity of observing that which is no more than a symbol, even when they are told that it is a truly significant symbol. Those Christian denominations which believe and teach that the Lord is literally present at their worship have no difficulty with Sunday attendance. The others find their communicants frequently averring that the Lord is equally present on the golf course.

I am not dealing in anachronisms, my assertion about symbols is attested to by Philo. He laments in one passage, *De Migratione Abrahami* 89ff, that some of his fellow Jews have ceased to observe the specific laws. These people, Philo says, are right in regarding the specific laws as allegorical elements of spiritual truth, and they really understand the spiritual truths quite well; but they ought not to abandon the literal observance of the law. Philo applauds them for regarding the laws as symbols; he chides them for having ceased to observe the symbol.

Or, if we will view Philo's argument from a different angle, he is contending that the Law of Moses is not of the same substance, and not at the same eminence, as the law of nature. In Philo's view the Law of Moses is not the fundamental principle, but only secondary.

It is at this point that Paul and Philo share the basic element common in their respective approaches. To neither of them was the Law of Moses the primary principle. Each in his own way sought for what he regarded as primary. We must insist that Paul's assessment of the Law as secondary (it was mediated, he says, by the angels!) preceded his conversion. It was this assessment, coupled with his own personality traits, that produced in Paul the inner disturbance which only his conversion allayed.

For both Philo and Paul, the essence of religion could not be merely a memorial and a product of long ages ago. Not what God told our forefathers, but what he continues to tell us even in our day, is for Paul and Philo the crucial element. They unite in asserting, as if in direct denial of a rabbinic contention, that revelation continues into the present; there is no trace in either of them of the rabbinic view that prophecy—God speaking directly to man—had ceased with Ezra in the fifth pre-Christian century.

Indeed, as I have said before, Paul and Philo have many elements in common. Both of them view the Bible as a vehicle for individual salvation. Both are pre-occupied with the question of how the individual can enable his mind (or soul; the words are interchangeable) to triumph over his body. For both of them, man, the mixture of the material and the immaterial, plays host to the struggle within him between the enlightened mind and the aggressive senses and passions. Both of them ask similar questions: Will the appetites of the body conquer man's reason? Or will man, through his reason, regiment his bodily desires?

But striking as are the common elements in Paul and Philo, even more striking is the point at which they diverge, for they tend to reverse each other's process. To Philo, the Law of Moses is the formula whereby the individual enables his higher mind to achieve domination over his body, lets his soul rise out of his body, and achieves immortality. The observance of the Law of Moses, according to Philo, can bring a transformation of man from a bodily creature into a spiritual creature—and it is likely that Philo means an actual transformation. Refracted by Philo's allegory, the details of the Law of Moses specify what the senses are and how many they number; what the passions are, and how they gain domination over man's soul. Such preoccupation with man's make-up we in our day would classify as psychological, rather than philosophical. Or, to put it more precisely, the philosophical hodgepodge in Philo is the array of explanations of the relationship between higher mind or soul and body, while the psychological facet in him moves beyond mere explanation into the exposition of how they can and should function. Philo is interested in telling us what we should do, for he is a preacher; in the telling he has recourse to philosophy only to explain the supposed significance in what he wants us to do. To indulge in still another anachronism, Philo deals with the problem, how in this troubled Hellenistic age can man achieve peace of mind? (A goal, of course, far beyond what such literature in our time claims to offer, for nowadays it deals with only the level of personal or social integration.) Philo gives us advice which we can paraphrase into the formula: "Observe the Law of Moses, and thereby you will be transformed into the spiritual being who lives by the law of nature. Do you want to know what the senses and passions are? Read my allegory of Gen.14 and you will know. In fact, you will find there how to have your mind control the senses and passions. Read me on the rest of Genesis too. Here in the Bible, indeed in its laws, is a blueprint, a program for you to follow; here are things you must do!" The key word is "Do."

But for Paul, by contrast, there was a personal problem: he

could not do those things which the Law and Philo would have said he must do. Paul needed beforehand the peace of mind to do that which Philo asserted would bring peace of mind to a person.

To Paul the Law of Moses was a revelation which came at one particular time in history—that is, there was a period of time in history before it was given—and it could therefore be supplanted by a revelation more recent in history. Moreover, the Law of Moses was in Paul's mind not a direct echo of God. Of its origin, he tells us that it was "ordained by angels through an intermediary" (Gal. 3.19; see also Acts 7.53, and Hebrews 2.2; perhaps a similar intent underlies II Cor. 3.12ff.). The scholars have searched desperately, and so far in vain, for some ancient source from which Paul may have drawn this unusual idea, but they have had to be content to note that the nearest approach to it is a scattering of rabbinic passages which tell that angels were present when the theophany at Sinai took place; but surely there is all the difference in the world between mere presence at an event and crucial participation in it. We need to be content to proceed, at this stage in our knowledge, without finding the supposed source of this thought. It is not essential that we recover the source, however, for Paul's meaning is quite clear. In the statement he asserts his belief that the Law of Moses is at best the product of a second-rate revelation. It seems to me likely that the background of Paul's thought, if there is any (that is, if the matter of angels and intermediaries is not a *tour de force* of his own creation), is this: God is transcendent, yet Moses, living within this world, received the Law from Him. The intervening angels supply the bridge over the gap across which the divine Law passed from God into man's possession.

Paul's assumptions that the Law was subject to time and that it was not a direct revelation of God Himself combine to suggest its innate limitations. Paul is searching for God Himself; the Law of Moses, in his view, is a function not of the divine realm of heaven, but only of this world, and it is too far removed from God Himself for it to be vivid and compelling.

The Law, furthermore, is not something internal in man, such as motive or inspiration, which impels him to a line of action; it is rather an external towards which man, if he wants to observe it, needs to impel himself by means of some inner force. Not that, in Paul's eye, the Law does not contain worthy things. But these things of worth, Paul argues in Romans 2.14-15, are attainable without the Law, as when Gentiles obey the Law without having a Law; they exhibit the effect of the Law but by a law written by nature in their hearts.

Against this background, the difficulties and contrary arguments in Romans 7 become much simpler to understand. The individual who lives by the law of nature, Paul argues, has become transformed into a spiritual being and has an inner motivation. The untransformed person, however, remaining unmotivated, struggles vainly in his effort to observe the Law of Moses. Transformed, and given an inner impetus, the person can achieve the full intent of the Law without difficulty and without the problems of its complex details; untransformed, however, he does not possess the inner strength or resources to cope with that incentive to transgression which inheres in the mere mention of them in the Law.

Romans 7, I have suggested, is hardly an abstract argument, but rather recounts Paul's personal difficulties. It reports the unsettlement and the disturbances within him when he was still within his inherited Judaism. It records what he left behind him when he became a "Christian." He became a "Christian," indeed, when he had the conviction that he had encountered something beyond what had been handed down from subordinate angels and then through an intermediary; he became a Christian when he had the vivid sense of the closest and best possible experience of God. This experience brought him the release from his tension.

Paul's matured attitude towards the Law has unjustly exposed him to the charge of inconsistency. We can be aware of the injustice of the charge if we follow Paul's thought sympathetically. First, since the Law was a product of a revelation, though a second best one, it was a part of Paul's heritage of continuing revelation. Therefore Paul will speak in praise—grudging praise —of the Law. But, second, because it was only a second-rate revelation, Paul will contend that there are limits to the Law. And third, out of a combination of an at best grudging regard for the Law and his conflicts—at Antioch, in Galatia, and elsewhere—a bitterness creeps into him, and in its wake an unfairness about the Law. When these matters are kept in mind as part of the many elements which Paul's mind holds in equilibrium, then one does not rush prematurely into the mistaken judgment that Paul was full of contradictions. There are no real contradictions in his multi-faceted attitude towards the Law.

When we review the rabbinic doctrines about the nature of the Torah, we can see most clearly how the rabbis and Paul take antithetical stands. From the rabbis' standpoint the Torah was eternal, extant even before Moses, so that the patriarchs observed it in advance of Sinai. In Moses' time there was a double revelation, the one in writing, the Pentateuch, and the other oral, and both were equally valid. The oral was in the nature of a supplement to the written; it filled in and it clarified. Whatever growth it seemed to undergo in the millennium and more between Moses' time and the period of the rabbis was not change but merely the extension of the original revelation. The Torah which Moses had received at Sinai he had transmitted to his successor Joshua, and Joshua to his successors, the elders. Thence it had come to the prophets, who gave it to the enigmatic group known as "the men of the great assembly," from whom it was transmitted to several proto-rabbinic pairs of sages, and finally to the rabbis. This accrued revelation consisted in exhortation and injunction; from its legal aspect, the total of the commandments, statutes, and the like numbered, according to rabbinic tabulation, six hundred and thirteen. Of this figure, 365 were prohibitions, or negative commandments, and the remaining 248 were positive.

From whatever stage in the long road from Moses to the rabbis some single law came, that made no difference in its character as revealed law; the totality of the 613 was either explicit or implicit in the revelation at Sinai. Only the negative commandments were obligatory on women; all were required of men. In light of the specification of so many items, God could expect a perfect effort on man's part, but not a perfect performance. Transgression, of omission or of inadvertence, even of commission, was to be expected. Therefore repentance, redress, and atonement were envisaged as means of restoring man after some dereliction. Central to the return to good status was the annual period of penitence, culminating in the Day of Atonement. On the climactic day the individual Jew went through the rites and ceremonies which were designed to bring him back into good standing. The book of Leviticus specifies the rites for the period when the Temple was operative and the priests were presiding over animal sacrifices; after the destruction of the Temple in 70, the rites were altered to prayer, confession, and the like.

Man repented, man atoned and, it was believed, God graciously pardoned. The initiative came from man; he solicited and God responded. The atonement was not for man's general character, not for his sinful*ness,* but for his specific, individual sins. So much for the rabbis.

An initial distinction between Paul and the rabbis is that they use the word sin in quite different senses. Whereas the rabbis mean some specific act which a man may have done, Paul means by sin man's innate condition of being a mixture of body and spirit. One can repent for one's actions; but repentance is hardly to be envisaged for one's innate being. Repentance is a word which occurs in Paul so seldom (Romans 2.4 is virtually the only passage) that the scholars have noted that Paul not only ignores repentance but by implication seems to deny it. Where the rabbis deal with man's repentance and God's gracious forgiveness, Paul deals with man's helplessness and God's gracious redemption.

Christianity took over some holy days from the Jewish calendar—Pentecost, for example. But Yom Kippur, the Day of Atonement, does not enter Christianity. Indeed, its sole mention in the New Testament is in the Epistle to the Hebrews, where it stands in a context of a type of Jewish atonement made by man on his own behalf, completely superseded by the Christian type, in which atonement is made for man by the Christ.

One must not let the circumstances that Paul is a Jew or that he is, in his own way, loyal to the Jewish Bible, obscure the truth, that Pauline Christianity and rabbinic Judaism share little more than a common point of departure, the Bible. They use it, of course, but in manners totally divergent—so much so that they might as well not have had the common point of origin. Indeed, had Christianity followed Paul without deviation, its overlapping with rabbinic Judaism would have been even less than it is. In the sense that to Judaism the Law remained conceived of as thoroughly divine in origin and eternal, and in Paul as limitedly divine and cancellable, one can almost set Pauline Christianity and rabbinic Judaism down as antitheses to each other.

Rabbinic Judaism assumed that the ancient revelation of Law required the subsequent age to be faithful to the revelation by applying its principles and its details to every conceivable situation. Paul, on the other hand, saw the ancient revelation to Moses not as a crucial, decisive event, but as a single milestone in a long road of revelations, whose climax came in Paul's own time. For the rabbis, the climax was in Moses, and Sinai to them was the highest mountain; for Paul, Sinai was only a hill, which had now sunk below the horizon. For Paul revelation was a continuing matter; and as something continuing, its loftiest peak needed to be something in the recent present, or awaiting a near-at-hand future. The rabbis said: God's greatest revelation in the past obligates you to observe His laws; Paul said: Moses revealed a pretty good Law, but there had been a revelation of God to Abraham better and earlier than to Moses, and a revelation in Christ Jesus better and later than to Moses, and Moses' Law is no longer binding.

Certainly with respect to what one would call "the nature of religious experience," Paul and rabbinic Judaism are poles apart. While Judaism did develop its own type of emotionalism, and its own mysticism, these centered about and proceeded from the assumption of the preciousness and the validity of the ancient and abiding revelation through Moses. Paul, on the other hand, proceeded from an assumption of personal communion with God, and of a recent and *a continuing communion* with him.

Insofar as Pentateuch religion provides the main lines of rabbinic thought, and amounts to a kind of principle of religious living, Paul must be credited with either creating or else, at the minimum, re-creating a new and startlingly different principle. In his own eyes, he departed not from Scripture, but from the Law encased in it, for the revelation contained in Scripture had not come to an end, but it had lasted until Paul's time and had come to him too.

Paul the Convert

i. the word convert

In the previous chapter our focus was on Paul's relation to the Jewish ideas from which he was departing. Now we need to look at this transition in a focus on the new conceptions into which he was entering. I shall take the reader to and through some of these conceptions, not for the purpose of giving an exposition of them, but because we can understand Paul the man only in the light of these conceptions.

For many would-be students a traversal of Paul's conceptions is difficult, even to the point of impossibility. Some have tried the journey and quietly given up. Others, on completing the journey, confess that they might as well have stayed at home. Alfred North Whitehead, the late professor of philosophy at Harvard, has said, ". . . The man who, I suppose, did more than anybody else to distort and subvert Christ's teaching was Paul. I wonder what the other disciples thought of him—if they thought anything. Probably they didn't understand what he was up to, and it may well be doubted whether he did himself . . ." *

Paul's thought certainly contains complexities and perplexities. The difficulty in understanding Paul is threefold. First, there is the double presentation of him in the New Testament, once in his genuine Epistles, and a second time in Acts and the Pastoral Epistles. When we separate these two presentations, the task becomes easier.

Second, the difficulty is often not so much in understanding Paul as it is in re-creating the atmosphere and climate of the times. The challenge here involves not so much a capacity to understand as it does a willingness to study a period which is remote from us and greatly different. The results of such study as I have myself pursued it are partly reflected in the preceding chapter; this present chapter provides another part.

The third difficulty is in the nature of the sources, that is, in the kind of materials his Epistles consist of, and in the nature of the circumstance that these chance writings came to be Christian scripture. What I try to do in this chapter is to set forth for the reader a broad view of some relevant portions of Paul's thought. I will need, accordingly, to talk about Paul's views on such subjects as the Christ and "spirit" and the like. The information about these views comes from his Epistles and I shall presently review some significant characteristics of Paul's letters.

But first a caution is necessary before examining what it is that Paul handed down to us. We need to recall, even if again and again, that, aware as he was that there had been a decisive change in his outlook, Paul does not believe that he has departed from Judaism. Rather, he believes that he and those who have come along with him are the authentic Jews; those who have not come along are inauthentic Jews, even though they are Jews by birth and by physical descent from Abraham. Those

* *The Dialogues of Alfred North Whitehead*, p. 307.

who are Jews merely by birth, Paul believes, have undergone both blindness which is temporary, and also a rejection by God scheduled to last for some limited duration, after which God would revert to them.

Accordingly, to speak of Paul the "convert" is to use an uncertain word and to trespass into some ambiguities. It is well to clear these up. In general, modern Jews and modern Christians do not mean precisely the same thing by the word "convert." Jews usually understand conversion as the act of changing from one denomination to another; for example, John Doe, born a Protestant, "converted" to Catholicism. Christians, on the other hand, especially Protestants, stress in conversion not the external act of changing affiliation, but rather the inner religious process; this process may result in a change in formal affiliation, but that is secondary, and it need not happen at all. For as some Protestants use the term, conversion is the process through which one passes from a merely formal and superficial affiliation into a vivid sense of personal belonging. Accordingly, a person may be born a Methodist and be reared in a Methodist Sunday School and church; but when he undergoes "conversion," he does not leave Methodism, but rather he changes from being a Christian by accident of birth into being one through an act of personal experience of God.

From the vantage point of almost two thousand years, perhaps we can conclude that Paul did change his formal affiliation, as it were, from Judaism to what came to be called Christianity. Yet from Paul's own standpoint, he has remained completely within Judaism. From his own vantage point, his "conversion" was not a change of affiliation but a personal experience of God. It was kindred to the sense of personal communion with God which marked the ancient prophets of Israel. I defer until the next chapter recounting Paul's narration of that experience. At this point I only give some of the setting and some of the implications of the experience, but not the experience itself.

Whether one believes or doubts the statement that Paul had

an experience of God, the statement itself is not hard to understand. But between Paul and our understanding of his vivid sense of that experience, lies the paradox of his Epistles: these Epistles constitute both the path we must tread to understand Paul and at the same time their innate character establishes them as obstacles in our course.

What sort of writing are his Epistles? They are, for the most part, the quick and urgent notes dictated by a traveler. The "conversion" experience yielded a compulsion in Paul to have others benefit from his experience and example, so he traveled about exhorting people. He found himself saying things which he needed to explain. This latter was especially the case when he was either not fully understood or else misunderstood. The Epistles are one side of a two-sided correspondence. They are largely the answers to questions which were put to him by people of one place after Paul had left that location and arrived at a second place. The precise questions put to Paul have not survived to our day; we try to infer from Paul's answers what these questions were.

In the answers which his Epistles give to questions, Paul inevitably touches on issues of metaphysics, an area laden with difficulties. To understand today the particular metaphysics of a remote period would be difficult enough if we dealt with direct and straightforward exposition. Paul's Epistles are not straightforward exposition. If we are properly to assess the content of Paul's experience and of his statements, we need to remind ourselves that the Epistles represent random answers to random questions. We need to recognize, as is now uniformly the scholarly conclusion, that Paul was not a theologian. That is to say, he was not primarily a systematic thinker, not a definer of terms, and not a classifier of the views, opinions, and expressions of either contemporaries or predecessors.

Many interpreters have tended to make undue inference from Paul's utterances and this often has led them into extravagances. Principally, the error has been to make Paul seem to say things which Paul did not say, and which he could not possibly have meant.

It is regrettable to report that in the interpretative literature, terms which he uses casually are scrutinized from various angles and facets, as though Paul chose them from a list of synonyms; untenable distinctions in words and phrases are elaborately set forth; and the great apostle is made to mean as many different and contradictory things by modern scholars as he was by ancient church exegetes who put no curb on their fancies. It is no exaggeration that were Paul to have available in translation into his native Greek some of the expositions of his thought as these appear in English, French and German (and Scandinavian), he would not understand them. The error that such studies uniformly make is that they go from the legitimate effort to explain the sense of this or that term into the illegitimate discovery of subtle deductions and distinctions which were foreign to Paul's thought and intent. The custom of committing him to some supposed precision of expression has arisen; the elementary consideration is overlooked that Paul's letters were, except possibly in the case of Romans, not premeditated, not tracts designed for eternity, but simply business letters dealing each with some concrete situation and specific question. In addition, the Epistles were mostly dictated—and that means that they were not elaborately edited and re-edited as though they were essays by a stylist. Moreover, as a random collection, they reflect only a portion of Paul's total thought, not all of it.

Whenever one reads a systematic study of Paul's doctrine, the system is that of his interpreter; it is never Paul's own. Paul had no metaphysical system.

Yet it chances that Paul in his responsive Epistles does touch on aspects of some major problems in theology; the solutions which he offered came in part to be authoritative when his writings came to be regarded as Scripture. Hence there is the paradox about Paul that although he was not himself a theologian and certainly not a systematic one, he is the prime source of

Christian theology. Indeed, even more than that. He is the early source of later views some of which were to be regarded as orthodox, and some of which were to be denounced as heretical.

As I have said before, I am persuaded that in Paul's mind there was never any basic inconsistency. Yet that which is involved in any exposition and explanation of the Christ-Jesus is inevitably apt to be bound up in potential inconsistency. Paul, in his Epistles, was attesting to his experiences or advising churches what to do about or in certain situations. Therefore Paul's "theology" is indirect and coincidental. When it is fragmentized by commentators, its coincidental quality yields, to the unrestrained commentators, more distinctions than Paul ever could have thought of.

But even when we can hear Paul's voice above the din of the centuries which adulated him, his thought itself contains the difficulty inherent in metaphysics in general, and in Graeco-Jewish metaphysics in particular. The Christ-Jesus, to Paul partly God and partly human, is central to whatever theology there is in Paul. The metaphysical paradox of the "God-man" idea is sufficient in itself to yield a harvest of apparent (but unreal) contradictions. It is in the Christ-Jesus that Paul believed he had encountered God. A natural question arises: just what does it mean that "Paul encountered God, specifically in Christ-Jesus"? This question is inevitably bound up with what is basic in Paul, and, though its answer is necessarily complex, we must not shun it.

ii. the Christ

In an age in which Greek thought had relegated God to some position outside the world, and in which Jewish thought, in the matured view in the Bible, had declared that God was invisible and imperceptible to the senses, Paul struggles with the problem of how man can get to God Himself.

The answer for Paul is found in his view of who, or rather what, Christ was, and it involves a distinction which we can make, even though Paul himself does not make it explicitly. It is the difference between the *function* which the Christ serves in Paul's thought, and the *nature* of the Christ in it. I understand enough of the function of electricity to be able to use it. I turn on a light, I plug in a razor, I watch television. Perhaps others understand the *nature* of electricity, but, being neither a scientist nor an engineer, I do not. But I know how electricity functions.

Let us first try to understand Paul's view of the nature of the Christ—that is, just what was the Christ? Paul inherits from his Christian predecessors the view that there was a man Jesus who was more than a man. To be sure, Jesus had a human existence, but that was merely the human phase of a being which was essentially divine and which had, for a period of time, become man. The Christ, then, was that divine being which became Jesus.

The first description to which we turn is the celebrated kenosis ("emptying") passage in Philippians 2.6-11: "Though he [the Christ] was divine by nature, he did not snatch at equality with God but *emptied* himself by taking the nature of a servant; born in human guise and appearing in human form, he humbly stooped in his obedience even to die, and to die upon the cross. Therefore God raised him high and conferred upon him a Name above all names, so that before the name of Jesus every knee should bow in heaven and earth and under the earth, and every tongue confess that Jesus Christ is Lord, to the glory of God, the father." * Here, in telling us about the Christ, Paul is indulging in, or quoting approvingly, language which is mythological; the obscure reference in the passage seems to scholars unmistakably to be a motif found in other writings too, that of the primeval rebellion of the evil angels against God. The Christ, Paul is saying, was a divine heavenly being, but not so haughty a rebel as were the evil angels. The Christ was lower than God and became the man Jesus. As a divine being, the Christ was a "spirit"; on be-

* The Holy Bible, translated by James Moffatt. Harper & Brothers, 1925.

coming Jesus, the Christ took on a physical human body. "Incarnation" means to change into a body. *The* Incarnation is the customary term for describing the change from the divine spirit into the physical Jesus.

So far, then, we see Christ in a passage from Paul with mythological overtones. In addition to the mythological, Paul also uses metaphorical language. This is the case when he speaks of the Christ as the Son of God. Paul does not mean that Jesus was God's son. He means that the Christ (which, in a phase, became Jesus) was an "off-shoot" of God. Did Paul envisage some difference between the "emptying" divine being, and the "son"? I doubt it! These are simply two different ways of describing the same thing, and there is still a third way which Paul uses—and even a fourth and a fifth.

The third term Paul uses is the inherited Jewish term Christ, but in a new and different sense. The Hebrew word means "the anointed." Anointing meant nothing to Greeks; it was a Semitic practice, a rite used in appointing someone a king. The "anointed one" was without either meaning or significance to Greek pagans; Paul, though he retains the ancient Jewish term, used it not so much as a term, but as a title; it is very much the equivalent in his thought of a fourth term, Lord. To the term Lord we will return.

Furthermore, if the Epistle to the Colossians is by Paul, or a reflection by a close disciple of Paul's thought, then Paul also uses as a fifth term the philosophical term *logos* in application to the Christ. (Or, let us say, even though the word is absent from the genuine Epistles, the concept is at least partly present.) *Logos* is neither simple to explain nor to understand. Perhaps an example may clarify matters.

There is an electric light within my room, and it serves my needs. A power plant is located on the Ohio River about eight miles from my home; I have never visited it, for it is quite remote from me. I myself have no direct contact with the power plant, but only with the electricity which comes into my home; and within my home there are available the effects of what the power plant can supply.

Now let us imagine that the power plant occupies the place of God, who has been conceived of as remote from this world; the electricity entering into my home is an off-shoot of the power plant. It is not the same as the power plant, but for me it serves in lieu of the power plant. So, in the time of Paul it was conceived by some that God Himself was remote from this world, but an aspect, or an offshoot of God, was within the world, just as electricity is within my home.

This immanent ("within this world") aspect or offshoot of God is called by Philo and by others the "Logos." If you start with the belief that God is remote (like the power plant), you deal with or encounter God in the facet which is immanent (like the electricity in my home).

Perhaps now the intent of Paul can be grasped, though there is still one step more to take. At this point the reader should understand that there are areas of great similarity in Paul and Philo's approach. To my knowledge Philo has never been called "un-Jewish" for holding to this metaphysical view of God and his Logos. What is different in Paul and what leads to the adjective un-Jewish is his assertion that the "off-shoot" took the human form of Jesus—and in consequence the Christ Jesus was really a divine being. To Jews this latter step has almost invariably meant an un-Jewish deification of a man. *Paul has no such deification view in his mind at all.* Such views are found in Christian writings but they are not Paul's. Incarnation, in fact, is the opposite of deification, for it supposes that a divine being has become human. That the man Jesus, being the incarnation of a divine being, was for the period of the incarnation super-human, smacks of deification, and contributes to a broad misunderstanding. But Paul does not deify Jesus; rather he humanizes the divine Christ.

Philo, in at least one passage, somewhat similarly humanizes beings which he believes are divine. He tells us that three visitors who came to Abraham (in Genesis 18) were divine beings who had become incarnate. The incarnation of divine beings, then, was not limited to Paul. The Hellenistic ideas in him are not usually assessed in as balanced a way as are those of Philo; in reality, however, they have as much or as little a Jewish matrix as Philo's own thought. The matter can be put in this way: Paul believed that Philo's logos had had an interval on earth in the form of Jesus. To the divine offshoot of God which Philo called the logos, Paul gives in this new sense the traditional title Christ.

In holding the view which subsequent generations have called un-Jewish, Paul himself never had any sense other than that he was fully within the frame of reference of his inherited Greek Judaism. It is not the one idea of the Incarnation alone which accounts for the separation after Paul's time, and through Paul's work, of Judaism and Christianity. These other ideas we shall consider in due course, though the principal one, the abrogation of the Law of Moses, we have already discussed.

The point here is that, in spite of some differences, Paul's Christ and Philo's logos have a clear relationship to each other. There is, of course, at least this significant difference: Philo's logos is a metaphysical abstraction, not a reality. On the other hand, the Christ for Paul was a real being, who, though eternal, came into a historical series of events as Jesus.

Now Paul shifts his figure from mythology ("kenosis"), to metaphor ("son of God"), or to metaphysics ("Logos"), without any sense of saying something contradictory or inconsistent. What he is trying to describe is by its very nature almost beyond description. Some of the titles which Paul applies to the Christ, such as "son of God," Philo applies to the Logos. We need not be surprised, therefore, that a mind such as Paul's which was not that of a rigid philosopher chose a variety of media for expressing its content. When Paul tells, as he does in several different passages, that he saw the Risen Christ, he is telling us that he had the most feasible vision of God which the metaphysics of his day provided. To have seen the Risen Christ is virtually equal in effect to having seen God, for God Himself was invisible. Paul's conversion was not so much his being persuaded by the emissaries of the new movement that they were speaking the truth. Rather, his conversion was his sense of personal experience of the Christ whom the emissaries talked about.

Because Paul had this sense of experiencing God, he felt that there were some far-reaching consequences. In his preaching he set forth these consequences, and in passing we get both clear and also blurred reflections of his mental processes.

It seems quite clear, for example, that Paul's thought keeps Christ distinct from God (just as we can keep distinct the electricity in our home and the remote power plant). God he speaks of by the Greek word *Theos,* God. The Christ, however, he terms Lord* (*Kyrios* in the Greek). Paul conceives of the Christ-Lord-Logos-Son of God as a pre-existent being who became incarnate and had in Jesus a human career, and who had reverted after the crucifixion to the side of God, to await the coming occasion of the universal judgment. So much for the nature of the Christ.

Now though it is unmistakable that for Paul the Christ seems to be some entity both connected to and yet distinct from God, I would insist that in the totality of Paul's thought, it is quite a subordinate matter just what or just who the Christ was. The issue in the time after Paul was, What was the nature of the Christ? Respecting Paul, though, the real issue is what function the Christ fills. The answer we have already seen. Christ (or the Lord, or the Son of God, or the Logos) is the vessel through which Paul attains what for him is the most feasible and the

* These words derive from the Greek translation of the Bible, and in it they are interchangeable and synonymous, just as they are for Jews and many Christians today. The synonymity is evident in the Jewish affirmation "The Lord our God the Lord is one." On the other hand, though, Philo makes a distinction between the words God and Lord, yet not the same distinction which Paul makes.

fullest communion in the world with the God who is remote and outside the world. There are laborious discussions in the interpretive literature as to whether there is in Paul a "Christ-mysticism" or a "God-mysticism." These discussions are totally meaningless. For Paul there is no viable distinction. And, accordingly, the interpreters who embrace one side in the partisan discussion of whether Paul's thought was "Christocentric" or "theocentric" are discussing a matter at which Paul would have snorted. To Paul theocentric mysticism was attainable only in the form of Christ-mysticism.

At the risk of belaboring the point about God and the Christ, I shall try to illustrate my meaning by two examples. First, if I do not know German, the only medium through which I can know Goethe is a translation. I may express some random judgments on the character of the translation which I am using, but my basic choice is to use the medium or not to know the source. The transcendentalism of Paul's environment made it inescapable that he should need a medium, the Christ, by which to get to God. But I would insist that it is God, not the medium, which concerns Paul.

Christ to Paul is not interchangeable with God; Christ is subordinate to God. But he is not a "mediator," in the sense of one totally and essentially different from him on whose behalf he functions; he is, rather, the agent who is virtually the same. The mythological language which Paul uses, especially "Son of God," and the sense of separateness of Christ from God, are deceptive; Paul intends a certain distinction: he consistently maintains a differentiation between God and Lord. But an understanding of the totality of Paul's thought is a corrective against misinterpretation at this point.

Let us dispose of "mediator" once and for all. The genuine Epistles of Paul never use the word *mesites* of Christ, but only of Moses, Gal. 3.19-20.

The term is found in Hebrews 8.6; 9.15; 12.24 and I Tim. 2.5 referring to Christ—but these writings are not from Paul.

While there is from the standpoint of modern analysis an obvious mediatorial function to the Christ in Paul's conception, such intermediation falls considerably short of his regarding the Christ as a mediator. He does not. It may appear to us that in Paul's view Christ acts *for* God; but in Paul's thought God acts *in* Christ. It is in the post-Pauline period that "Christ the mediator" is born and developed; the seed is unconsciously present in Paul, but as yet the seed is far from sprouting.

Perhaps this discussion is reducible to a semantic problem. But I believe that it is much more than that, though I concede it partakes of semantics. Perhaps I shall accomplish the objective of my argument if I make it clear that in my judgment the Christ is in Paul's mind the vessel through which divine salvation takes place here on earth; but the Christ is not in itself, or himself, if one prefers, the autonomous dispenser of that salvation. Or, let us say, it is not Paul's belief that Christ has saved him, but rather that God has saved him through Christ. The light bulb is in my room; it gives me light; it, in turn, obtains from the power plant the electricity by which it sheds the light. That is, the electricity, an off-shoot from the power plant, comes into my room and in the form of a bulb gives me light. Let the lead-in wire be severed, and the bulb does not function.

Our second example in clarifying God and Christ in Paul's thought concerns Exodus 3.4, when God was revealed to Moses in the burning bush. Let us set up a proportion so that we can see the relation of the revelation of God to the instrumentality through which it is performed: God (in Exodus) is to the burning bush, as God (in Pauline thought) is to Christ. The burning bush is not God; it is distinct from him. The bush is the vehicle in which God is revealed.

I may become only mildly curious about that bush, or else pre-occupied with it. I may want to know its botanical name, its classification, whether it grows from a seed or bulb, whether it produces buds or flowers or propagates in some other way—in short, I may seek all kinds of information about it. I may obtain this information and thereafter I may convey it. In doing so I may occasionally use the technical language of botanists, or the adjectives of aesthetes, or even try to paint a picture of it. If Paul was interested in setting forth a plain and clear statement of the metaphysics of God and Christ, his Epistles, alas, chance to lack such a classification. It seems clear that this was not his intention. Similarly, Exodus includes no effort to classify the burning bush; there it was merely the instrument of revelation. It is in this sense of an instrument of revelation that the burning bush and the Christ have a facet in common.

Paul, to repeat, at no time in his preserved Epistles stops to give us either a full, or precise, or accurate description of the Christ; he tells us only things which occur to him in other connections. It was the generations after Paul who became, as it were, the botanists and who plunged into their laborious, and often polemical, analyses of the precise nature of the Christ.

The burning bush was only one minor instrumentality in which revelation took place. From Paul's vantage point, this was long years ago. The Christ, to him, was the major, indeed the climactic, vehicle of revelation; this was both in the recent past and continued into the present. The bush was a mere shrub, related to other earthly shrubs; the Christ was a pre-existent, divine being, primarily related not to earth, but to God.

The Christian tradition, even within the New Testament, began to let its fancy play around the definitions and significations of the Christ. The New Testament literature later than Paul became more clearly explanatory, but it did not exalt the Christ beyond Paul's own exaltation of him. When we move beyond Paul's time, we do encounter extensions of the "doctrine of the Christ." We do not, however, move into any higher Christology ("conception of the Christ"). We move into the more theosophic, as in John, or the more idiosyncratic, as in Hebrews (Christ as a Priest). Ultimately, outside and later than the New Testament, the full resources of Neo-Platonism and of Stoicism were to enter in to define the Christ as indeed the logos of traditional Greek thought, as in the Alexandrian Fathers. But New Testament literature begins, in the Epistles of Paul, with the highest Christology within the New Testament.

It is of no great importance that in speaking of the Christ Paul uses interchangeably the language of Greek Judaism, or Stoicism, or myth, or philosophy, or the mystery religions. He is not thereby guilty of illogic or wavering. The aspect of now this form, now that form in which he couches his expression falsely suggests a conflict or indecision in Paul's mind. His terminology may imply inconsistency, but there is a full and total integrity in his mind.

For fundamental is the circumstance that the Christ is not for Paul a matter of definition, but a matter of his personal experience. The theologian is under the obligation to define and explain, to elucidate and classify the abstraction of his dialectic. The mystic, however, deals with what he has personally encountered. The theologian sorts, classifies and synthetizes ideas; the mystic only attests to experience.

iii. the mystic experience

Paul was a mystic who encountered God—in the form of Christ. Paul's "conversion" is the change wrought in him because of that experience. As a result of it, Paul sees what to him are new and heightened insights within his inherited and precious Judaism.

Now we must be more specific about the character of this heightened insight. In my judgment, no term better serves initially to classify the convert Paul than the word "prophet." Paul had the sense of a call from God, of communion with him, and of a commission from God.

When one reflects that mysticism and prophecy always emerge from some specific context, then the true way to assess Paul becomes clearer. In the older prophets, we understand Amos in the light of our knowledge of the eighth pre-Christian century,

Isaiah in the light of the portentous appearance of the Assyrians on the horizon in that same century, Jeremiah in the teeming days of the Deuteronomic Reformation and the Babylonian invasion a hundred years after Isaiah. Amos deals with the accrued social injustice of the settled agricultural north, as witnessed by a shepherd from the pastoral south; hence the substance of Amos' message is that God disapproves of the conduct rampant in Israel, especially of the extravagances of cult. Isaiah, fervently convinced that Israel should trust in God and not in alliances, sets forth that God will punish Israel for its infidelity by bringing in a destructive foe—a foe which is a tool of God, and not at all its own master. Jeremiah's early message dealt with Israel's faithlessness to Yahve in its pre-occupation with Baal practices; when the destruction came, and again he prophesied out of a specific context, he spoke about a new and better covenant; the tone of his addresses changed from that of doom to that of encouragement.

Perhaps the above is sufficient to indicate what is meant by the substance of the prophet's message being conditioned by his own time. Paul's activity was between 35 and 55 in Grecian lands of the Roman Empire. We must not expect the eighth century Amos to say precisely the same thing which Jeremiah said after the Babylonian invasion in 597; nor shall we anticipate from Paul some message akin to what Haggai and Zechariah taught about 516. The substance of what Paul says is determined by his time and place; the form of his communion with God is shaped by it; but the essence of his experience is quite unchanged from that of the whole succession of Old Testament prophecy.

As Amos (9.1) saw God standing on the altar and as Isaiah (Chapter 6) saw Him seated on the high and lofty throne in the Temple, and as Jeremiah reported (1.4-10) his dialogue with God, so Paul experienced God in terms of Paul's own environment and personality—God as revealed in Christ Jesus. Like the prophet, Paul wanted people to know about his experience, and, if possible, to share in it.

Paul's tremendous labors as a missionary are to be understood as the consequence of his sense of experiencing God. It is wrong to think of him as a traveling missionary who had mystic experiences; it is correct to think of him as a man who conceived his prophetic-like commission to be that of a traveling missionary.*

It is characteristic for the mystic who believes that he has encountered the God of a historic faith to feel that the external worship in that faith is relatively unimportant and dispensable. In this latter regard, Paul is in line with the prevailing trend of the pre-exilic prophets of Israel.†

Accordingly, we need to modify what we have said above about Paul and the Law of Moses. The matters of natural law and of specific laws, of the Unwritten and Written are merely the environmental factors which supply the form in which Paul's justifying arguments are expressed. Paul represents a return to older Hebrew prophecy.

Paul confronts a situation different from that of Amos, Isaiah, and Jeremiah. These pre-exilic prophets denied the validity of ritual ceremony or of a written code at a time previous to the existence of the Pentateuch, for the latter, in spite of its traditional ascription to Moses, is a post-exilic compilation, coming no less than a century after Jeremiah's time, and almost five centuries before Paul's. But by Paul's time the Pentateuch had become

* In the same way in which it is unyielding to press Paul's writings in their theoretical aspects into some elaborate structure, it is also unyielding to bog down in petty details about the geography of his missionary labors. While it is obvious that a normal curiosity about his travels should excite those who study him, one need only glance at the endless reams of paper filled with expositions of the North Galatian hypothesis and the South Galatian hypothesis to see how futile is the straining to recover from the limited and contradictory evidence what the true facts are about the Galatian sojourn. That Paul used theological terms and that he traveled about and that he founded churches are petty concerns compared with the recognition that Paul is in the line of Old Testament prophets, and that he believes that he has had an experience such as they had.

† Notice, too, how the Quakers, for whom religious experience is primarily illumination by the Holy Spirit, have done away with virtually all the externals of religion.

the very center of his religious heritage. Amos could ignore it, for it did not exist; Paul (and Philo) must deal with it and account for it.

Paul's denial of the validity of the Pentateuchal legislation is akin to Amos' denial of ritual sacrifice (5.21-22) and to Jeremiah's denial of the existence of any valid written code (7.21-22). The impetus in all the cases was identical; the end result was the same: Communion is the only essential, and ritual is useless. What is different is only the environment and the particulars confronted.

What is a prophet? He is someone who believes, or is believed by others, that he communes with God. In ancient times one way of expressing this kind of belief was to speak of the prophet as having the "holy Spirit" within him or "poured out" on him.

The word spirit has become by our time a vague and ambiguous word. In our day we usually use it in the sense of something which is intangible, "immaterial." The adjective spiritual in our time appears in contrasts such as this: "It is all right for a business man to be concerned about money and property, but a preacher (or a rabbi) ought to be interested in spiritual things." Often, by spirit or spiritual we have in mind things which are not only not material, but which have no genuine, tangible existence.

To take another example, we no longer believe in ghosts, even on Halloween. Such a "ghost"—for which the word *spirit* is a synonym—is certainly without a body, yet it is in some way regarded as a discrete entity. To put it in another way, such a ghost (if he were still believed) is not in a body, as you and I are, but is disembodied; yet, though disembodied, it is still something. In our usual speech and thought, though, by spirit we mean a thing which is nothing material.

It was quite otherwise in the ancient world, for the ancients stood at approximately the place where we should stand if we believed that ghosts, though not material, were something. Basic to the meaning of "spirit" was the sense of "breath"—and it is to be remembered that on cold mornings we can see our breath.

Ordinary people, of course, breathed ordinary breath. But there was in addition the breath of demons or the breath of God. The former would be an evil spirit, the latter the Holy Spirit (or, as it used to be known, the Holy Ghost).

It was believed that if either of these extraordinary types of spirit came into a person, the man was thereby bound to be different in his action from his usual behavior. Irrational or insane men were thought to have been entered by some evil spirit. On the other hand, pious men had been entered by the Holy Spirit; such, for example, were the prophets of old.

The influence of the spirit (evil or holy) on the individual was clearly to be discerned in that person's actions. Accordingly, when a person was entered by the Holy Spirit, he was transformed from his former conduct into something different; such a transformation was almost as if the person was born anew. "Rebirth," indeed, came to be a characteristic term to describe such a transformation; the Gospel According to John 3 records that naivete of one Nicodemus who on being urged to undergo "rebirth" replies that a man, full grown, can hardly enter his mother's womb to be born again; Nicodemus' "misunderstanding" is the point of departure in the Gospel for a monologue on "spiritual rebirth."

iv. the transformation

A "convert," in Paul's view, is one who has undergone this "spiritual rebirth." He is no longer the man he used to be, whose actions are predicated on his senses and passions; to use Paul's phrase, such a man is one who "has died to the body." If a person has "died to the body," then it stands to reason that he is now "spiritual." Such, indeed, is Paul's own boast—though at one point, Philippians 3.10-12, modesty compels him to deny that he has as yet quite achieved full spirituality or full perfection.

How seriously, that is, how literally, did Paul think of his transformation from the material to the spiritual? There can be no mistake about it; he means it with the utmost literalness. Or, to state it negatively: It does not mean merely that Paul is more moral than before, or more ethical, or that his opinions have been altered, or that his views have been modified. No, in the plainest sense of the terms Paul means that the very substance of his being has been changed. He is no longer the physical, and thereby mortal vessel of clay; rather, he is now the immortal being of spirit. His soul is still encased within its prison the body—but that impediment, which will disappear at death, can be modified and thereby overcome while Paul is still alive.

This transformation, conceived to have taken place literally, occurred in, and is to be equated with Paul's experience of Christ; his missionary activity is directed towards persuading those who hear him to imitate his own example, of imitating Christ, and to become spiritual as Christ was and as Paul has become. A man with the plain, ordinary spirit within him is a simple, ordinary man ("psychic man" is Paul's term, I Cor. 15.45ff.). But when this man has the Holy Spirit infused within him, he becomes something quite other.

In Paul's view, such was the experience of Jesus. For Jesus was a man born of woman; when infused with the Holy Spirit, Jesus became the Christ Jesus. Or, to alter the figure, as Paul himself did, Jesus became the Lord Jesus, or the Lord, or the Son of God. As the man Jesus could become the Christ Jesus, so Paul, or one of his hearers, could become a Son of God.

Now if the mathematical equation of man plus Holy Spirit equals a transformed and hence spiritual man, then equally mathematically the transformed man minus the Spirit is the ordinary mortal man. The Spirit, then, is a kind of entity which can be added to a man. In Paul's thought, the term "Christ" is at times only another metaphor for the Holy Spirit. The "Christ Jesus" is Jesus plus the Holy Spirit. But when Paul speaks of "Christ is within you," he obviously has in mind no such incongruous matter as some physical being contained within another; and when he speaks with great frequence of someone being "in Christ," he has in mind no similarly far-fetched image.

Paul's thought touches on matters about which later theologians quarreled, and which became issues in church councils, namely: what was the relationship between the man Jesus and the Christ? But Paul does not exhibit any impulse to define the relationship. It is beyond mistake, however, to recognize that sometimes when Paul speaks of "Christ" he means no more than Holy Spirit; sometimes he means the particular combination of Holy Spirit with Jesus. When he speaks of the Christ dying for us, he obviously means the combination of Jesus and the Holy Spirit. And when we understand the rough equivalence of Christ to the Holy Spirit, the metaphorical language that he used, such as the term Son of God, becomes clear. Paul does not in any sense mean that Jesus was the Son of God; it is always the Christ Jesus who fills that role. Obviously, if the language is only metaphor, there could be in Paul, as we have said, no semblance of what developed after his time, the doctrine of the virgin birth of Jesus. This latter motif, which is widely paralleled in pagan literature, in part represents metaphor turned into supposed reality, and in part it is one of several discordant answers found in the New Testament to the post-Pauline question: Granted that Jesus was the divine Christ, just when did he become that? That is, just when did the Christ and Jesus merge into one? The answer in the Gospel of Mark suggests that the occasion was his baptism, at which time Jesus was "adopted" as the Son of God. Luke and Matthew suggest that it was at the moment of birth; John gives the answer of "Incarnation": that is to say, in John's view there never was a union of the Christ with the human Jesus, but rather the pre-existent Christ, a spirit, became for the time transformed into the man Jesus.

The view of the Incarnation in Paul is near to John's. Either adoptionism or the virgin birth suggests that Jesus became the Christ. Incarnation, on the other hand, suggests that the Christ *became* Jesus, and seems to me to be quite remote from Mark and Markan "adoptionism"; it is equally remote from Luke and Matthew in whose Gospels we find the virgin birth. But this is to speak in negatives; what affirmatively was Paul's thought about the Incarnation?

The answer to the question requires the preliminary word that in Paul's Epistles there seems little reflection of any need or desire to explain Incarnation, neither with respect to when it took place in the career of Jesus, nor how it took place. There seems, indeed, to be only one passage which touches the question, Romans 1.3-4: ". . . His son, who was descended from David according to the flesh and designated Son of God in power according to the Spirit of holiness by his resurrection from the dead." The passage is difficult and is assessed with great variety among the interpreters. An extreme position denies that the verses are genuine. An intermediate position declares that the earliest view, of Palestinian Jewish Christians, was "adoptionist," that the latest view, that as in John, was incarnationist, and that our passage in Romans represents a way station from adoptionism to incarnationism, and is Paul's harmonization of his own view with those of his predecessors. Still another view focuses its attention on the Greek word rendered by "designated," and distinguishes between what the Christ *was* and what the universal *recognition* was.

Though Paul makes it very plain that the Christ was a preexistent spiritual being who (or which) became incarnate in Jesus, Paul does not tell us enough about Jesus, in whom he believes the Christ became incarnate, for us to know very much about Paul's view of Incarnation. He had made the decision, according to II Cor. 5.16, to stop regarding Christ from a human point of view; this decision effectively prevents us from knowing whatever Paul may have thought about the Jesus in whom he believed the Christ was incarnate. Later on we shall ask why Paul made this decision.

Indeed, to go a step further, that Gospel which is most

nearly in accord with Paul's view of Christ as a pre-existent being is the Fourth Gospel. It says not one word about virgin birth, or the baptism of Jesus, or the temptation; that is to say, it omits, or does not know, these things which the Synoptic Gospels, Mark, Matthew, and Luke, provide as the information about the Jesus in whom the Christ was Incarnate. In its own way, the Fourth Gospel, like Paul, abstains from telling us many matters which arouse our curiosity.

Then, to ask the question again, what was Paul's view of the Incarnation? The answer is that we know from Paul's Epistles only one side of it, the side that became incarnate, and we do not know very much about that into which it became incarnate. We know from Paul about the Christ; but he tells us almost nothing of Jesus.

To revert now to the main line of our argument, the Holy Spirit plus the man Jesus, total up as the Christ Jesus. This Holy Spirit, however, exists apart from its occasion of Incarnation in Jesus. It has also come into Paul and hence Paul's eminence. Or, to alter the figure as Paul himself does, Paul is a man "in Christ." This latter phrase, which is frequent in Paul's letters, is an expression which often means roughly, "being infused with the Holy Spirit."

A glance at a few other passages is the necessary preliminary to the conclusion to which we are tending. In Gal. 2.20 Paul says: "I have been crucified with Christ, and it is no longer I who live, but Christ who lives in me." That Christ, or Lord, means "Spirit" is expressly stated in II Cor. 3.18: "The Lord means the Spirit, and wherever the Spirit of the Lord is, there is open freedom." Or, let us select the most striking verse from an entire chapter which deals with the matter, Romans 8.9: ". . . You are in the Spirit, if the Spirit of God really dwells in you. Anyone who does not have the Spirit of Christ does not belong to him." And finally, on several occasions Paul uses the word *fellowship:* ". . . God who called you to this fellowship with his Son Jesus Christ the Lord" (I Cor. 1.9); "The cup of blessing which we bless, is it not a fellowship of the blood of Christ? . . ." (I Cor. 10.16); and II Cor. 13.14 with its closing salutation, ". . . The Fellowship of the Holy Spirit be with you all."

When Paul speaks, as he does frequently, of his transformation, what he means is that at one time he was a plain, ordinary, common sort of man. He cannot, nor does he want to, deny his human origin. But his present status, and his future destiny, are no longer mortal. To put it in one way, but to mean it with utmost seriousness, Paul has become a "Christ-like being"; or, to use a phrase from the pagan literature, Paul has become a "divine man." The experience of Jesus in having become the Christ, is Paul's experience too; and as Paul has imitated Jesus, so should his own followers imitate him and become "divine men" whose destiny is no longer death and whose bondage is no longer the human subjection to the demands or the tyranny of the body.

By imitation of the Christ, Paul means something more than a substitute or a later experience; perhaps a better English equivalent, in place of "imitation," is "sharing." The ritual experiences which Paul confirms as being authentic and valid are two, baptism and what came to be called the Eucharist. In baptism one not only imitates, but shares in the experience of the Christ Jesus who died; we read in Gal. 3.27: ". . . All of you who were baptized into Christ did put on the Christ"; or as Moffatt translates Romans 6.3-4: 'Surely you know that all of us who have been baptized into Christ Jesus have been baptized into his death. Our baptism into his death made us share his burial . . ." As for the Eucharist, we have already noticed the passage in I Cor. 10.16 that the "cup of blessing" is a "fellowship" with the blood, and the broken bread, with the body.

To keep our perspective on the significance of these two ritual acts, we must recall that, of the festival and ritual occasions of Paul's inherited Judaism, which includes the Sabbath, the New Year, the Day of Atonement, Hanukka, Purim, Tabernacles, Passover, and Pentecost, only the latter two are preserved and propagated in early Christianity. The Christian Pentecost is marked by an event with the end result that a Jewish occasion was taken over, re-interpreted into Christian experience,* and then preserved. So, too, did Passover in a sense become Easter. Paul in his Epistles mentions the occasion of Pentecost, probably in its Jewish sense, in I Cor. 16.8, respecting his intention to remain at Ephesus until that time. He uses the word "Passover" in I Cor. 5.7, but it is likely that he means there the title of the sacrifice for the festival and not the festival itself.

The Pentecost and the Passover abide in Christian tradition, for they become "Christian" by virtue of symbolizing events which transpired recently, and within Christian experience. But the purely Jewish festivals, recalling very ancient events, recede and disappear from Christianity. Surprisingly, the holy days are virtually lacking in Paul the Jew. In their place, Paul emphasizes the two ritual acts—baptism and the Eucharist—both of which are more than mere memorials. They are rather a medium for mystic sharing in the experience of the Christ.

That Paul instituted baptism and the Eucharist is hardly to be maintained. Not only did Judaism contain such rites, or at least similar ones, but we know that pagan religion also possessed them. When Paul contends, as he does in I Cor. 11.23, that the information about the Eucharist which he has passed on to the Corinthians came from the Lord, it is unthinkable that Paul is making the claim that these ceremonial acts are the result of his own initiation. The sense of what he means by having "received from the Lord" requires some explanation. It is reasonable to suppose that Christians before Paul observed these ceremonies. But the significance of these ceremonies underwent a transformation with Paul. It is, then, the significance of these ritual acts which can reasonably be attributed to Paul and which he states was a revelation. The older Jewish baptism was either a direct act of washing or a symbolic washing away of sins; with Paul,

* Acts 2 relates that on Pentecost the Holy Spirit, appearing like tongues of fire, rested on the Christians in Jerusalem.

baptism is transformed into a symbol of dying with Christ. The wine and the bread were the ordinary Jewish ways of beginning a festival dinner; with Paul, they become the mystic sharing in Christ's death. It follows, of course, that the Gospel passages Mark 14.22-25, Matthew 26.26-29, and Luke 22.14-33* are post-Pauline and are dependent upon the passage in I Corinthians. These passages describe Jesus as instituting and commanding the Eucharist with precisely the meaning and import which Paul had created for it.

Now, though Paul conceives of the Eucharist in part as a memorial of the Lord, the function of these quasi-sacramental acts is mystic. They are in perfect accord with Paul's thought and intuition, that he is in direct communion with God. The commentators have noted that the same Paul who denied the efficacy of the Jewish ritual endorsed the nascent Christian ritual. One school of commentators has attributed inconsistency to Paul—and on the surface it is certainly present. Another group has deemed it desirable to protect the great apostle from the devastating insult, and has resorted to tortuous and ingenious arguments which deny even the surface inconsistency. It seems to me that we accomplish a double purpose by recognizing the different planes on which the respective ritual acts were conceived. It acknowledges the presence of inconsistency, and at the same time it explains and justifies it, if one will accept Paul's premises: Those ceremonies, part of the Jewish heritage, which were only memorials, only echoes of the actions of God in the remote past, are to Paul ineffective; but those which in their execution bring present communion with the living God are both worthy of observance and of perpetuation. The memorial aspect of ceremonies is of little concern to Paul; it is the union with God here and now which excites him.

Accordingly, when Paul alludes to some revelation respecting the Eucharist, he does not have in mind the initiation of the

* A textual, and therefore procedural, problem exists in Luke.

rite, but rather his own intuitive transformation of it from the mere memorial into the vehicle of communion with God in Christ.

v. the benefit

We need now to consider some of the elements concerned with the dying with Christ, and the participation in his "blood" which was shed, or in his "body" which was broken. The important thing to remember is that, in Paul's view, when the death of Christ took place, the union of the spirit of God with the man Jesus came to an end. The spirit did not die, but ascended to heaven to await the proper point in the vague and variable timetable when it would return.

In Paul's view, the death of the Christ Jesus was an Atonement. This term is used in religion in general as a description for the process of shedding sinfulness. To understand Atonement, one first needs to determine what is meant by sin. We saw above that for the rabbis a sin was an individual wrong act; we saw that in Paul's thought sin was a state or condition of man, resulting from man's simply being a man. In Paul's thought Atonement required a change in man's state or condition. Moreover, man, in his view, had no power to effect this change; rather, it had to be accomplished for man, and by a power sufficiently great to achieve the objective. Man could not atone for himself; God must atone for man.

The death of Christ Jesus is for Paul the divine Atonement. When the union of the divine Christ and the human Jesus ended at death on the cross, the humanness of Jesus ceased, but the spirit-Christ lived on. If a man could similarly "die," his body would be dead, but his spirit would live on. As a result of such a "death," man would no longer be "body"; rather, he would be spirit. If man is spirit and not body, he is no longer subject to the passions and senses of the body. Thereby he no longer faces an inability to do that which he should do, or to abstain from what he should not do. If one could only "die" as Christ did, or "die with Christ," one would reap the benefit of the Christ's Atonement.

Paul believed that the Christ's Atonement had brought to Paul the transformation which he wanted and needed.

The Atonement of Christ was in the past. There is in Paul the double scheme of which we have spoken, the initial preparatory coming of the Christ, and the Second Coming, destined for the near future. In this interval, a man could become "spirit" like the Christ, by "dying" in respect to his body, just as Paul had done. A man thus transformed into spirit would remain here on earth until the Second Coming, and at that time, he would go up into heaven where the Christ had been in the interval, and where the Christ truly belonged.

But an understanding of Paul's thought is possible only when we understand the patterns which he confronts. Paul on one occasion, in I Cor. 15, addressed himself to the situation of the living who would presumably still be alive at the Second Coming of Christ. In I Thessalonians 4.13-18 his attention, on the other hand, is directed to a consideration of those who have already literally died. To the latter, Paul has no difficulty in asserting that they will be resurrected. Yet to hold out resurrection, in the light of an expectation that the Second Coming would take place soon, would have been equivalent to promising his hearers that prior to resurrection they would have to undergo literal death.

Paul makes no promise of such a dubious good fortune. Rather, he asserts that for those alive at the time of the Second Coming, their living transformation from flesh into Spirit would be the equivalent of the death and resurrection of the deceased. To put it into a phrase, he holds that the living can go into resurrection without dying.

When Christ Jesus died and rose to heaven, the Christ part of the compound left this mortal world and returned to the immortal; access to the world of immortality was achieved by a literal dying in the mortal sphere. Yet, the transformation of a living person involved not a real death but a figurative one.

Accordingly, the death of the already deceased and the transformation of the still living would bring both to the same situation. "We who are alive, who are left until the coming of the Lord, shall not precede those who have fallen asleep. For the Lord himself will descend from heaven with a cry of command, with the archangel's call, and with the sound of the trumpet of God. And the dead in Christ will rise first; then we who are alive, who are left, shall be caught up together with them in the clouds to meet the Lord in the air; and so we shall always be with the Lord" (I Thess. 4.15-17).

When Paul speaks to the living about resurrection, as in I Cor. 15, he finds the need to make it plain that he does not mean by resurrection simply a restoration to the life which just ended, but rather a rising from the old existence into a totally different and better one. In part his comments on resurrection in I Cor. 15 are motivated by some of his hearers who misunderstand his view. Paul begins by asserting that resurrection is a correct and true belief. But you might, if you misunderstand Paul, suppose that he is telling you that resurrection means that one gets a second life, similar to what he had before. But if the goal of one's religious living has been to escape from the body into communion with ultimate reality and to avoid death, then all that similar resurrection could do is to put one right back where he did not want to be in the first place. In the passage in I Cor. 15 Paul tells what resurrection is like; that is, he defines the nature of the resurrection "body," rather than resurrection itself.

The resurrection body, Paul assures us, is different from the living but mortal body.* There is a physical, mortal body on the

* So, too, the stock exchange, attributed in the Gospels to the Sadducees and Jesus. Since he believes in resurrection, they ask him about a woman who married a succession of seven brothers, marrying anew on the death of the predecessor. The climactic question is this: At resurrection time whose wife is she? The reply asserts that at resurrection time there is no marrying, for the resurrected are like angels in heaven (Mark 12.18-27; Mt. 22.20-33; Luke 20.27-38).

one hand and there is an immortal spiritual body on the other. Involved in death and resurrection is the transformation of the physical body into the spiritual; in this Paul is quite clear. Yet he clutters things up by wishing to emphasize the process of this transformation, so that he tells his hearers that the process of transformation involves "death." He gets into some bad botany by a comparison, invalid to us but valid to him: a seed, he tells us, needs to die in order for it to sprout as a plant!

Nevertheless, the passage makes Paul's point quite successfully. Only, Paul scarcely sticks to what words really mean. In the beginning of the passage, Paul is genuinely talking about resurrection; he continues to use the word, but when he is midway in the passage, it is scarcely resurrection anymore. For what Paul confronts is this, that primitive Christian tradition focuses centrally on resurrection, and probably in the sense of being restored to the same old life; this centrality of the term in tradition commits Paul to its retention. Respecting the already dead, it is a gratifying term for their survivors to hear. For the still living, however, Paul must make the assurance of some comparable benefit ultimately to be attained, yet without the trouble of the intervention of literal death. In I Cor. 15, in dealing with the living, Paul plays with the term resurrection in such a way that it amounts virtually to immortality.

What is the difference? It is this: resurrection supposes that death occurs, but thereafter a restoration to life ensues. Immortality supposes that death does not take place; one can by transformation move from mortality into immortality.

The failure to understand that Paul deals with both the really dead and with the living whom he wants transformed has led to extravagant misunderstanding of I Cor. 15. For 50 verses Paul plays with the term "resurrection," but since he is dealing with the living, he does not really mean "resurrection." In verse 51 he suddenly exclaims: "Lo! I tell you a mystery. We shall not all sleep, but we shall all be changed, in a moment, in the twinkling of an eye at the last trumpet. For the trumpet will sound, and the dead will be raised imperishable, and we shall all be changed. For this perishable nature must put on the imperishable, and this mortal nature must put on immortality." When the living Christian, as Paul sees it, "shares" in the death of Christ, he is in the process of moving from the realm of mortality into the realm of immortality. One crosses from the mortal sphere into immortality by "dying."

Not everybody manages to make the crossing from mortality to immortality. It is only the "saved" who are able to cross. They do it, not alone, but in company with the dying Lord. And in "dying" with the Christ Jesus, one becomes like the Christ, an immortal being who has passed through this life with its death into immortal life with its eternity.

A variety of terms can describe the experience of "dying" and of "rising," and vagueness often supplants clarity in the description of how it takes place. There is such vagueness in Paul's terms. Rather than give a formulation of the steps in the process, he tells us, for example, that "faith" is the vehicle by which to gain the great benefit, but he does not define faith for us. The one thing which we can see clearly is that he does not mean by faith a creed or platform, but rather some kind of inner experience. Or, he describes the end result of the beneficial process as "justification," but without defining the word for us.

My own feeling is that these words of Paul have no special meaning and specific connotation. The general connotations derive from the dominant theme in Paul of mystic communion; the words retain traces, but only traces, of their etymologies. Accordingly, there is some sense of "believing" in Paul's use of the word faith, but it is the direct object of "believing" (that is, what it is that is believed in) which supplies the connotation; in short, one must first *believe* that Christ died for one's sins in order for one to become sinless like Christ. Faith is the combination of believing in Christ and of becoming like him.

As for justification, its juridic sense of acquittal means in the Pauline context the transformed person. Previous to justification, the individual is subject to the disabilities of his body, with its senses and its passions, and prone to sin; justified, he holds his senses and passions in subjection, thereby living on the level of divinity—innocent, now, of sin as is the Deity, but with this qualification, that the Deity has never sinned, but man needs "acquittal" from sin.

Paul uses three other terms to describe the benefit derived from the atoning death of Christ. "Reconciliation" (Romans 5.10; II Cor. 5.17ff.) would seem to mean, if it indeed has some inherently specific meaning, that the final step in ending an estrangement has taken place. Initially there would have been harmony, or relative identity; then departure; and finally, now restoration. Perhaps the background of this figure of speech is to be supplied from Philo and from the Stoics, that man, in being born into a body on this earth had left his proper homeland, heaven, and for a time has been away. The true sage, these tell us, is a stranger here on earth. The identical motif is found in the Epistle to the Hebrews. The underlying notion may be rephrased in this way: man's soul left the celestial realm and in the consequent alienation was ill at ease in this world; now, however, the soul has become *reconciled* by ridding itself of bodily encumbrances. The Stoics and Philo unite in viewing this attainment as possible by man's exercise of the powers which lie in him; for Paul, however, this attainment comes through the grace of the sacrificial death of the Christ.

"Adoption" (Romans 8.15 and 23; 9.4; Galatians 4.5) is somewhat similar in its import. It focuses on man's estrangement from God and man's human and mortal nature. Now, as transformed through the death of the Christ, man has left his human limitations; he is a son of God not through literal propagation, of course, but through "adoption."

"Redemption" (Gal. 3.13; Romans 3.24-25) has the sense of "ransom," of giving something so as to effect someone else's release. This release is, of course, from bondage to human limitations: ". . . The redemption which is in Christ Jesus whom God put forward as an expiation by his blood."

All five terms, justification, atonement, reconciliation, adoption, redemption, revolve around one and the same concept. They are not descriptions of five different processes, but five descriptions of one and the same process. They deal with the present benefit of the past action of the Christ, namely, that as the Christ at crucifixion left this world and went back to heaven, so man, dying symbolically, can become a "citizen of heaven," rather than a poor earth-bound creature.

Now we have noted that one pole of Paul's thought revolves around the incident in the recent past, that the Christ came and died; the second pole looked to the immediate future, for Paul believed that the Christ was soon to return. We need to assess what these related but separate items meant to Paul.

The Second Coming was part of Paul's conviction on the subject of the future final judgment and End of the world which the technicians have called "eschatology." * Since the time of Schweitzer's New Testament writings, shortly after the turn of the century, eschatology has had a considerable vogue.† Indeed, the word has very often become devoid of meaning for it finds its place into sentences in such a way as to render them both ponderous and meaningless. It is one thing to emphasize the reality that Paul looked forward to the Second Coming as an event of great nearness, and as a high point even above what had taken place in the first coming. But it is another thing to suggest that Paul's thought was totally future-oriented, totally eschatological.

Indeed, along with the future, Paul deals with the present, for

* Eschatology means "a study of the last things," that is, of what is to happen at the end of time.

† Schweitzer denied that the historical Jesus could be recovered, and he retained as the primary reliable heritage from Jesus an "eschatology attributed to him." Why this one item should alone have escaped the thoroughgoing skepticism of profoundly skeptical students remains a mystery to me. But a by-product since Schweitzer's time has been an extremism which has interpreted almost everything in the New Testament as "eschatological."

if he had not done so, the Church as a continuing institution could not have found his Epistles still usable even after it learned that Paul was wrong about the immediacy of the end of the world. Indeed, while almost all Christian denominations still pay some kind of lip service to an eschatological item in the Creeds, it is only the more enthusiastic churches which revive the immediacy—and become proved wrong. Were Paul's writings as exclusively eschatological as the one-sided interpreters declare, Paul would hardly continue to elicit the empathy which he does in modern Christendom.

Indeed, apart from the letters to the Thessalonians, eschatology enters into Paul's Epistles only tangentially. Paul's expectation of the end was vivid; but there was in his mind an interval of time still to be lived through between the now and the coming event.

Paul spends more words on what the Christ had *already* done for him and fewer on what the Christ would do in the future. The initial coming of the past has been preparatory; its purpose was to transform the elect, so that when the end came, they could escape the disaster and enter into the future glory. Regeneration, justification, reconciliation—these were benefits already available.

When decades went by and the Second Coming failed to take place, there arose the need in the developing Christendom to translate the preparatory into the permanent. This was done by either winnowing out the eschatology, as did the Fourth Gospel, or by retaining the doctrine and ignoring it, as most of modern Christendom does.

Paul's thought is deeply conditioned by the interval between the present and the future, for his Epistles deal with the present practical matter. The term often applied to Jesus, "interim" ethics, is well applicable to Paul. Now it may be argued that some facet of Paul's well-known opposition to marriage* reflects the

* I Corinthians 7.1-7 and what follows: "It is well for a man not to touch a woman. But because of the temptation to immorality, each man should

conviction of only a brief interval remaining, and perhaps Paul means that a permanent arrangement such as marriage is ill-advised in view of the transitory nature of things. Yet it is equally possible that Paul finds the physical basis of marriage inconsistent with the "spiritual" being, for the former involves succumbing to passion and the senses. Therefore, even had Paul not conceived that only a short time remained, perhaps he would still have opposed marriage. In a word, then, Paul's opposition to marriage does not necessarily indicate that the End of the world is near. The later church departed from Paul with respect to marriage, making it a symbol of the mystic union between Christ and the church. It declared an over-rigid abstention from satisfying bodily needs to be wrong and heretical; this heresy is known as "encratism." A counter-balancing fostering of monasticism and celibacy by the church owes some debt to Paul. Celibacy and monasticism are justified in the church as a proper way of present life, and are not necessarily bound up with an expected early End of the world.

Thus, too, even when we make due allowance for the Pauline view of the transitory nature of the world, and allowance for his exaltation of the future coming of the end of the world at the return of the Christ, we must not overlook the importance to him of the present, for the first coming, in his view, did tremendous things.

Between the two poles of the first coming and of the future second, the weight or direction of Paul's intent in certain given passages may not always be certain. Yet it is clear that he conceives of immortality as a state which the devout can enter even prior to the Second Coming.

---

have his own wife and each woman her own husband . . . Do not refuse one another except perhaps by agreement for a season, that you may devote yourselves to prayer; but then come together again, lest Satan tempt you through lack of self control . . . To the unmarried and the widows I say that it is well for them to remain single as I do. But if they cannot exercise self control, they should marry. For it is better to marry than to be aflame with passion . . ."

To return now to our main thread: what is essential for Paul is that his nature has been transformed. This he believes has been accomplished for him through the three major incidents in the earthly career of the Christ: Incarnation, the Atoning Death, and the Ascension of Christ. Though all three are relevant to Paul, which of these is the most relevant to him? The Incarnation, though of the recent past, is of the past; the Resurrection of those literally dead is bound to the Second Coming, which is a future. The present transformation from a physical (he says "natural")* man into a spiritual (he says "pneumatic") is both Paul's abiding experience and it is also the state into which he wants to induct his auditors. Thus, as has been noted by the scholars, the emphasis in Paul is neither on the Incarnation nor on the Resurrection, but rather on the Atoning Death. "We preach Christ crucified . . ." (I Cor. 1.23); "O foolish Galatians! Who has bewitched you, before whose eyes Jesus Christ was publicly portrayed as crucified?" (Gal. 3.1; see the sequence of verses in Romans 6.1-11.) Although neither Good Friday nor Easter existed as early as Paul, the argument may be clearer if it is put in this way: Good Friday would have meant much more to Paul than Easter.

Now baptism symbolizes both the Atonement and the Resurrection, but the Eucharist is, in Paul's words, a proclamation of "the Lord's death until he comes." That is to say, in Paul's thought the Resurrection of the Christ is so thoroughly subordinated to the expected Second Coming that it is not important in itself. The Resurrection of the Christ (and that which was later known as his Ascension to heaven) is the nexus, the connecting chain between the Atonement of the past and the Second Coming of the future. But Resurrection is not in itself a pre-occupation of

* There is no need to recapitulate or even briefly to reflect the divergent views on Paul's "anthropology." Least of all is there need to delineate it either as "Jewish" or, contrarily, as "Hellenistic." This brief comment is in order: In most Grecian writers a contrast exists between "soul" and "body"; in Paul there is a contrast rather between "body" and "spirit," but "soul" seems to be a third element, and to be partly akin to body and also akin to spirit.

Paul. It is rather the rock bottom foundation of his thought, the great axiom which is so patently Paul's basis that he does not need to return to it constantly, anymore than does the mathematician to the theorem that the whole is equal to the sum of its parts. That Christ had been resurrected and ascended to heaven, awaiting there the time of his return to earth, is as intrinsic to Paul's thought as that God exists. One does not state and restate axioms; accordingly, the Resurrection and the Ascension to heaven of Jesus fail to receive in Paul's surviving letters the attention which he does pay generously to the Atoning Death. We read at the close of the Gospels according to Matthew and Luke, and in the beginning of Acts, about the Ascension of the Risen Christ. Paul does not tell us about the Ascension in itself, but only about it in the light of his having seen the Risen Christ. Accordingly, it is not the Risen Christ himself which is Paul's topic, but rather who it was who saw him.

This is what Paul's conversion amounts to in his eyes: the conviction of transformation from a material (and therefore mortal man) into a spiritual (and therefore immortal) being, as a result of the vision of the Risen Christ and of continuing communion with God in Christ.

Before Paul, Christianity was a typical version of Judaism, without subtractions, but to which was added the belief that Jesus was in some way God's agent, and was destined to return.

In Paul, Christianity becomes notably altered. He believes that as a result of his experience of God, a new revelation has taken place. God, whose action in the ancient past has been the core of Judaism, was available in the present, for a new understanding of Judaism had come into being. The Law of Moses had served its day and was no longer needed, for God himself was now available. Man, before, had been helpless in an alien world; the death of the Christ, if man shared in it, could transform man from body into spirit. Man had become estranged from heaven; now, man could, like the Christ, become reconciled and again a citizen of heaven. All this, plus some details which I have deliberately omitted, is the essence of Paul's transmutation of Christianity. Jesus and his imminent return were virtually all that Paul received from the Christendom into which he came. The transmutation was the new idea which he on his own added.

Paul believed that in his personal transformation there lay also the opportunity for others to become similarly transformed; consequently, he sought out hearers with whom to share his experience.

The foregoing at which we have just looked represents what Paul believed he had experienced and what he wanted his hearers to share with him and also to experience. But more than that, his hearers were to be the converted and Paul was to be the converter. There was a very special role which Paul believed that he himself played and he was well aware of that role. Hitherto I have used as the descriptive term for Paul the epithet prophet. The term, though, which Paul uses for himself is a different one. We turn, accordingly, to see what Paul meant when he described himself as an "apostle."

IV

Paul the Apostle

The basic meaning of the word apostle is one who is sent out. A modern word, which is a near equivalent of the term, would be "messenger," or "emissary," or "missionary." Yet none of these words connotes what the Greek word Apostle meant to Paul (and to other New Testament authors).

When Paul gives us a list of "inspired" leaders in the church, his list is arranged in descending order. He speaks first of apostles, then of prophets, and then of teachers, workers of miracles, and so forth. There can be no doubt in the light of the whole passage, I Cor. 12.1-14.28, that an apostle is supreme above all other persons. Indeed, in the conclusion to the passage, in 14.39-40, Paul exhorts his hearers to become prophets and speakers-in-tongues; but he says not one word about their becoming apostles. Did he believe that apostleship was an eminence which an individual could not attain by striving, but needed to be divinely appointed for it?

Paul certainly holds that God has called him to be an apostle (I Cor. 1.1); not only has God called him, but He has set Paul apart for that purpose (Rom.1.1). Paul tells us that his work as an apostle is not the result of an appointment by human beings, but from God (Gal.1.1, 12-15).

Most of the citations in the preceding paragraph come from the salutations which usually open Paul's letters. That old formula, the ancestor of our modern "Dear Sir," is the most natural place for the writer to identify himself, for customarily the writer of the time began his letter with his name and the credentials which went along with it. Hence there is the clustering of the citations from the salutations. But it will presently be seen that the assertion found in the salutations is carried through consistently in the body of the letters.

There may be some connection between Paul's sense of his having been called by God and the enigmatic description of himself in II Cor. 12.1-5. Paul there speaks of himself as a "man in Christ who fourteen years ago was caught up in the third heaven." Scholars dispute as to whether this passage does or does not reflect Paul's initial "call." Such may be the case, but the evidence is not sufficiently clear to justify a conclusion so specific. Accordingly, it may possibly not reflect Paul's initial call; but surely it is the rare person who will narrate about himself in all seriousness that he was caught up in the third heaven and shown things about which he cannot speak. Even if the passage is not to be interpreted as Paul's initial call, it depicts at least Paul's belief that he experienced a special revelation from God.

In the same Epistle, when Paul feels called upon to defend the authenticity of his claims to the office, he recalls that in his preaching he did not use mere arguments based on logic, but rather that he relied on "proof supplied by the Spirit and its power." This statement is more than a description of the bare emotionalism of his exhortations. That he did not preach calmly, but in something of a frenzy, is to be taken as obvious and not worth stating. The significance of the passage lies in its attributing the frenzy to the "Spirit." Moreover, according to Paul, God has revealed the "Spirit" to him (2.10); and it was from God that Paul had received the Spirit.

An apostle in its basic meaning, we have said, is someone who is sent. In Paul's view, however, the Apostle is simultaneously called and sent. All too often apostle is misunderstood through over-accentuating the "being sent" at the expense of the "call." Paul argues that he has been sent primarily on the basis that he has been called. He contends that the purpose which he serves in the work which he is doing is not something which he elected for himself. To the contrary, he believes in both a general and a specific predestination: Those who believe were predestined to believe and those whom God "predestined He also called" (Rom. 8.29-30). Again, "How are they to believe in him of whom they have never heard? And how are they to hear without a preacher? And how can men preach unless they are sent?" (Rom. 10.14-15).

Since all this applied to him personally, Paul simply states in Romans 1.1 that he was "called to be an apostle, set apart for the Gospel of God." In II Corinthians 1.1 he terms himself an apostle "by the will of God."

Two very clear passages are found in Galatians. In the first of these, Paul contends that he was not only called through God's grace, but that God "had set me apart before I was born . . . to reveal his Son to me, in order that I might preach him among the Gentiles" (Gal. 1.15-16). The second passage, Gal. 2.7-9, concedes, if but for the moment, that Peter had also been set apart, though for the purpose of preaching to Jews; but God worked through Paul for the Gentiles, and the leaders of the Jerusalem church "perceived the grace" that was given to him.

Such contentions, we should note, are by no means small

ones, and the commentator must choose whether Paul meant them seriously or was only indulging in oriental exaggeration. I see no alternative but to take them seriously.

Paul precedes his account of his having been caught up in the third heaven with the statement (II Cor. 10.8): "For even if I boast a little too much of our authority . . . I shall not be put to shame." He continues (verse 13): "But we will not boast beyond limit, but will keep to the limit God has apportioned us . . ." He cites in II Cor. 11 some of his personal vicissitudes designed to show that he is authentically an apostle: "Five times I have received at the hands of the Jews forty lashes less one. Three times I have been beaten with rods; once I was stoned. Three times I have been shipwrecked; a night and a day I have been adrift at sea; on frequent journeys, in danger from rivers, danger from robbers, danger from my own people, danger from Gentiles, danger in the city, danger in the wilderness, danger at sea, danger from false brethren; in toil and hardship, through many a sleepless night, in hunger and thirst, often without food, in cold and exposure."

This record, his argument seems to run, bears out the validity of his claims to apostleship. It is after this earnest and moving account of his vicissitudes that Paul makes the crowning contention that when he was caught up in the third heaven "he heard things that cannot be told, which man may not utter" (II Cor. 12.2-4).

When Paul asks the emotion-laden question, "Am I not an apostle?" (I Cor. 9.1), he promptly replies, "Have I not seen Jesus our Lord?"

In still another passage (I Cor. 15.2-5), Paul makes the claim of having personally seen the resurrected Christ. In this passage Paul defends the credibility of the doctrine of resurrection. His defense in part maintains that the death and resurrection of the Christ were in accordance with Scripture; but he moves then to appeal to the record of a succession of resurrection appearances. These appearances he lists in the order in which they presumably took place: first to Cephas, then to the Twelve, then to 500 of the brethren, then to James, and last of all to Paul himself. That is to say, Paul's contention that he is truly an apostle rests primarily on his claim to having seen the Risen Christ.

Is Paul in this latter passage telling us that he is the last to have seen the Christ and does he attach a special significance to his being the last? Nowhere does Paul say so directly. I confess to having read and reread the Epistles without inferring that he has such an intent. When this interpretation of his intent occurred to me, I quickly reverted to more re-readings. I found, on the one hand, that there is nothing at all in the Epistles which stands in the way of such an interpretation; and, on the other hand, many passages and nuances and issues, previously vague, now took on a bold clarity.

As I now interpret Paul's intent, he believes that his vision of the Risen Christ is both the most recent and more climactic than the visions afforded to his predecessors. A curious Greek word accompanies Paul's reference to himself as the last of all. A single word, it requires a phrase to render it into English: "to be born out of due time." The word customarily refers to an abortive or premature birth. Exactly what Paul had in mind in this colorful word is admittedly elusive; it is most likely a figure of speech for suddenness or abruptness. As joined to his statement that the Risen Christ appeared to him last of all, this figure of speech seems to support his contention that God had predestined him, even to the point of granting him a resurrection vision suddenly and abruptly.

This conviction that he was the last to see the Risen Christ affords Paul the opportunity to play two seemingly opposite roles. On the one hand, as we have seen, he believes that God has predestined him. On the other hand, this same conviction permits Paul to continue in a humility—a humility which in reality is directly the opposite of both his conviction and of his line of argument: "Last of all, as to one untimely born, he appeared also to me. For I am the least of the apostles, unfit to be called an apostle, because I persecuted the church of God. But by the grace of God, I am what I am, and his grace toward me was not in vain."

Indeed, this is an understatement, and this humility is the opposite of what Paul really means. He is in no way conceding that he is the least of the apostles. We read in II Corinthians 11.5 his contention, in a caustically sarcastic passage, "I think that I am not in the least inferior to these superlative apostles." And in 11.23 he says it explicitly: "Are they servants of Christ? I am a better one . . ." And next, out of other passages that might be selected, there is the statement in Galatians 1.11-12: "For I would have you know, brethren, that the gospel which was preached by me is not man's gospel. For I did not receive it from man, nor was I taught it, but it came through a revelation of Jesus Christ." And, finally, the very opening words of Galatians: "Paul an apostle—not from men nor through men, but through Jesus Christ and God the Father. . . ."

These assertions of Paul—that he was not acting on his own, but only filling a role designed for him before birth by God; that God had called him; that his eminence as an apostle was second to nobody's; that it was to Gentiles that he was to preach; that he was the minister of a new covenant; that the content of what he preached was revealed to him by God; that his Gospel was different from what others were preaching, and intended for different personnel, Gentiles not Jews—all these total up to a remarkable contention of far-reaching importance.

Paul's striking set of contentions is obscured in the usual interpretive literature. It assumes, incorrectly, that in Paul's view the acme of the history of Jewish revelation, which began with Abraham, was reached with Jesus. This is incorrect. Jesus was not, in Paul's conception, a mere man to whom revelation might come or might not come. Jesus, or more properly, the Christ Jesus was a divine being whose incarnation was the final step in the long progress of divine revelation which came to man.

Modern interpreters who, under Unitarian influence, deny the divinity of Jesus, seem inclined to classify Jesus as a prophet. This conclusion they support from some apt passages; the tenor of other passages they unhappily ignore, even those at some pains to deny that Jesus was merely a prophet: * *"And Jesus went on with his disciples, to the villages of Caesarea Philippi, and on the way he asked his disciples, 'Who do men say that I am?' And they told him, 'John the Baptist'; and others, 'Elijah'; and others, 'One of the prophets.' And he asked them, 'But who do you say that I am?' Peter answered him, 'You are the Christ.' And he charged them to tell no one about him"* (Mark 8.27-30). Similarly the parallel accounts, Matthew 16.13-17 and Luke 9.18-20, deny that Jesus was a prophet.

For a prophet in the biblical tradition is a man to whom the Deity appears. Thus, Amos 9.1 relates that Amos "saw the Lord standing upon the altar"; and Isaiah 6.1 tells that in the year of death of king Uzziah, Isaiah saw "the Lord sitting on a throne, high and lifted up." Genesis is replete with accounts of the Lord appearing to Abraham, Isaac, and Jacob.

There is not one single account of God's appearing to Jesus in any of the Gospels, not in the four found in the New Testament, nor in the "apocryphal" gospels which failed of inclusion. It would have been illogical for such an account to appear, for it would have been in contradiction to a cornerstone of the New Testament. The New Testament contention, however, is quite clear. It is that God revealed himself not to Jesus, but *in* Jesus. The opening verses of Hebrews make the New Testa-

NB

* Other passages too imply that Jesus was a prophet: Mark 6.4; Matt. 13.57; 21.11, 46; Luke 13.33; 24.19; John 6.14. But Luke 7.16-27 and John 7.40-41, like Mark 8.27-30, deny it. The epithet, thus, was only tentative, applicable, if at all, solely to the human career of the Christ, who was divine and hence more than a prophet. In 19th century scholarship "prophet" was a term of praise, "priest" of dispraise. Those who emphasized that Jesus was a prophet usually chose to ignore that Hebrews (2.15; 3.1; and 5.1-10) specifically makes him a priest.

ment contention plain: "In many and various ways God spoke of old to our fathers by the prophets; but in these last days he has spoken to us by a Son."

To revert now to Paul's contention, it is this, that the pinnacle of the form of the history of revelation is *in* Jesus, but it is to Paul, and not *to* Jesus that the high-point was vouchsafed. Curiously, Paul omits Abraham, Isaac, and Jacob from consideration; in his eyes revelation began with the disclosure to Moses of the Law. Revelation, now however, as Paul sees it, has come not in the form of the Law but of the Spirit, and it has come to Paul in its climactic occurrence.

This final idea is the gist of II Corinthians 3.

In this chapter Paul draws a contrast between the Law of Moses and the Spirit. He speaks of the Law of Moses as the "ministration of death, carved in letters on stone." The reference is clearly to the Decalogue, the account of which is contained in Exodus 19-24.* In that account, Moses ascends Mount Sinai, and then returns to declare the Decalogue and other laws to the people. Thereafter, Moses reads to the people (Exodus 24.7) a Book of the Covenant; at that point, the people reply that they will hearken and will do.

The "ministration of the Spirit" is, by contrast, one of life. Paul, in his own eyes, is the minister of this new covenant, as Moses was the minister of the old.

There can be no mistaking Paul's intent of comparing himself and his eminence to Moses, this to Moses' disadvantage. The old covenant (and let it be recalled that the Greek word *diatheke* three centuries ago was invariably translated "testament") was instituted by Moses, the new by Paul. The passage says clearly that the new was superior both in its content and also in its minister: "It is not that I am personally qualified to form any judgment by myself; my qualifications come from God, and he

* It is frequent in Paul's Epistles that a contrast is drawn between the Law of Moses as "death" and the Christ as "life."

has further qualified me to be the minister of the new covenant . . ." (James Moffatt's translation).

Paul's belief in his own special and decisive role was unquestionably a function of his intuition. Yet it should not escape our notice that Paul not only volunteers this contention, but it is also part of his response when his right to be an apostle is challenged. In a setting in which Paul made the claim of being an apostle, he heard that opponents said, "Paul is not an apostle at all." Paul retorted, if one may put words into his mouth, "I am not an apostle? Indeed! I am *The Apostle!*"

His Epistles, unhappily, do not tell us clearly who his opponents were—his addressees knew without being told. Yet two relevant circumstances, when they are understood, throw good light on this matter.

The evidence is clear that Paul had opponents. The Corinthian correspondence revolves on the issue of whether or not Paul is justified in calling himself an Apostle, and in preaching his particular message. We know that at Corinth there were, by Paul's attestation, four parties, those of Paul, Apollos, Cephas, and Christ. The text does not identify what it was that separated one party from another, and for modern scholars to suggest the bases of the separation is only speculation. The existence of the parties suggests not harmony, but conflicts. The Corinthian Epistles bear out this conclusion. Moreover, there were those at Corinth who denied that Paul was legitimately an Apostle.

To understand this denial, let us move on by asking a question: Why did Paul make the important decision he mentions in II Cor. 5.16 not to speak of Jesus "after the flesh"? Or, to rephrase the question, why did Paul decide to avoid in his preachment references to things which Jesus had done or things which Jesus had said? The Gospels record things which the Church believed that Jesus had done and said, and their content is quite bulky. Paul, however, gives us only one quotation from the statements which it was believed that Jesus had made, namely, he cites Jesus' opposition to divorce. Of the parables and aphorisms, there is not one quotation.* Of the denunciations of the Pharisees and Sadducees attributed by the Gospels to Jesus, there is not one word.

As to the incidents mentioned in the Gospels, Paul alludes to the Crucifixion and to the Resurrection, but he abstains from narrating any incident but one. He makes one other reference which we will turn to in a moment. From Paul's Epistles alone we should not suspect even the mere existence of the incidents and discourse of which the Gospels are composed: The miraculous birth of Jesus, his baptism at the hands of John the Baptizer, his temptation in the wilderness, his numerous cures and exorcisms, his rejection at Nazareth, Peter's confession at Caesarea-Philippi, the triumphal entry into Jerusalem, the overturning of the table of the moneychangers in the Temple, the trial before the Sanhedrin, the part played by Herod and by Pilate in his condemnation.

While the allusion to the Crucifixion and the citation of Jesus' attitude towards divorce are unmistakable proof that Paul knew some things about Jesus, we need to confess that we have no idea of precisely what he knew and how much. On the one hand, we cannot be sure that everything knowable actually reached Paul; on the other hand, legend about Jesus kept growing and some of the material now found in the Gospels came into being after Paul's time. This kind of uncertainty is illustrated by a passage in Paul which defies definite understanding. It is in connection with the single incident which Paul relates that of the institution of the "Eucharist." Paul precedes his account of the "Lord's sup-

* Scholars have occasionally found echoes of Jesus' teachings in Paul's words, though usually without raising the question of whether these are echoes of Jesus in Paul or, as many of us would hold, echoes of Paul in the Synoptic Gospels. But this point is of no importance; whichever way one wants to interpret the echoes, the fact remains that Paul *only once* directly quotes Jesus. Why did not Paul on page after page and in paragraph after paragraph appeal to the words of Jesus as authority for what he was advocating? This question will be dealt with shortly. The fact to be noted here is that he did not so quote.

per" with these words . . . "For I received from the Lord and also I handed over to you that the Lord Jesus on the night when he was *handed over* took bread etc." The italicized words are rendered by some scholars by "betrayed"; other scholars contend that betrayal is a motif which developed long after Paul's time and that it is an error to read "betrayal" into Paul's neutral word. These scholars point out that nowhere in his Epistles does Paul mention any specific "betraying," and Judas the "betrayer" is totally missing from Paul's pages.

We cannot, then, be sure just how much of the material now found in the Gospels was in existence in Paul's time, and how much of that material had come to Paul. Nevertheless, the noticeable absence of material about Jesus in Paul's Epistles is in striking conformity with what he himself declares became a part of his procedure.

Why did he so decide?

Several motives seem to have entered in. Of these, a chief one, perhaps even the chief one, was this: Paul had never known Jesus and had never been a disciple of his. To have quoted constantly from Jesus and to have referred frequently to events in Jesus' life outside the Crucifixion and Resurrection would have amounted to the concession that these were important, and that to have been an eye-witness to them was important. In short, it would have amounted to Paul's conceding that his opponents who had been Jesus' immediate followers had those great credentials which he himself lacked.

Moreover, these opponents, if they were immediate followers of Jesus, had been in the movement before Paul's time; and it would be from such people that the epithet of a Johnny-come-lately would have emerged. For Paul engendered opposition both to himself and to what he was doing—and therefore he was forced to defend the validity of his unique preachment and his claim to apostleship. If we will imagine some words from an opponent of Paul, we will see more clearly what it is that Paul claims. The opponent says: "This man Paul is preaching something which he himself devised; he didn't get what he is preaching from us, or from Jesus. He wasn't in on things at the beginning. He's not one of the founders of our movement. He has no letter of credentials. He isn't to be listened to."

To this Paul replies: "My career shows that I am an Apostle. Look at what I've suffered. Five times I received the thirty-nine lashes. Three times I was beaten with rods. Once I was stoned. It's true that what I preach I didn't get from my opponents. I got it from God."

The opponents retort: "Paul never knew Jesus, Paul never saw him."

Paul responds, "I never saw Jesus, but I saw the Risen Christ. That exceeds by far simply having known Jesus when he was alive. As for your calling me a Johnny-come-lately, my reply is this, that God picked out the time for me. He chose me before I was born and he predestined me for what I am doing, and he revealed to me what I am saying. And if you are raising the time factor, then don't raise it with me, raise it with God."

The opponents retort, "Paul is not an Apostle; our leaders in Jerusalem did not send him out."

Paul replies, "Exactly right. I was not sent out by any men. It is God who sent me. He sent me as the minister of a new covenant of my inherited Judaism for a new people."

The foregoing reconstruction will, I trust, help clarify some conclusions I am about to summarize. Paul came into Christianity early; but others had preceded him. He came in early enough, however, that had he been a Palestinian, he could well have known Jesus. He entered Christianity in the Greek dispersion of which he was a native. First he had persecuted the movement, but then he had espoused it. Not only had he espoused it, but he felt a sense of divine appointment to spread this movement to Gentiles. To that end he traveled, exhorted those who would listen to him, and shaped his followers into a series of local churches. This missionary activity brought him into conflict with missionaries who had been dispatched from the "mother church" in Jerusalem. The conflicts centered on two related but different items. One conflict was on the content of Paul's message. The other was on Paul's authentic right to be called an Apostle. Respecting the latter, opponents denied that Paul was an Apostle, both because he had not been sent out by the church at Jerusalem and because he had not known Jesus. Respecting the former, he was teaching wrong things—so they said. Paul responded that this appointment had come from God and that the content of his message had come from God. True, he had not seen Jesus, but he had seen the Risen Christ; indeed, to him had come the most recent vision. In view of God's revelation to him, he was not only genuinely an Apostle, but the revelation made by God to him was the crowning act in the long history of God's revelation to Israel. Paul never quite takes another step which he might well have taken, and which others took. That is, he might have gone on to say that his not having known Jesus was totally unimportant. That is, in defending his right to apostleship on the basis alone of having seen the Risen Christ, Paul might have denied the right of his opponents. He does not go that far. Though he limits apostleship among his opponents strictly to those who have seen the Risen Christ, he does not proceed to attack those who personally knew Jesus. He does not attack them, but disparages them, this in the light of his own greater mystic experience. However strange it may seem to modern men, in Paul's day there were rivalries on the comparative issue of having known the Risen Christ versus having known the human Jesus. To Paul, the former was the crowning credential, and the latter only trivial.

Had Paul been a leader or teacher ignored in early Christianity, his contentions of being the minister greater than Moses of a new covenant greater than the old could have been dismissed as an aberration, as the grandiose views of a marginal personality. But Paul was noticed and Paul had followers, and his

Epistles, though written for the moment, became enshrined as Scripture. Paul, in short, represents a deviation which came to be a dominant theme.

While Christianity obviously begins with Jesus and derives its initial impulse from him, there is a second beginning of Christianity in Paul and a new impetus derived from Paul.

A minority of scholars have pointed out repeatedly something which most of Paul's interpreters overlook. It is that Paul is fully as much an iconoclast and rebel against the Christianity which had developed up to the time of his entrance into it as he was to his inherited Judaism. Indeed, the personal opponents of Paul, when they are Jews by birth, are *Christians,* and the bitter controversies reflected in his Epistles are not with Jews but with Judaizers. A "Judaizer" is not a Jew, but rather a Christian who advocates and practices Jewish observances. Although Paul is, of course, critical of his inherited Judaism, his criticism of it is a matter of abstract theory; but Judaizing, on the other hand, confronted Paul as a vivid and real issue, impinging on the very work which he was daily doing. The angry tone of Galatians emerges not because Judaism, with a total denial of the Christ, had infected a church of Paul's own creation, but because Christian Judaizing had infected it.

Or, to put the issue in another way, Paul has frequent occasion to regret that a blindness, as he sees it, had overtaken Jews, with the result that they have not come into the new movement. Yet his quarrels and disputes and partisan conflicts arose, rather, with people within the movement. Paul wanted Jews on their becoming Christians to leave their Jewish ways behind them; Paul objects that these, now Christians, have brought Jewish practices along with them. He wants Gentiles not to absorb these practices, but Judaizers encouraged them to do so.

Paul passes judgment on whether or not a Jew is accomplishing anything worthwhile in observing the Law of Moses; but this is not in the orbit of his true concern. When a Christian, on the other hand, is observing the Law of Moses, and is requiring Gentile converts to Christianity to do so, Paul becomes agitated and personally involved.

Paul's deviation from the Christianity as it was when he came into it took the form of a unique preachment which set forth a plan and vehicle for communing with God in Christ. It altered, reinterpreted, and reshaped the Christian message which Paul himself had heard. It was directed towards Gentiles, not Jews. And all this was justified on the contention of its having been revealed to Paul as a designed climax by God. This is what is meant in the assertion that in Paul Christianity undergoes a second beginning.

But might it not be more proper to assess this turn of events in some less extreme way? Would it not suffice to say that Paul was no more than the author of some special version of Christianity which branched off from the main stream? Or should the matter be put in this way, that Christianity became bifurcated in Paul's time?

Provided one confines his view to the restricted decades of Paul's period of activity and life-time, either of these two forms of description is as apt as the one which I have chosen. However, when we look at developments after Paul's time, we begin to see, as it will be my task in subsequent pages to point out, that Paul's view, far from remaining a deviation, became instead the mainstream of Christianity. The figure of bifurcation is scarcely the apt figure of speech for a tree which has two branches, one of which shrivels and dies while the other thrives and grows. Pauline Christianity grew and flourished; the Christianity of his Judaizing opponents died out. When deviations develop after the time of Paul, it is from what is essentially Pauline Christianity that the deviations, at least those reflected within the New Testament, take place.

No, in the perspective of the subsequent history of Christianity, the Pauline version of it is something more than a mere branch resulting from bifurcation; and it is something much more than a mere deviation. To describe the contribution of Paul to Christianity as a second beginning does not overstate the case.

Born a Jew, in a Greek environment, converted to Christianity, Paul's particular doctrines are the refraction through his cosmopolitan eyes of Judaism, Hellenistic religion, and his acquired Christianity. Respecting the latter, he has received traditions and he passes them on, but only after they have been revolutionized by the magic of his intuition. One of his main legacies to Christianity is his stand towards the Law of Moses. But even more, with him begins the process of seeing in Old Testament passages prefigurations of the Christ which go beyond mere proof-texting.* As for his Hellenism, there is in Paul a resounding echo of popular philosophy, popular religion, and both the attitudes and the sense of arrival which characterized the Greek mysteries. This latter statement is in no sense a derogation of Paul; surely we are in a position now to recognize that Christian and Jewish denunciation of the Greek mysteries is partisanship, and that the mysteries contained, in addition to rites which we can regard as abominable, a religious quest which is universal and exalted.

These three strands, Hellenism, Judaism, Christianity, are blended in Paul. If somewhat imperfectly, or incompletely blended, they are nevertheless rather thoroughly intermixed with each other. Yet if they are the basic ingredients, then we must still remember that the special flavoring of the batter is that of Paul's own personality.

When transmuted Christianity emerges from Paul, we deal

* It is mere proof-texting, for example, to contend that Jesus was of the stock of David and then to quote a passage which speaks of the stock of David, and then to supply the absent bridge that the passage applies to Jesus. At a different level is Paul's contention that Christian baptism took place in Moses' time and that Israel was "baptized in the cloud and in the sea," and that in the wilderness period Israel "ate the same spiritual food and drank the same spiritual drink. For they drank from the spiritual Rock which followed them, and the Rock was Christ"; I Cor. 10.1-4.

no longer with whatever primitive Palestinian Jewish Christianity may have been, for we are mostly in the dark about that. We have little direct data on what Christianity was before it encountered Paul. We can guess at what it was by the process of noting what it was that Paul changed, and by inferring from the changes what it was that was changed; and we can check the inferences by comparisons with what we know about Judaism. The pre-Pauline "Christianity" I have described above as a rather usual Judaism to which there were added conceptions about Jesus, but without any accompanying deletions.

No records have come down to us directly from early Palestinian Christianity. Mark, Matthew and Luke are not safe guides to it. With Paul we have moved from a Jewish Christianity into a "gentilized" one. Unless this is so, there is no substance to Paul's repeated contention that his special mandate from God was to be the Apostle to Gentiles. And the particular Gentiles to whom Paul preaches are Grecian; they are not the Babylonians among whom Jews had had a long dispersion, nor are they the Ethiopians among whom the Negro Falashas still survive as a relic of still another Jewish dispersion. At least in this sense, Paul's Christianity represents a Hellenized version.

Respecting Philo the curious situation exists that Jewish scholars steeped in rabbinic literature are prone to emphasize the "un-Jewish" character of Philo; while classicists, whom I have known, have told me that Philo seems to them very much "un-Hellenic." It is the Jewish in the blend of Philo which makes him seem strange to classicists, and the Hellenism in Philo makes him strange to rabbinists; and moreover, Philo is always individualistic. So with Paul, his heritage of Old Testament and of apocalypticism gives him a Jewish tinge; his conformity to Greek religion and mysticism makes him seem strange to rabbinists. The reading of him in the light of the rest of the New Testament, much of which is directly or coincidentally devoted to paring him down, adds its own perplexity.

Of the immediately personal accomplishments of Paul I shall

speak in the last chapter. The general accomplishment is that in him Christianity becomes Hellenized, transformed in terms of the environment of the religious genius who was the transformer. Paul did not create Christianity, he re-created it.

Hellenized and made appropriate for Gentiles, the Gospel as he preached it was, he felt, the product of divine revelation, and that divine revelation was a continuing factor. It was not the inherited bits of revelation of long ago as in Judaism, or the inherited bits of incidents about or words from Jesus of a short time ago, but rather revelation as an ever continuing manifestation which characterizes the transition in Paul from Law to "Grace."

But in the realm of human beings can there be unified action without some kind of regulation? When Paul abrogated, as it were, the Laws of Moses, he deprived the Church of a ready-at-hand form of regulating itself.

Perhaps Paul is right that proper attitude, if we may so paraphrase him, will yield the proper conduct. Paul's way of saying this is to speak of "fruits of the Spirit"—that is, that the right spirit produces the same beneficial end result which the Law aims at but fails to produce.

It is certainly true in a city that if every citizen had the proper attitude, and lived by that attitude, there would be a need neither for laws, nor, surely, for the enforcement of them. But where is the community which would annul prohibitions against speeding, against going through a red light, against parking near a fire hydrant, and rely instead on proper attitude?

Judaism, and the Church up to Paul's time, regulated itself through the Law of Moses. Paul denied that the Law was needed; Paul advocated instead reliance on right attitude.

It needs to be clear that Paul is concerned with the means of attaining an objective, not with the objective itself. Paul is not advocating lawlessness or unrighteousness, but to the contrary, a righteousness no less exalted. His ethics, in a word, remained unchanged both in fundamental belief and in the details of ethical standards. His ethics is persistently Jewish—not Greek. He bequeathed to the Church an opposition to idolatry, to sexual irregularity, and immorality as Judaism had expressed and defined these things.

But the repeal, as it were, of the Law of Moses amounted unintentionally not so much to a better way for righteousness to rule triumphant, as to a means for license to arise and for anarchy to prevail.

There is as a consequence this paradox: through Paul's activity the Church was growing, but the more that it grew because of Paul, the more difficult it was for its gains to be consolidated. When Paul did away with the authority of the Law of Moses, he failed to replace it with some other authority which could be *viable* and *effective*. The growth of the Church after Paul's time, and in Paul's image, required that this deficiency in authority be made good. Long after Paul, the Church took the attitude towards the Law of Moses that only its ceremonial requirements were obsolete; its ethical requirements were held still to be binding law.

But in the period immediately after Paul, these arose inevitably a supreme need for some vehicle or device for inner regulation. We can best understand what much of the subsequent literature deals with when we ask the questions: Can a church grow and be organized, be preserved and be perpetuated without some authority, vested either in a person or in a sacred Scripture or in a tradition or in regulations? If conduct is the matter of divine inspiration, then is not a community somewhat at the mercy of the non-conformist who justifies his actions on the basis of a divine revelation?

Paul is the great source-book for the non-conforming individual. It is no accident that it was to the Epistle to the Galatians that Martin Luther turned in the sixteenth century to justify his defiance of the Catholic Church. Luther invoked the authority of Paul to demonstrate that one need not bow to authority. The fragmentation of Protestantism in the United States into its approximately 280 denominations derives ultimately from the precedent and the teaching of Paul.

In his own life-time Paul found the need to clarify his intent and to distinguish between liberty and license. We might define license as the liberty somebody *else* unjustly takes, and liberty as license when we ourselves take it. For when one does away with some objective yardstick of conduct, such as the Law of Moses, then anarchy or even chaos can exist.

Paul had no intention of creating anarchy. A fifteenth century Jew, of the sect of the Karaites, Isaac Troki, points out what seems to him to be an inconsistency in Paul, namely, that in one breath he denies the validity of Law and trusts to inspiration, but in another breath he feels impelled to advise people what to do, as for example his counsel about marriage.

The growing church after Paul's time, when it came to the threshold of becoming crystallized in its institutional forms, needed inescapably to become well organized and immovably stable. Paul's legacy was of little benefit to this need, indeed, he provided a great obstacle to such a stabilization.

In any stable church it is prudent to exalt the prophet only when he is a heritage from the remote past. A contemporaneous prophet is inconvenient to an established church. One recalls Joan of Arc. In I Corinthians 12-14, Paul discusses "spiritual gifts" as these pertain to leaders in the church; chief among the leaders are the apostle and the prophet. This is in accord with Paul's non-conformity. On the other hand, in I Timothy, written a century after Paul's time, we read about bishops and deacons, and in Titus we read about bishops and the need for the faithful to be submissive to rulers and authorities; in contrast to Paul, the Pastoral Epistles (I and II Timothy and Titus) do not provide at all for the existence of prophets.

The leading characteristic of Paul was that he regarded himself as an apostle, indeed the Apostle, the prophet par excellence;

his experience of God was like that of the pre-exilic prophets; he preached and taught to the end that his hearers should become, if they could, prophet-like too. They also were to commune directly with God, for a supreme and recent revelation of God had come through him. He could assure them, as he did, that what they needed was not the Law of Moses, but the Holy Spirit.

Paul's message was an effective one. It touched the hearts and minds of people. It won him followers. It enabled the Church to grow and expand. The Church followed Paul's way.

The Church could, and did glory in its heritage from Paul. But not everything which Paul taught and advocated lent itself favorably to the increasing need for stability.

To borrow a figure, the Church could not take Paul straight.

V

Paul and the Acts of the Apostles

In First Corinthians 15 Paul speaks of Resurrection appearances to Cephas, then to the "twelve," then to more than five hundred "brethren" at one time, then to James, and finally to Paul. In his Epistles Paul mentions co-workers of his, Barnabas, Timothy, Titus, Silvanus; he also mentions a colleague, Apollos. It is a noticeable circumstance that of all these leaders, writings in the New Testament are attributed only to James and to "Peter," but not to any other of this aggregate of 512 persons. The writings in the New Testament total twenty-seven; thirteen of the twenty-seven bear the name of Paul as the author.

Modern scholarship believes that no more than ten of the thirteen Epistles in the New Testament attributed to Paul are truly from his hand. It is remarkable that both fact and tradition combine to ascribe to Paul virtually half of the New Testament. Why does this preponderance cluster about Paul?

Did few of Paul's other contemporaries, the other 509, write? Or, if they wrote but their writings were not preserved, then was it accident that so many letters of Paul survived, and that certain letters not by him came to bear not just any name but his name in particular?

Both the Christian tradition and the modern scholarship attempt, if only indirectly, to give answers to this startling preponderance of Paul's Epistles in New Testament literature. Tradition and modern scholars do not coincide in their answers, for scholarship, especially as pursued by Protestants, has considered it inescapably necessary to challenge the tradition in many small and even large matters.

In raising the question of Paul and the New Testament literature, we deal with a kind of mystery, and the scholar who attempts to solve it must, like a detective in fiction, examine clues and sift them; he must listen to testimony and evaluate it, and then set forth a probable theory, test it and assault it—and then perhaps the detective is ready for the case to be presented to a grand jury. Many a good detective story gained in suspense (or else protracted the narration) by announcing prematurely that the case is solved, only to have something upset the applecart, and then the detective must begin again to array the facts and to try to draw the proper and compelling inferences. Premature announcements of the solution have occurred in New Testament scholarship. But let us look at the case.

The New Testament consists of four Gospels (According, respectively, to Matthew, Mark, Luke, and John). It has one book of history: Acts of the Apostles relates the events about the church from the time of the Ascension of Jesus to heaven until, as Acts narrates it, Paul arrives at Rome. To Peter are attributed two Epistles; to a Jude one; to a John three; to a James one. An anonymous Epistle bears the title "To the Hebrews." Lastly, there is a curious book, likewise attributed to "John," known both as The Apocalypse and also as Revelation.

The Gospels, as is universally known, deal with the earthly career of Jesus. When presently we look at them, it will be only from the restricted viewpoint of their impingement on Paul. These four, dealing with the early events of nascent Christianity, carry the narrative of Christian history up to the point where Acts picks it up, the Resurrection appearance of Jesus. Acts is by the author of Luke, but it is also in a sense the sequel to all the four Gospels. No other New Testament writing pretends to be a survey of history. The Gospels give us the supposed beginnings, the events of the time of Jesus, Acts carries the history on, but it ends abruptly and inconclusively. All the other literature lacks the purpose of relating what is supposedly history. The Epistles deal with theological or practical problems of the time of their writing, and Revelation purports to tell what will transpire when the great judgment comes at the End of the world.

Accordingly, the New Testament noticeably lacks historical information respecting its own period. Much that we claim to know about early Christian history is derived obliquely rather than being stated expressly. An example may clarify this distinction between oblique inference and direct statement. Acts of the Apostles tells us a little about the mother church in Jerusalem; in Paul's Epistles, such as Galatians, there are passing references to it, as we have seen. But as far as New Testament writings are concerned the church in Jerusalem simply vanishes from notice without its later history or its ultimate disappearance ever being recorded. From the absence of any mention, we could obliquely infer that the church at Jerusalem had come to an end. It is not until the fourth century that any writer undertakes to tell us what happened to the Jerusalem church.

Similarly it was in the vicinity of Damascus that Paul appears to have become a convert, and presumably there was a church there; we have not one syllable in the New Testament about the founding of the church at Damascus. In the second century there was a flourishing church at Alexandria in Egypt, but we do not know who founded it, or when. Indeed, there is no account in the New Testament of the beginning of the church at Rome. For every fact the New Testament offers, there are ten it fails to provide. For every fact we know, there are ten we do not know.

New Testament literature writings come from the range of about a century, from about 40 AD to about 150 AD. There are some Christian writings which did not achieve a place in the New Testament (a collection known as the Apostolic Fathers, for example), which come from within this same general period. Nevertheless, even the use of material outside the New Testament fails to dispel the darkness that largely covers the historical events of early Christianity.

But the silence of the sources about things which we would wish earnestly to know is only half of the problem. The other half is this, that what the literature does tell us is not always reasonable or believable. This is not to imply that the authors of New Testament writings were necessarily deliberate falsifiers. Like the Old Testament historiographers, they played with history as though it was one of the arts. To expect pure history from Old or New Testament writers is to expect something which they did not intend to furnish.

Some authors, in Old Testament as well as New, could not distinguish between what they wished had happened and what did happen. The piety of a religious writer was often a barrier between him and accurate history. He told of things as he believed they should have been. We need in fairness to examine an author's intent rather than his performance. If the end result seems to us to be distortion and mis-statement, we are by modern laws convicting ancient writers for what in ancient days was not a crime.

In sum, since we in our day understand by history a meticulous accuracy in the narration of past events, we need to adjust ourselves to a changed expectation in the quasi-historical writings of either Old or New Testament.

The need, then, to assess and weigh and sift the statements in the documents is an inescapable necessity. Moreover, a similar need extends to the literature later than or outside the New Testament which refers to the New Testament.

For example, a fourth century writer quotes a second century father to the effect that the Gospel According to Matthew was written in Hebrew and then translated into Greek; but the Gospel According to Matthew found in the New Testament today cannot, in the view of virtually all modern scholars, possibly be the result of translation, but instead it was necessarily written in Greek. This is their conclusion, based on the conviction that Matthew used and rewrote Mark, following Mark's Greek in many places so closely that his dependency on Mark is one of the assured results of Protestant scholarship. The second century father was misinformed, or else he was distorting things.

I essay in this chapter and the next the role of detective. I set forth the considerations which can be presented to the grand jury of my peers touching on Paul and the New Testament literature. I shall cite the evidence of certain witnesses—in this case New Testament authors—and then I shall call on certain experts, New Testament scholars, to help in sifting the evidence and in setting aside some of the testimony usually offered. There is a purpose in this endeavor. Paul fits somewhere in the history of early Christianity, his Epistles fit somewhere in the New Testament literature. If we come to see clearly where Paul's Epistles fit into New Testament literature, this will help us to understand Paul the man.

To participate in this search, the reader needs to begin with a certain willingness, or else this effort, on his part and mine, is futile. He needs to be willing to approach the literature of the New Testament without some preconception as to its unfailing inerrancy. The writings in the New Testament (as in the Old) come from men, and they have all the potential grandeur and foibles of which human beings are capable. Without such a willingness, the reader may be limited to the attitude of the Christian traditionalist toward the New Testament writings. By disposition the traditionalist accepts the testimony in Scriptural documents as historically correct and sound, and to him the suggestion that the documents may contain errors is unacceptable. The bare intimation that there are contradictions and discrepancies is often beyond his capacity to observe and to recognize. For example, the fact that there are four Gospels means to him that there are four different but *equally reliable* reports about Jesus. Where one Gospel gives data that another lacks, or gives them from a slightly different perspective, such things are the unimportant result of the style or disposition of the particular evangelist (the author of the Gospel), and these considerations in no way affect the historical reliability of what is being narrated. The material about Jesus in the Gospels is to him historically correct, and the material in Acts is historically correct, and the ancient church traditions about the authorship of the Gospels and of Acts are historically correct. To such a traditionalist, there is no difficulty in harmonizing the birth narrative found in Luke and the totally different narrative found in Matthew; and he is not troubled by the circumstance that neither Mark nor John related the birth of Jesus. He can take in his stride Matthew's narration that the resurrected Jesus appeared to his disciples in Galilee, and Luke's that he appeared in the vicinity of Emmaus near Jerusalem.

The traditionalist gives his testimony about problems such as the one we are looking into with full earnestness and conviction; he believes firmly what he is testifying to.

The difficulty is that the modern scholar has been giving testimony also, for almost a hundred and fifty years, and his testimony clashes sharply with that of the traditionalist. Both the traditionalist and the modern scholar cannot be right; one must be set aside and discarded.

But even the modern scholarship, with its varieties and schools of emphasis, and its factions, is itself not to be taken literally. Its testimony too needs sifting. To understand Paul, we need to look as critically at the fairly-well agreed upon conclusions of modern scholarship as at the traditional explanations.

The chief difference between the traditionalist and the modern scholar as it affects an understanding of Paul is this. The traditionalist assumed that the materials in the Gospels about Jesus are historically reliable, regardless of when the Gospels may chance to have been written. It is agreed by all, modernists and traditionalists, that Paul's Epistles were written before the Gospels. Where there are items in Paul's Epistles, such as his account of the beginnings of the "Lord's Supper," which are found also in the Gospels, the traditionalist would believe that Paul derived his information from the earliest oral traditions about Jesus. The modern scholar, on the other hand, would suggest, believe, or insist that the date of the writing of a document is of almost equal importance as the content, and that, accordingly, it would be conceivable that Gospels written after the time of Paul contain echoes and reflections of Paul's teaching and doctrine. The usual modern scholar would not suggest that every single thing fits mechanically into such a chronological arrangement; he would, rather, hold that each particular item needs its own and separate scrutiny. He would give not a blanket judgment but one item by item, after each item has been studied and pursued as carefully and as fully as prudent investigation can go.

Insofar as one can generalize about modern scholars on the Gospels, two rather standard conclusions mark them off from the traditionalists. The first of these conclusions has to do with the relationships of the Gospels to each other as literary documents. After countless hypotheses which tried to explain the acknowledged phenomena, one has stood the test of time. It is this, that Mark is the earliest of the Gospels, and that Mark is a written source utilized by both Matthew and Luke. Mark could scarcely have been an Aramaic document written by a disciple of Jesus.

Secondly, there are many passages found in both Matthew and Luke which so agree with each other in wording that they have some literary relationship to each other. Many of these passages are absent from Mark; Mark therefore could not be the source of these particular passages.

There are roughly three possibilities in explanation of such similar passages in Luke and Matthew. Possibly Matthew used Luke as a source. Or possibly Luke used Matthew. Or possibly both Luke and Matthew independently used some now lost source which each copied independently of the other. The German word for source is Quelle; its first letter, Q, has become in New Testament study the symbol for this presumed source in addition to Mark which Matthew and Luke utilized. The main line of scholarship follows the judgment that there was indeed such a now lost source, and it discards the possibility that Luke may have used Matthew, or Matthew Luke.

The "priority" of Mark to Matthew and Luke, and the use of the former plus Q by the latter are virtually axioms in New Testament scholarship.

Now let us point out, as typical, one single implication of the difference at this point between the traditional scholarship and the modern. Matthew, Luke, and Mark all relate that Jesus was baptized by John the Baptist. Traditionalists would assert that we have here three testimonies; but modernists would say that we have three versions of the one testimony. To modernists the circumstance that Matthew and Luke corroborate what Mark says is the result of their copying Mark, it is not independent corroboration. (The Fourth Gospel, John, does not exhibit a close literary relationship to the other three.)

Next it was noticed by a scholar about forty years ago that in Mark the connecting material between episodes is very vague. The transition from one episode to another is unaccompanied by any clear explanation of the lapse of time or an accurate report of the change of place. A consequence of noticing this peculiarity in the connective material was the hypothesis that a Gospel such as Mark was the result of joining together small episodes about Jesus which had previously existed in some detached form, possibly written, but probably oral. Each episode conceivably had its own history of oral transmission before being incorporated into the written Gospel. Moreover, in the process of oral transmission the content of an episode may well have been influenced or altered by the transmitter. If such influence or alteration took place, then a proper study of the episode could possibly disclose some information about the alteration or about the alterer; an episode ostensibly designed to tell us about Jesus may coincidentally tell us also about the church quite some time after Jesus. This conclusion, standard among scholars, is, of course, at war with the traditionalist who ascribes complete historical accuracy to each and everything in the Gospels.

If the church's attitude about Jesus in the time after Jesus is discernible in the Gospels, then Pauline doctrine and influence could also be discerned in them, on the reasonable basis that Paul's Epistles were written before the Gospels, and Paul's message was in circulation before the earliest written Gospel was composed.

To the beginner what is at stake here is often a mental hurdle that is difficult to overcome. The novice notes that the Gospels are about Jesus and about the earliest events in Christian history; it is hard for him to reshape his thinking so as to recognize that the documents purporting to tell the earliest events carry unmistakable echoes of times and situations much later than the events being narrated. The truly crucial thing to understand about the Gospels is that they more adequately reflect the rather late date in which they were written than they do the early events which they relate.

What we shall do, as we go along, is to look at the New Testament writings, especially the Gospels, for those things which pertain to Paul. (Were our subject a broader one, we would, of course, look more broadly. It is the narrow one of matters relating to Paul so that we can look from a restricted facet.)

Ultimately our pursuit is to be chronological, to look at New Testament literature in the order in which it was written. Yet, we cannot begin in that way. We must, first of all, look at The Acts of the Apostles. A mapreader must orient himself; The Acts of the Apostles will help us chart our course; and thereafter we can come to a chronological development. We need first to summarize what Acts has to say about Paul.

Written by the same hand which wrote the Gospel According to Luke, Acts begins by setting forth that Jesus, after his Resurrection, spent forty days with his followers in Jerusalem before he ascended to heaven. Peter emerged as the leader of the "brethren" who numbered about a hundred and twenty. It was necessary to appoint a successor to Judas, the disciple who in the Gospels had betrayed Jesus; according to Acts, Judas died through falling head-long and bursting open in his middle, though Matthew relates that Judas hanged himself (Mt. 27.3-10). It was necessary to designate as a successor a man who could meet two qualifications: one, he must have been a follower of Jesus from the time of the Baptism to the Ascension; two, he must have seen the Risen Christ ("be a witness to his resurrection"). Two candidates were put forward; one of these, a Matthias, was chosen (Chapter 1).

Next comes the narration of miraculous events on the festival of Pentecost. The Holy Spirit rested on the entire community, so that Jews from all over the world visiting in Jerusalem heard the believers, supposedly Galileans, addressing them wondrously in their various native tongues. Peter made a conversionist speech and three thousand converts were brought in. The enlarged community had all their possessions in common; they attended the temple every day (Chapter 2).

Peter (with John) healed a man who had been lame from birth, and made another speech in the portico of the temple (Chapter 3). Two thousand more converts were added by this second speech. The priests and the captain of the Temple and the Sadducees arrested the two and put them into custody until the next morning. Then, at an assembly of rulers, elders and scribes, some wished to punish them, but a fear of the people yielded their release. The company of believers numbered not one needy person, for all sold their possessions and brought the proceeds and laid it at the feet of the apostles (Chapter 4).

A certain Ananias kept back some of his proceeds, this with the knowledge of his wife Sapphira. Peter knew that they were lying to the Holy Spirit. Promptly Ananias fell down and died. Three hours later Sapphira similarly died.

Meanwhile people gathered from the towns around Jerusalem, bringing the sick and those afflicted with unclean spirits, and they were all healed. The Sadducees arrested the apostles and put them in the common prison, but an angel of the Lord opened the prison door that night, and at daybreak the apostles entered the temple and taught. The council (Sanhedrin) was assembled and the apostles brought before it. A Pharisee named Gamaliel defended them. He said, "If this plan or this undertaking (of the apostles) is of men, it will fail; but if it is of God, you will not be able to overthrow them" (Chapter 5).

Now some dissension arose within the Church between the Greek-speaking and the Hebrew-speaking members over the daily distribution (of food) to the widows. Seven men were appointed to "serve tables."* The number of disciples greatly increased in Jerusalem, and a great many priests joined the new faith.

Stephen, one of the members of the Church, got into a dispute with some Jews from Grecian lands, and they falsely charged him to the authorities with having spoken blasphemous words against Moses and God (Chapter 6). Brought before the council, Stephen made a long speech which infuriated his auditors. He gazed into heaven and saw Jesus standing at the right hand of God; he announced what he was seeing. His auditors rushed upon him, cast him out of the city, and stoned him. The witnesses against Stephen laid down their garments at the feet of a young man named "Saul." Stephen died of the stoning, and Saul, we are told, "was consenting to his death" (Chapter 7 and verse 1 of

* The Greek word for distribution is that which in English yields "deacon"; it means "to serve the needs of the people." The seven are known in Christian lore as the earliest "Deacons," though that title is not applied to them in the passage.

chapter 8). Here, then, we encounter Paul for the first time in Acts, though here under the name Saul.

As a result of the stoning of Stephen, a great persecution of the Christians arose, and the church, except the apostles, scattered throughout Judea and Samaria. Saul entered house after house and dragged off men and women and committed them to jail.

Of the scattered, Philip went to a Samarian city and there cured the paralyzed and lame. Even a man named Simon, who had previously practiced magic, was numbered among the many converts.

Philip's converting required completion by having the Holy Spirit conferred on the converts. Peter and John were sent to Samaria to lay hands on the converts and thereby to pass the Holy Spirit on to them. Simon, however, offered money to have the Spirit-giving hands laid on him. (Let us notice this man Simon Magus; we shall need to refer to him much later.) Peter rejected this offer, telling Simon that he was not to have part in the matter.

Philip then went towards Gaza. On the road he met and baptized an Ethiopian eunuch (Chapter 8).

Meanwhile, back in Jerusalem, Saul went to the high priests to ask for letters to the synagogue at Damascus so that he might bring in bonds from there to Jerusalem any Christians he might find there. On his way, a light from heaven flashed on him and he fell to the ground. He heard a voice: "Saul, Saul, why do you persecute me?" He asked, "Who are you, Lord?" He was answered, "I am Jesus whom you are persecuting. But rise and enter the city and you will be told what to do."

His companions were speechless, for they could hear the voice but could not see any one. For three days Saul was sightless.

In Damascus a second man named Ananias saw Jesus in a vision. Jesus commanded him to visit Saul and to lay hands on him so that he might regain his sight. Ananias replied that Saul had done great injury to the saints in Jerusalem, and that he had brought to Damascus authority to arrest all the Christians. Jesus said, "He is a chosen instrument of mine to carry my name before the Gentiles and kings and the sons of Israel; for I will show him how much he must suffer for the sake of my name." So Ananias did as he was commanded and Saul's sight was restored. Thereafter Saul preached about Jesus in the synagogue in Damascus and "confounded the Jews . . . by proving that Jesus was the Christ." The Jews plotted to kill him, but Saul's disciples took him by night and let him down over the wall, lowering him in a basket.

Saul returned to Jerusalem. The Church at first shunned him, but he told them how he had seen the Lord on the road, and how he had preached boldly in Damascus. So he was accepted by the group at Jerusalem. Next Saul fell into dispute with the Hellenists, that is the Graeco-Jews present in Jerusalem, and his life was endangered, so that the "brethren" sent him to his native Tarsus.

The church meanwhile was building up in Judea, Galilee and Samaria; now we follow Peter to Joppa and Caesarea. At this latter city in a thrice repeated vision Peter was taught that there are no valid food prohibitions; and then he converted one Cornelius, a Gentile officer, centurion of the Roman army. Then the Holy Spirit fell on the Gentiles who were with Peter (as on Pentecost it had fallen on the Jewish Christians in Jerusalem). Peter confirmed this baptism by the "spirit" with baptism with water (9.31-10.48).

When Peter returned to Jerusalem, the so-called "circumcision party" took him to task for eating with the uncircumcised. Peter thereupon told of his visions at Caesarea, and his opponents were silenced. The church had meanwhile spread to Antioch. Barnabas was sent there from Jerusalem to look into matters. Satisfied, Barnabas went on to Tarsus, where he found Saul and he brought him back to Antioch. There the two labored for a year. In Antioch the name "Christians" was first applied to the believers (11.19-26). A prophet, Agabus, predicted in

Antioch that a famine would take place in the time of the Roman emperor Claudius (died 54 AD). The Christians determined to send relief to Judea and to do so by the hand of Barnabas and Saul (Chapter 12).

Next, persecution broke out in Judea, resulting in the death of James, the brother of John, and in the arrest of Peter during the Passover. An angel of the Lord enabled Peter to escape from his captors (12.1-24).

At this point Acts turns back now to Barnabas and Saul.* The Holy Spirit bade them to do the work for which they had been called. In brief, they sailed to the island of Cyprus, and then to Paphos; they moved to Perga and to Pisidian-Antioch. In the account we are told briefly (13.9) that Saul was also called Paul. At Antioch it was Paul, not Barnabas, who spoke in the synagogue on two successive Sabbaths, and he attracted initially both Jews and Gentile converts to Judaism. On the second Sabbath, however, the Jews stirred up the community leaders who drove Paul and Barnabas out of the district (12.25-13.52).

Next at Iconium, the Jews again stirred up the populace. Paul and Barnabas fled to Lystra (where Paul healed a cripple) and to Derbe, and from there ultimately they sailed to Antioch (14.1-28).

At this latter city difficulty ensued with some of the "circumcision party" within the church. Paul and Barnabas were appointed, with others, to "go up to Jerusalem to the elders and apostles about this question." At Jerusalem there was a great debate. Then Peter rose to defend the abstinence by Gentile converts from circumcision. He disclosed to those assembled that in the early days God had chosen him from among them as the mis-

* Acts 12.25 is textually uncertain; the last mention of the two supposed that they were in Antioch. Some manuscripts read that they returned to Jerusalem, raising a difficulty in what ensues, which supposes that they were still in Antioch; others read *from* Jerusalem, and its difficulty is that the book has not described any trip to Jerusalem, so that we cannot understand the *from* there.

sionary to the Gentiles, that "by my mouth the Gentiles should hear the word of the Gospel and believe."

Then Barnabas and Paul related the signs and wonders which they had done among Gentiles. James rendered a verdict against the need of circumcision; but he proposed a continuing validity of three prohibitions* (15.1-29). This set of prohibitions may be referred to as the "apostolic decree."

Thereupon two men, Silas and Judas, accompanied Paul and Barnabas to Antioch, the four of them carrying the decree in a letter from "the apostles and the elders." This letter would be confirmed orally by Judas and Silas, and would enjoin "no greater burden than these necessary things: that you abstain from what has been sacrificed to idols and from blood and from what is strangled and from unchastity."

The congregation at Antioch was gathered, the letter with the decree was read, and there was rejoicing.

Barnabas declined to accompany Paul on a return to the cities which they had earlier visited, so that Paul went off with Silas (15.30-41).

The remainder of Acts deals with Paul as the central character.

Paul was joined at Derbe and Lystra by a half-Jew named Timothy. Paul circumcised him because the Jews in those places knew that Timothy's father was a Greek (16.1-5). As Paul and Timothy traveled in those cities, they delivered to their hearers for observance the decisions reached by the apostles and elders at Jerusalem. They passed through Galatia, and then into Europe. They were on their way to Macedonia.

The narrative up to this point has been in the third person. Now (16.10) there is an abrupt shift to the first person: "Imme-

* For our purposes we need not go deeply into the textual problems of what was prohibited. In most texts of Acts they are summarized as pollutions with idols, unchastity, and blood. A manuscript tradition, the so-called Codex Bezae, has a different and longer reading; a vast literature exists about this "apostolic decree." It is repeated in Acts 15.29 and in 21.26. See also Rev. 2.14 and 20.

diately it sought to go into Macedonia," concluding that "God had called *us* to preach the gospel to them." Four such "we-sections" are to be found in Acts.* Paul exorcized a demon from a slave girl who had a spirit of divination. Her owners brought charges that Paul and Silas, Jews, were disturbing the city by advocating customs unlawful for Romans to accept or practice. They were jailed. A midnight earthquake broke their fetters and effected the conversion of the jailer. When the magistrates wished to summon them for trial, they learned to their dismay that Paul and Silas were Roman citizens, so they came and apologized to them (16.6-40).

At Thessalonica (now Salonica) Paul argued with the Jews for three weeks, proving his contentions from Scripture. Some Jews, many Greeks, and some leading women became converts. The other Jews assembled a rabble at the home of their host, Jason. Paul and Silas escaped to Berea. There they converted the noble Jews who welcomed them and also some Greek women of high standing. However, the Thessalonian Jews arrived and stirred things up. Paul departed alone for Athens. Silas and Timothy remained at Berea. At Athens Paul preached on Mars Hill (Areopagus), taking his text from an inscription which he saw: "To an unknown God." He declared that he was proclaiming this God to the Athenians. The speech went well until his audience of philosophers heard the doctrine of resurrection. Some mocked, but others wanted to hear him again. A few became converts (17.1-33).

Paul journeyed next to Corinth. There he met two Jews, Aquila and his wife Priscilla. They were from Rome, from which the Jewish community in its entirety had recently been expelled by the emperor Claudius. Aquila was a tentmaker and so was Paul (18.1-4). It was at Corinth that Paul reached the climax of his harassment by Jews. Silas and Timothy arrived there to find Paul preaching and testifying to Jews that the Christ was Jesus. The Jews opposed and reviled him. Paul shook out his garments and

* They are at 16.10-17; 20.5-15; 21.1-18; and 27.1-28.16.

said to them: "Your blood be upon your heads. From now on I will go to the Gentiles" (18.5-7). Paul remained at Corinth for a year and a half (18.11).

At that time the Jews made charges against him with the proconsul, Gallio. Paul, they said, was persuading men to worship God contrary to the law. Gallio declared that the uproar "is a matter of questions about words and names and your own law . . . I refuse to be a judge of these things" (18.12-17).

Paul later moved to Cenchreae; there he cut his hair in accord with a vow.

He left Aquila and Priscilla at Ephesus; he sailed on to Caesarea, and then went to Antioch, and after that through Galatia and Phrygia. At Ephesus, Aquila and Priscilla encountered an Alexandrian Jewish convert named Apollos. This Apollos was not well informed on the baptism of Jesus so that Priscilla and Aquila expounded things to him more accurately. Apollos crossed over to Europe, going to Corinth (18.18-28).

Paul now came to Ephesus. He encountered disciples there who had received "John's baptism," but who had not received the Holy Spirit. They were baptized in the name of the Lord Jesus; then when Paul laid his hands upon them, the Holy Spirit came on them. Thereafter Paul preached in the synagogue, but after three months of failure with Jews he withdrew and went to the hall of one Tyrannus. There he preached daily for two years (19.1-10).

Among the extraordinary miracles done by Paul at Ephesus, there were healings and exorcisms accomplished merely by bringing his handkerchief or apron to the sick. Exorcists themselves, seven sons of a Jewish high priest named Sceva were trying to emulate Paul's exorcisms; they were pronouncing the name of Jesus over an evil spirit in a man. The evil spirit answered these seven, "Jesus I know, and Paul I know, but who are you?" The man possessed by the evil spirit leaped upon them and they fled naked and wounded. As a result, the practice of magic in Ephesus, which even believers had been guilty of, ceased. The magicians brought their books to be burned, though these were valued at 50,000 pieces of silver.

One Demetrius was the maker of shrines of the Greek goddess Artemis. The craftsmen of Ephesus were associated with him. These were losing trade because of the growth of Christianity. Indeed, Paul was turning people all over Asia Minor away from gods made by hands. The devotees of Artemis rioted. The populace rushed into the town theater, dragging two companions of Paul there. Paul was persuaded by friends that it was dangerous for him to venture into the theater. The riot was quelled, however, by the town clerk. This official challenged Demetrius and the craftsmen to take to court anyone against whom they had complaints.

Paul next went to Macedonia and then to Greece. Then he sailed from Philippi to Troas with many companions. (Here another "we-section" begins.) At Troas, as Paul prolonged a speech, a young man named Eutyches ("Lucky") fell asleep and tumbled from the third story. He was thought to be dead. Paul bent over and embraced him, saying, "Do not be alarmed for his life is in him." The boy lived (Acts 19.21-20.12).

Paul and his companions sailed to Mitylene, Samos, and Miletus. At the latter place Paul summoned the Ephesian elders to him. Paul confided to them that he was on his way to Jerusalem and that "imprisonment and afflictions await me" (20.13-36).

Several laps brought Paul to Tyre; there the Christians told Paul not to go to Jerusalem. Renewing the voyage, Paul arrived at Ptolemais, and after that at Caesarea. There at the home of one Philip the evangelist, the prophet Agabus* took Paul's girdle and bound his own feet and hands, and said: "So shall the Jews at Jerusalem bind the man who owns this girdle and deliver him into the hands of the Gentiles" (21.1-15).

At Jerusalem Paul was greeted gladly. He was advised that it would be prudent to appease the Jews, who knew his reputation

* Is he the same Agabus whom we met before? Probably. But he is introduced here as though he is as yet unknown.

of having nullified the Law, by purifying himself along with four men who were under a vow. Accordingly, Paul purified himself, and went into the Temple with the men. Jews from Asia saw him in the Temple. They stirred up the populace to seize Paul. The Roman soldiers, observing the great tumult, rescued Paul. He was brought into the barracks for questioning, for the uproar made investigation out-of-doors impossible. Indeed, the mob outside was shouting "Away with him!"

Before Paul was brought into the barracks he received permission from the tribune to address the people. He did so in Hebrew. The crowd was noisy until they heard him speaking Hebrew. This quieted them.

Paul told them that he was a Jew of Tarsus, brought up in Jerusalem at the feet of Gamaliel. He had had a strict upbringing and was a persecutor of Christianity until the Road to Damascus. This event he related with embellishments. "When I had returned to Jerusalem and was praying in the Temple, I fell into a trance and saw him [the Christ] saying to me, 'Make haste and get quickly out of Jerusalem, because they will not accept your testimony about me.' And I said, 'Lord, they themselves know that in every synagogue I imprisoned and beat those who believed in thee. And when the blood of Stephen thy witness was shed, I also was standing by and approving, and keeping the garments of those who killed him.' And he said to me, 'Depart; for I will send you far away to the Gentiles.' "

At this point there was a renewed uproar, and shouts full of danger to Paul, so that Paul was brought into the barracks.

To find out why the throng was so opposed to Paul, the tribune wanted to examine him by scourging. They got as far as tying him up; at that point Paul informed the centurion that he was a Roman citizen whom it was illegal to scourge. The centurion reported this to his superior, the tribune. The tribune had bought his citizenship for a large sum; Paul was born a citizen. Paul was unbound; the tribune summoned the priests and the Council (Sanhedrin) to meet.

The next day Paul was brought by the tribune before the Council. The high priest Ananias commanded by-standers to strike Paul. They did, and Paul reviled the priest. Asked if he would revile God's high priest, Paul said, "I did not know that he was a high priest, for it is written [Exodus 22.28], 'You shall not speak evil of a ruler of your people.' " Paul now perceived that before him were Pharisees and Sadducees. He cried out that he was a Pharisee, and that he was on trial about the hope and the resurrection of the dead. Promptly a dissension arose between the Pharisees and Sadducees, the former of whom now defended Paul. In the midst of the dissension the soldiers brought Paul back to the barracks.

At night the Lord appeared to Paul: "Take courage, for as you have testified about me at Jerusalem so must you bear witness also at Rome" (23.1-11).

The Jews conceived a plot to kill Paul, but his nephew heard about it and warned him. The information came to the Romans and the tribune dispatched Paul to the governor Felix at Caesarea.

Five days later the high priest Ananias and a spokesman Tertullus arrived at Caesarea and there accused Paul of being a ringleader of the sect of the Nazarenes, and of an effort to profane the Temple. In rebuttal, Paul pointed to his having attended the Temple peacefully twelve days previously. He said, "This I admit to you, that according to the Way, which they call a sect, I worship the God of our fathers, believing everything laid down by the law or written in the prophets, having a hope in God which these themselves accept that there will be a resurrection."

At this point the governor decided to put off the case until the tribune Lysias would come down. Paul was kept in custody, but was allowed some liberty and also some visitors.

Felix with his Jewish wife Drusilla later visited to hear Paul speak about justice, self-control, and future judgment. Felix hoped to get money from Paul and he conversed with him often. But two years elapsed; Felix was succeeded as governor by Porcius Festus, and Paul was still in prison (23.12-24.27).

The Jewish leaders tried to prevail on Festus to send Paul to Jerusalem so that they could ambush him on the way. Festus refused; instead they were to come to Caesarea to accuse him there.

They came, and with many serious charges which they could not prove. Paul said, "Neither against the Law of the Jews, nor against the Temple, nor against Caesar have I offended at all." Paul went on to appeal to Caesar himself; Festus replied, "You have appealed to Caesar; to Caesar you shall go" (25.1-12).

A few days later Festus laid the matter before Agrippa and Bernice, the Jewish king and his sister, who expressed the wish to hear Paul. Festus stated that he was reluctant to send Paul to Caesar without some definite charge to accompany him.

Paul spoke before the king and Bernice, telling of his youth spent in Jerusalem, of the strictness of his rearing as a Pharisee, of the Road to Damascus, and of his proclaiming "throughout all the country of Judea, and also to the Gentiles, that they should repent and turn to God and perform deeds worthy of their repentance. For this reason the Jews seized me in the temple and tried to kill me. . ." Paul challenged Agrippa: "King Agrippa, do you believe the prophets?" Agrippa said to Festus: "This man could have been set free if he had not appealed to Caesar" (25.13-26.32).

We come now to another "We" section. Paul was delivered to a centurion named Julius. They set sail—the account in Acts traces the route—and found themselves along the coast of Crete, where a tempestuous northeaster put them into great difficulties. Paul comforted the crew and passengers with the word that "This very night there stood by me an angel of the God to whom I belong and whom I worship and he said, 'Do not be afraid, Paul; you must stand before Caesar.' " The ship went aground on an island which turned out to be Malta. The natives see a viper on Paul's hand and expect him to swell and suddenly fall down dead; when this did not happen they said that he was a god (27.1-28.6).

The chief man of the island, Publius, entertained Paul and his companions. Publius' father was healed of a fever and dysentery by Paul's prayers and by his putting his hands on him. Then Paul cured the rest of the diseased people on the island (28.7-10).

Three months later, after putting in at Syracuse (in Sicily), they finally arrived at Puteoli (near Naples). There they found brethren who welcomed them, and they stayed for seven days. Then they came to Rome and were met by brethren who met them at the Forum of Appius and Three Taverns and escorted them into the city. Paul was allowed to remain alone with the soldier who guarded him (28.11-16).

Paul summoned the Jewish leaders of Rome and told them of his status. They answered that they had received no letter from Judea about him, and no evil word had reached them. They appointed a day on which they would hear him expound his views. They came to his lodging in great numbers. Paul tried to convince them about Jesus both from the Law of Moses and from the prophets. Some were convinced, some not. Paul quoted to them Isaiah 6.9-10: "This people's heart has grown dull, and their ears heavy of hearing, and their eyes they have closed . . ." He concluded: "Let it be known to you then that this salvation of God has been sent to the Gentiles; they will listen" (28.17-28).

The book ends with the statement that in the next two years Paul welcomed all who came to him, "preaching the kingdom of God and teaching about the Lord Jesus Christ quite openly and unhindered" (28.29-31).

This, then, is the testimony of Acts. We need now to ask ourselves whether or not it is reliable testimony; does it agree or disagree with what Paul tells us about himself, his doctrines, his accomplishment? Or is a different conclusion inevitable in view of the contradictions and discrepancies.

First, Acts tell us that Paul spent his youth in Jerusalem, that he was present at the stoning of Stephen, that after his conversion on the Road to Damascus, he spent time in Damascus preaching, proving that Jesus was the Christ, that he escaped from Damascus by being lowered over the wall in a basket, that he came to Jerusalem to join the apostles, who were afraid of him, but Barnabas sponsored him (Acts 7.58; 8.1; 9.1-27). But, to the contrary, Galatians contains Paul's assertion that he had never been in Palestine before his conversion near Damascus. Gal. 1.15-24 reads: "But when he who had set me apart before I was born and had called me through his grace, was pleased to reveal his Son to me in order that I might preach him among the Gentiles, I did not confer with flesh and blood, nor did I go up to Jerusalem to those who were apostles before me, but I went away into Arabia; and again I returned to Damascus. Then after three years I went up to Jerusalem to visit Cephas and remained with him fifteen days. But I saw none of the other apostles except James the Lord's brother. Then I went into the regions of Syria and Cilicia. And I was still not known by sight to the churches of Christ in Judea; they only heard it said, 'He who once persecuted us is now preaching the faith he once tried to destroy.' "

Second, in very many passages in the Epistles, Paul asserted that the Law of Moses, having been superseded, needed no longer to be observed; he even argued that it was wrong to observe it. In Acts, however, he was willing to spend seven days at the Temple in fulfillment of a vow. In Galatians, he contended that he had steadfastly refused to circumcise his companion Titus. In Acts he circumcised Timothy.

Third, Paul told in Romans (chapters 9-11) that practically no Jews had become Christians and that God had accepted the church as the new Israel, displacing the old. Acts, on the other hand (21.20), tells us that on the occasion of Paul's last visit to Jerusalem there were many tens of thousands* of Jews among those who believed.

* The King James, the Revised Standard Version, and Moffatt read in English "thousands" in place of "tens of thousands," but my comment on the discrepancy is not altered by accepting the incorrect rendering.

Fourth, in Galatians Paul had insisted that he was an apostle from God and not from man. Acts concedes, by the account of the incident on the Road to Damascus, that Paul had seen the Risen Christ. But Acts tells us that Paul, after being led sightless to Damascus, needed to have Ananias lay hands on him and fill him with the Holy Spirit, and then Paul arose and was baptized. (Paul's Epistles do not relate or allude to his having been baptized.) Moreover, Acts tell us that when Paul came to Jerusalem it was through the help of Barnabas that he became acceptable to Apostles there.

Fifth, throughout his Epistles Paul insisted that he was preaching a unique Gospel. We spoke of this above; the key references are Galatians 1.6-11 and Second Corinthians 11.4. Similarly, when Paul wrote in his Epistle to the Romans of his wish to visit his addressees, he spoke of his desire to "impart some spiritual gift to strengthen them . . . I want you to know, brethren, that I have often intended to come to you . . . in order that I may reap some harvest among you as well as among the rest of the Gentiles. I owe a duty both to Greeks and to barbarians, both the wise and the foolish. Hence the eagerness on my part to preach the gospel to you also who are in Rome." As the phrase "the rest of the Gentiles" shows, this church is a Gentile church; Paul's addressees here are *already* Christians. Yet Paul feels that his Gospel contains some element of special value even to those who are already within the church. Thus, his Epistles speak consistently of his having a unique, revealed Gospel. Yet at the scene of Paul's trial in Acts 23.6, we get the astounding declaration from Paul that all that is at stake in his preachment is the mere matter of the resurrection. Moreover, the author of Acts suggests that Paul made this incredible, mendacious statement deliberately, when he "perceived that one part were Sadducees and the other Pharisees."

And last, in this connection, is the disparity in the accounts of Paul's consultation with the leaders in Jerusalem. Acts 15 tells that dissension having arisen in Antioch between abrogators and maintainers of circumcision, Paul and Barnabas and some others *were appointed* to go up to Jerusalem to the apostles and the elders about it. Gal. 2.2, however, declares that Paul went up by a *revelation*. The second chapter of Galatians recounts Paul's insistence that he did not bow to the authority of the church in Jerusalem; he set before it the Gospel which he preached to Gentiles and he received from the "pillars" the right hand of friendship; they confirmed him, he reports, as the apostle to Gentiles, and Peter as the apostle to Jews. In Acts, however, the initial admission of Gentiles into the church was accomplished by Peter at Joppa and confirmed promptly at Jerusalem, and this at a time when Paul had ostensibly retired to his native Tarsus until summoned to Antioch by Barnabas. At the meeting, as matters are related in Acts, it is Peter who claims to have been the apostle to the Gentiles, and Peter who advocates that the Jewish law not be imposed on Gentile converts. The council then issues, according to Acts, a decree containing the requirements expected of Gentile converts, embodying three (some texts have four) points. About this decree the Epistles of Paul are completely silent. According to Acts, however, Paul himself helped broadcast this decree.

Now this problem of the relationship of Acts 15 to Gal. 2, with the glaring discrepancies, is, like the relationship of Acts to the Epistles, a very old problem. We need now to call on some of the "experts" to help us evaluate the problem. There have been roughly four different solutions proposed respecting Gal.2 and Acts 15. One of these tries to handle the inherent contradictions by asserting that the two accounts are not describing the same event, but two different events, and, accordingly, the discrepancies are of no moment. The event of Gal.2, such people contend, is alluded to in Acts 11.30. This verse tells no more than that Barnabas and Paul delivered alms to the elders in Jerusalem at the time of the famine predicted by Agabus. This solution has not commended itself to many students; Acts 11.30 says nothing that would suggest that a church council was held.

The total effect of this proposal turns out only to underline the discrepancies between Acts 15 and Gal. 2, for it comes out of an acute awareness that Acts 15 and Gal. 2 are beyond reconciliation.

A second proposed solution involved harmonization of the discrepancies. This is attempted by tabulating, as it were, the elements of agreement and disagreement in Acts 15 and Gal. 2, and then by concluding that the items of agreement are more numerous. This procedure results either in thereafter ignoring the discordant matters, on the basis that a sufficient number are in accord, or else, distinctions are drawn between the supposed subjectivity in Paul and the supposed objectivity in Acts. We are told, for example, that when Paul claims that he went to Jerusalem by a revelation, he is discussing the matter internally, as it affected him, while the author of Acts speaks externally. Or, we are told that Paul is being biased. These latter statements are no more than polite assertions that Paul is lying. If the event of the church council in Acts 15 and Gal.2 is the same, it is inescapable that we select one of the accounts as the tolerably correct one, and reject the other.

A third solution, which comes from the fringes of scholarship, stresses that the contradictions are irreconcilable. It declares that the account in Acts is the reliable one—goes on to assert that the Epistle to the Galatians is not really by Paul, but is, rather, a late and unreliable pseudonymous writing, designed to emphasize the rupture between Christianity and Judaism, and to repudiate the theme of Acts that Christianity was fully faithful to Judaism. Now neither I nor anybody else who turns aside from the traditional views about authorship of New Testament books is able conclusively to "prove" or "disprove" some particular authorship. Those who, like me, do not believe that Paul wrote the Epistles to Timothy which bear his name can scarcely "prove" that Paul did write Galatians. But my own judgment about Galatians is this, that the premise that Galatians is not by Paul ought to be accompanied by a cessation from trying at all to understand the New Testament. I know of no other writing in either Old or New Testament which elicits from me the unreserved feeling of genuineness and of a sense of personal contact with the author. Accordingly, if to prefer the Acts account about the Council over the Galatian account means to reject the Pauline authorship of Galatians, then we end up in a blind alley.

The fourth solution is that of Tübingen—a German university—scholars of over a century ago. In my judgment the "Tübingen school" was on the threshold of the correct solution. It did not reach the true solution because of its subjection to the "dialectic" of the philosopher Hegel which was central in the Tübingen approach. Hegel (1770-1831) supposed that in the history of any religious movement, once it is underway, one group in the movement continues in the line of the founding personality; rather soon, however, some other group or groups, though remaining within the movement, move with a pendulum swing to some extreme position; thereafter there arises a third stage in which the various opposing views are brought together and harmonized. These three stages are known as thesis, antithesis, and synthesis.

The Tübingen scholars correctly discerned that in Galatians there were reflected two positions extremely opposed to each other, the one of Paul and the other of Peter. They saw correctly that in Acts there is an easing of the tensions and that Paul and Peter hold similar views. The Tübingen scholars believed that Acts deliberately sought to show, especially through its chapter 15, that there were no substantial differences between Peter and Paul. This end result Acts accomplished by a double process: one facet was to make Peter conform to Paul by having Peter be the first to bring Gentiles into the church and to make the claim to be the apostle to the Gentiles and the first to abrogate the Law of Moses; the other facet was to bring Paul nearer to Peter by having Paul subservient to the Jerusalem elders and faithful to the Temple; and Paul preached in diaspora synagogues initially to Jews and only somewhat reluctantly thereafter to Gentiles and the like. In short, Acts seemed to the Tübingen school to be arguing on behalf of a unity and serenity in the church at some relatively late date, by romancing about its inner unity and serenity in the primitive period. So far, so good, in my opinion.

But the Tübingen school went on to fit this schematization into the pattern of thesis, antithesis, and synthesis. As they saw things, there emerged from the opposition between the Jewish Christian party of Peter (the thesis) and the Gentile Christian party of Paul (antithesis), the synthesis of early Roman Catholicism. Acts, by this view, is a late writing, designed to strengthen the synthesis of the two opposing parties, the Jewish Christians and the Gentile Christians.

The schematization by the Tübingen school has failed to persuade subsequent generations of scholars. The Hegelian pattern has seemed too artificial; the Tübingen school relied too extremely on some literature, not in the New Testament, known as the "Pseudo-Clementines." * But if anything at all has survived

* The Pseudo-Clementine writings are principally two works, *Homilies* and *Recognitions*, supposedly by a second century Roman, Clement. This literature relates to the matter here under consideration in this way, that it describes some events in which "Peter" bests Simon Magus in the series of disputes and contests. Curiously, Simon Magus is described as having many of the characteristics which New Testament literature attributes to Paul; and allusions in the Pseudo-Clementine literature to Simon Magus' career become clearer when they are interpreted as referring to incidents in Paul's life. It would be easy, accordingly, to interpret Simon Magus simply as a substitute name for Paul were it not that the literature is so manifestly from a century after Paul's time. Why attack Paul a century after Paul's day? A good many theories have arisen to explain "Simon's" similarity to Paul; for example, Simon Magus is interpreted to be not Paul, but rather the arch-heretic of the second century, Marcion, an extreme Paulinist.

There are great disputes about the Pseudo-Clementine literature. It is to be doubted, moreover, that these writings are the product of one hand and of one single date. In recent years there has been revived a tendency to see in this literature a good and reliable reflection of Palestine Jewish Christianity. There have been those who have wanted to build a bridge between this Palestine Jewish Christianity and the Dead Sea Scroll community. Somewhat similarly the Tübingen school of a century ago in-from the Tübingen school, it has been its recognition of some of the leading motifs and purposes of Acts.

To the problems of the conflicts between Galatians and Acts, the Tübingen answer would be that the Acts account is relatively late, without historical validity, and *tendentious*. This latter word may need some explanation beyond its dictionary sense. Its basic meaning is "written with a view to effect"; it means almost the same as "tendency," except that "tendentiousness" carries with it a connotation of deliberate and premeditated purpose, whereas "tendency" is less deliberate. For example, there is at first glance a tendency in Acts to declare that Jews, not Romans, caused the early church its difficulties; but further, intensive study shows that this motif is not historically reliable but is rather the objective of the *tendentiousness* of Acts.

The Tübingen school correctly noted each tendency *in* Acts, but it misread the real tendentiousness of Acts. The Tübingen school made it necessary for subsequent explainers to start with the notice that Acts and the Epistles contain discrepancies and contradictions which are beyond harmonization or explaining away. The attention of scholars focused, properly, on Acts as the problem. Acts is the puzzle which needs to be solved.

---

terpreted the Pseudo-Clementines as somewhat reflecting Palestine Christianity. In the Tübingen theory the Pseudo-Clementines became a prop in their structure of two simultaneous impulses existing in early Christianity.

The complex problems in the Pseudo-Clementines obstruct an easy answer to all the enigmas raised. Yet this much can be said in our context: The anti-Paulinism in the Pseudo-Clementines reflects not Palestine Jewish Christianity, but rather an arm or a segment of the Dispersion Gentile church. The Pseudo-Clementines are more interested in disparaging Pauline doctrine (and those who are conceived as overextending it) than they are Paul himself. Probably by this time Paul had become too sacred a character for a clear and direct attack on him to be made. It is as though the Pseudo-Clementines are saying: Villainous teachings have come into being in Christianity, these in the name of Paul; in reality, however, these teachings come from the scoundrel Simon Magus, and not from the respectable and respected Paul.

Other literature, from the same period as the Pseudo-Clementines, and even later, depicts "Paul" in triumphant contest with "Simon Magus."

We need to call on the experts and to see what they in turn tell us about Acts in its broad outlines; so far we saw the experts only in connection with the Jerusalem council. (I follow here the chapter by MacGiffert, in Foakes-Jackson and Lake, *The Beginnings of Christianity,* II, 363-395.) The attack on the trustworthiness of Acts was pre-eminently by F. C. Baur of Tübingen in 1838. He built his case on the earlier work of a Karl Schrader who had concluded that the purpose of the author of Acts was controllingly apologetic and that the historical trustworthiness was thereby seriously affected. Baur at first suggested that Acts was written by a Paulinist to defend the Apostle's mission to the Gentiles against the attacks of Jewish Christians by showing that Paul had everywhere preached first to the Jews and had turned to the Gentiles only after the former had rejected his gospel. Later on, however, Baur moved on to a different view, namely, that Acts belonged in a group of writings, including the Epistles of James, the goal of which was a reconciliation of the hostile opposing parties of Jewish Christians and Paulinists.

After Baur, Schneckenburger "agreed that the purpose of the author of Acts was primarily apologetic and not historical—to defend the apostle [Paul] against the attacks of Judaisers and to remove as far as possible the Jewish Christian prejudice against him—but he maintained that there has been no serious departure from historic fact . . . Luke . . . drew a detailed parallel between his [Paul's] achievement and Peter's . . . Paul uniformly keeps the Jewish law with meticulous care. . . . His recorded discourses . . . contain no trace of the gospel of freedom from law, which bulks so large in Paul's Epistles. Titus, his uncircumcised gentile companion, is not mentioned nor is his work in Galatia . . . The whole work is brought to a climax with. . . . Paul's declaration, 'Be it known unto you, therefore, that this salvation of God is sent unto Gentiles; they will listen.' . . . There is more Paulinism in the first half of the book than in the second, more in the mouths of the early disciples than in Paul's own mouth . . . Luke did not invent or falsify his facts . . . but simply selected his material in such a way as to produce the desired effect."

Albert Schwegler, however, reverted to Baur's unfavorable judgment of the historicity of Acts: ". . . Even though the first part at any rate, and the second as well, are based on older sources and narratives, when we remove the improbable, the impossible, the demonstrably unhistorical . . . there is extraordinarily little historical reality left. The complete historical trustworthiness of the Acts is impugned even by its numerous purposeful omissions and silences . . ."

Eduard Zeller built on all these predecessors. According to him, the chief aim of Acts was "to convince Jewish Christians that a free Gentile Christianity was legitimate. . . . by conceding the legitimacy of their own Jewish form of Christianity . . . 'The work is the peace proposal of a Paulinist who wishes to purchase the recognition of Gentile Christianity from Jewish Christians by concessions to Judaism and in this sense to influence both parties.' " Zeller added that a subsidiary purpose of Acts was to conciliate the Roman government and to prove the harmlessness of Christianity from a political point of view by showing that Paul was uniformly acquitted whenever he appeared before Roman authorities.

In sum, then, despite the variations, the Tübingen school and its adjuncts not only considered Acts a "tendentious" work but delineated the "Tendenz" as an effort by the author to reconcile the Gentile and Jewish Christianity of the author's own time.

Opposition to the Tübingen school came not only from the upholders of tradition (who still flourish in our day), but also from within the liberal scholarship. Bruno Bauer, for example, was sure that by the time Acts was written, the battle between the Judaizers and the Paulinists was already over; Acts, therefore, was not a proposal for future peace, but the expression of its past consummation. " 'The Acts first brought Judaism to recognition and control within the church. It helped to fasten the chains that bound the Church to the Jewish world, and the Church clung to Acts. . . . because it wished this bond with Judaism . . . The Judaism which was represented in the Acts and was reconciled to Paulinism was naturally not historic Judaism . . . Nor was it the Jewish Christianity of which recent scholars have so much to say.' " This modification of the Tübingen view is, in my judgment, most *à propos*.

A Frenchman, Ernest Renan, rejected at one and the same time both the Tübingen view and also the trustworthiness of Acts. Acts is " 'A dogmatic history written to support the orthodox doctrines of the time. . . .' "

Another rejection of the Tübingen view came from Overbeck. He too held that the book was apologetic, not historical. He saw in it " '. . . The attempt of a Gentile Christianity. . . . to explain its own past, particularly its own origin and its first founder Paul . . .' The author wrote in the second century, so long after the events recorded that he was largely ignorant of the situation. . . ."

Somewhat similarly Pfleiderer believed that the author of Acts, at a time in which Paulinism was already a changed thing, interpreted the conditions of the apostolic age in good faith and used his sources ingenuously on the assumption that the relation of Jewish and Gentile Christianity could not have been other in the days of primitive Christianity than it seemed in his own, a relation, namely, of mutual approximation and growing understanding and amity on the part of the saner elements in the two parties. . . .

In sum, the liberal scholarship found the Tübingen contention of tendentiousness correct, but could not agree that it was a proposal for the future. The scholarship, though rejecting the Tübingen view, remained skeptical about the trustworthiness of the historical material in Acts. The predominant view of nineteenth century scholars can be summarized in Jülicher's words: " 'In the Acts the Gentile Church of the beginning of the second century has codified its best knowledge of the first period of its history.' "

A more conservative view has gained considerable vogue from the eminence of its propagator, Harnack, as a church historian. Starting with the conclusion that Luke, the author of the Gospel, was also the author of Acts and that Luke was written rather early (in the first, not second century), Harnack pushed the date when Acts was written back to a time when Paul was still alive. While most scholarship has agreed with Harnack that the same author wrote both Luke and Acts, Harnack has persuaded only a minority of scholars of a relatively early date for Acts. The majority have clung to the Jülicher view.

Still another approach, and far different from anything offered before, was set forth by John Knox in 1942 in *Marcion and the New Testament*. It will be recalled that Marcion was the second century figure of some great eminence and influence. Born about 110 A.D., Marcion spearheaded a movement and a theology which resulted in his being denounced as a heretic. Marcion is known to us primarily through the denunciations of him in the church fathers. He has an oblique significance in New Testament problems in that it is usually held that it was Marcion's gesture which brought into being a more or less official New Testament. Marcion appears to have constructed a "canon" consisting of no more than one Gospel, probably Luke, and no less than ten Epistles of Paul. Since by Marcion's time other gospels and epistles were in existence, the concentration by Marcion on Paul was obviously the result of his conscious choice. Tertullian (born 160 A.D., died about 230) wrote five heated books (about 210) against Marcion, the fifth of which was an attack on Marcion's understanding of Paul. This need in the third century to attack Marcion so severely even after his death attests to the importance and size of Marcion's movement; it remained in existence in the regions of Italy for some three hundred years, and in the Eastern domains of the church some centuries longer.

Tertullian accuses Marcion (in Book V, section II) of having rejected the Acts of the Apostles, and he goes on to give what has since his time become the standard traditional reconciliations of the Epistles and of Acts. Tertullian's refutation of Marcion gives us some clues to Marcion's adulation of Paul, for it was the Paul of the Epistles, not the Paul of Acts whom Marcion took as the real person.

The full nature of Marcion's "heresy" need not concern us. Two facets merit our notice. One of these was Marcion's contention, which was much more widespread than Marcion alone, that Jesus was never a real person; he believed it incredible that God should become incarnate in a physical body. Tertullian says this of Marcion's view: "His Christ . . . was not what he appeared to be, and feigned himself to be what he was not—incarnate without being flesh, human without being man . . ." The broad denial of the physical reality of Jesus was termed "docetism"; the word means "to seem"; Jesus was not really a physical being, he only "seemed" to be.

The second emphasis of Marcion was that the God of the Old Testament was a false god, and that the Old Testament was false. In a word, Marcion wanted to sever completely any relationship between Christianity and its parent Judaism.

Respecting Paul, Tertullian accuses Marcion of mutilating Paul's Epistles so as to make them conform to Marcion's emphasis. Marcion, it would appear, had assembled what to others seemed too brief and one-sided a collection of Christian writings. Some twenty-five years after Marcion's hey-day there arose the first list which somewhat encompasses the full list as it is now found in the usual canon. The more or less accepted view is that the central church countered Marcion on two levels. It declared the Old Testament to be canonical for Christians and it countered his short list by a longer one.

Now it turns out that insofar as Marcion's Luke was concerned, it was shorter than our Luke (if indeed it was Luke). Early attacks on Marcion charged him with having shortened Luke, while scattered evidence indicates that the Marcionites denied the accusation and they in turn accused their opponents of having lengthened and thus distorted the true Gospel. Professor Knox revives a dispute, which had some vogue among scholars, about Marcion's Luke; Knox suggests that what the Church did was to adopt Marcion's short Luke and to lengthen and recast it, and to create the Acts of the Apostles to add to Luke.

The context in which Knox (p.115) believes the Church found the action necessary was this, that ". . . The more conservative churches (and this means Rome principally) in the middle of the second century were confronted with the necessity of a crucial choice as far as Paul is concerned: either they must canonize him or repudiate him (or at least seriously discredit him). . . ."

There are some keen observations in Knox's book, but I do not believe that its main thesis is completely right. Or, rather, I believe that its deficiency, as in the case of the others whom I have cited, lies rather in a failure to bring into proper focus and sequence the basically correct glimpses which it has. The crux of the matter which we have been pursuing has been this series of questions: Does Paul in Acts have the same character which he has in his Epistles? If it is a different character, which is the reliable one? What in the nature of Acts can help us choose between it and the Epistles?

For myself, I have no clear idea when Acts was written, except that I incline towards a second century date, not a first. I do not believe that most or any ancient writings had just one and only one purpose; I would suggest this respecting the Paul of Acts, that Acts deliberately handles Paul as it does, not because the author of Acts misunderstands him, but because he understands him very accurately.

The author's intent, if we may so speak of one bit of tendentiousness among several, is to divert us exactly from that understanding of Paul which I have tried to set forth in the preceding chapters. What Acts does in its anti-Marcionism is to change Paul from being a religious genius into being just one more missionary. Others, as indicated, have seen this in Acts too.

But I do not believe that this reduction of Paul was designed to bring about a reconciliation, past or future, between Jewish and Gentile Christianity, nor simply to serve as a retort to Marcion. It was done rather under the same necessity in which Amos, Isaiah, and Jeremiah are neutralized in the Old Testament by being set into the canon of a Scripture embodying in part ritual activities at total variance with the view of these prophets. The Pentateuch does not obliterate the pre-exilic prophets; it only neutralizes them. The New Testament does not obliterate Paul; it only neutralizes him. The chief tool in the neutralization of Paul is Acts. But Acts is not the only tool, for the other tools are the Synoptic Gospels, James, and the Pastoral Epistles. All of these writings come after Paul's time; all of them in considerable measure take their point of departure from Paul. The so-called Jewish Christians whom the Tübingen scholars saw as a wing of Christianity were, in my judgment, winnowed out of Christendom long before Acts was written. We shall see later that these so-called Jewish Christians are a tool in the neutralization of Paul.

The New Testament writings, apart from Paul, are all younger than Paul, are all in Greek, and all emerge from Gentile, diaspora Christianity. Let it be clear that some of these writings use earlier sources; for example, Mark is used as a source by Matthew and by Luke. Mark in turn used some sources, not only oral, but in the case of the "passion narrative," probably a written one. However, the experts have often been so preoccupied with this quest for supposed sources that they have been blind about the purpose for which the sources are used. This is exactly what has happened in recent New Testament scholarship, especially in the desperation to find, through isolating sources, some supposedly unshakable historical foundations.

Whatever may have been the sources of this or that New Testament book, the book itself is intelligible in its own right only if it is assayed in its totality. We are confronted in the New Testament by literature written invariably in Greek and the non-Pauline literature is invariably later than Paul's time. I believe that the New Testament literature not by Paul is virtually *all* influenced, and usually or occasionally shaped, both affirmatively and negatively, by Paulinism.

For if it is true, as I believe, that Acts reduces Paul from sole eminence into a shared eminence, of what utility was that gesture unless that eminence was of striking stature? If one wants properly to assess Paul, he must first redeem Paul from Acts of the Apostles. He must see that it is of very small moment whether the biographical details of Paul's life or of his journeys in Acts can be squared with the Epistles. It chances that they cannot, but it would make no difference if they could. Acts could have been accurate in these points rather than present us with conflicts; the real crux, however, is whether Paul was the inspired person whose genius was such that the church could scarcely withstand and contain him, or whether he only traveled in places different from other apostles and believed and taught nothing different.

It is my judgment that Acts not only errs egregiously in details in matters which are also found in the Epistles, but tendentiousness respecting Paul is so strong in Acts that it adds misleading and unreliable details about him. Among such details are these: it gives him a Jewish name, Saul. It makes him a former student of Gamaliel. It portrays him as speaking Hebrew. It depicts him as turning from Jews to Gentiles only after a series of bitter experiences with Jews; that is, his motivation is not principle, but expediency. The Road to Damascus is a romance; the determination to get extradition papers against the Christians in Damascus is pure fiction; the Roman citizenship is a pipe-dream. Some of these motifs are legendary accretions derived from details mentioned passingly in the Epistles; such, for example, are the details given in Acts of Paul's persecution of the

Church. The purpose of the fictitious items in Acts is to demonstrate that Paul was by residence as much a Palestinian Jew as were the native-born Palestinians; it is to deny that Paul was a Jew steeped in the Greek dispersion. These details are in conformity with similar motifs in the Gospel According to Luke: Christians never had any criticism of or disloyalty to the ancient Judaism, but did have trouble at the hands of Jews. Acts needs to be classified not with history but with legend.* The "we-sections" have been demonstrated by scholars to be stylistically identical with the remainder of Acts, and they too come under such a judgment.

But in reality it is not Paul the person against whom Acts is contending. After all, it depicts him as little different from the other apostles. But it is the Pauline doctrine which Acts is attacking. Acts' version of Paul is the vehicle through which Acts can accept Pauline doctrine as a correct basic doctrine of Christianity, and at the same time deny the clear corollaries and implications of that doctrine.

We saw above that the Tübingen school is the source of a distinction which scholars still make between the "Petrine" tradition, that is, Palestinian Jewish Christianity, and the Pauline tradition, dispersion Gentile Christianity.

The so-called "Petrine" tradition recorded in Acts is manufactured out of the whole cloth. The only real "quasi-Petrine" tradition in the New Testament is that recorded in Paul's Epistles, in Galatians and Corinthians, in the name of Cephas. The retort will be made promptly, how about the Gospels of Mark and Matthew? To this we reply that they in no way represent the Cephas-tradition of Galatians, as we shall see.

* That Paul was a martyr in Rome is the best known legend about Paul. It is not found in the New Testament, but appears first in Tertullian (160-230). A book called "The Acts of Paul" was in circulation as early as 210. A tradition is related by Jerome (427) that Paul and the Roman philosopher Seneca were friends and correspondents; this "correspondence" has survived to our day. Legends about all the disciples and apostles became legion.

The Petrine tradition in Acts and other New Testament writings is the hammer with which one blunts the sharp edge of Pauline doctrine. The Tübingen scholars conceived of a Petrine and a Pauline tradition existing simultaneously. It is here that the Tübingen interpreters made their error. The succeeding pages will illustrate my conviction that what the Tübingen school meant by Petrine tradition is in reality the impedimenta which the later church created and threw up against Paul. Acts is no more reliable for the "Petrine" tradition than it is for the Pauline. Indeed, were it not for Acts, one would scarcely have suspected even the existence of such a thing. Now there is a second century bishop, Papias, who tells us that the author of the Gospel According to Mark was the interpreter of Peter. But without Acts, and by discounting the misleading contribution of Papias, the so-called Petrine tradition becomes dissolved into nothingness, as it should.

Now it must be clear that Acts and other New Testament literature does not totally reject Paulinism; it is only the implications and the corollaries of his doctrine which are rejected. All New Testament literature begins with a quasi-Pauline base.

Accordingly, the modifications which Acts makes are chiefly of Paul. There are in Acts no significant or extensive pre-Pauline views. The scholars who have searched in Acts for its alleged sources have been more diligent in noting what presumable sources Luke used than in how he used his sources. There is on record a book, *The Apostolic Preaching and Its Developments,* by C. H. Dodd, which essays to winnow out of some of the improbable speeches in Acts the "primitive apostolic preachment." The contradiction discernible in the procedure is that, on the one hand, it is the unanimous testimony of liberal scholars that the speeches in Acts, like those in the Greek historian Thucydides, are what the author thought should have been made on the given occasions. They are in no sense stenographic reports of what was said. One therefore wonders how these, on the other hand, can be pared down to a solid stratum of virtually stenographic outlines. Most of the scholars who have undertaken the subjective quest of an author's supposed sources—a standard and debilitating subject for a Ph.D. thesis—have tended to assume that an author is nothing but a compilation of sources. They seem to assume that an author, who might conceivably have used a source, had little or nothing of his own to contribute in the way of viewpoint, emphasis, interpretation, style—and innate creativity.

Along with its tremendous legacy from Paul, the Church inherited some minor debits. His doctrines were abstract and metaphysical. Hence, they could scarcely appeal to the unscholarly mind. While it is likely that Paul himself was able to speak movingly and stirringly, the reading of his letters without the apperceptive mass of some nineteen hundred years of a favorable Christian disposition towards them could be only the reading of a fascinating but argumentative essay. We have the testimony of II Peter 3.16 that there are things in Paul's letters "hard to understand which the ignorant and the unstable twist to their own destruction." Moreover, complexity abides in them, for Paul, in Dean Inge's phrase, "grazes more than one heresy, or what the Church afterwards called heresies" (*Mysticism in Religion,* 32-33). The content of Paul's preachment and of the incidental doctrines are not the material with which a stable Church can become crystallized. Indeed, what is central in Paul, namely, an insistence that personal inspiration, or intuition, or the Holy Spirit, or the Christ can accomplish what age-old tradition and religious organization cannot do, amounts to an invitation to dissidence. In his own lifetime Paul faced the problem of those of his hearers who confused his preachment of liberty from the Law with their own disposition towards license.

The example of Paul, who broke with established Judaism, was preserved by the Church virtually against its own interests. When one canonizes a rebel, one enshrines rebellion. Paul preached a revolutionary doctrine that the inherited Jewish Law was null and void. It is a truly wonderful church which shapes itself solely after Paul's prescription in I Corinthians 13 of faith, hope, and love as sufficient "rules." However, a more realistic church, if it is to be organized, systemized and regulated, requires more humanly feasible vehicles, such as a constitution, regulations, and persons with authority.

With Pauline doctrine, the Church could, as it were, secede or be pushed out of Judaism. There was no other course available. But Pauline doctrine was a charter not merely for a new order but also for potential and continuing anarchy. The issue for the Church was this: how could it constructively channel Paul's striking contribution, and yet not be put into upheaval here and there by the rampant individualism implicit in that contribution? The Church in the Greek world dealt with the "problem" of Paul, not by repudiating him, but by neutralizing him. It accepted, on the one hand, that the Law of Moses was no longer binding. Paul wrote little in the way of providing some new form of authority. Acts made good this deficiency, for it set forth a theory of authority, resident not in Scripture, for there was as yet no New Testament, but in persons whom Jesus appointed, or whom Jesus' successors appointed. Acts even described how this authority was conferred, by the laying on of hands and the transfer of the Holy Spirit.

Acts set forth a view of the unbroken chain of this authority. It admitted Paul into that chain. But it diluted the sharpness of Paul's claim to personal revelation by showing him in Acts to have been an apostle from men as well as from God. Ananias laid hands on Paul; the apostles at Jerusalem accepted him; Paul obeyed them even to the point of transporting and disseminating their apostolic decree with its three prohibitions which we saw above (p. 134). Paul's Epistles show no knowledge at all of this decree. The decree is found only in Acts and nowhere else in the New Testament.* One reason for the silence is that

* Its content does seem to be alluded to in Revelation 2.14 and 20: the former (2.14) refers to the Hebrews in the desert, the prophet Balaam and his employer Balak who "put a stumbling block before the sons of Israel

the decree was not in existence in Paul's time or when the other New Testament literature was written, but only after them. The decree is a mean between two extremes, neither of which the later church could accept. On the one hand there was the heritage of the full regimen of the Jewish Law; on the other hand, there was the heritage of Paul's full rejection of the Jewish Law. The decree concedes, as though to Paul, that the full Jewish Law need not be observed; it establishes, however, a modified Law emerging from a Church council, which does need to be observed. The decree is a cornerstone of the conception that with the Old Testament law abrogated, there is now a new law, the Law of the Church.

By the device of the apostolic decree, the Church affirmed Paul's view that it was not to be governed by Jewish Law. At the same time, it denied Paul's intimation that inspiration and intuition alone were sufficient for regulation.

Acceptance and neutralization became the clues to much of the New Testament literature of significance after Paul's time. Acceptance and neutralization need to be held in good balance in our minds, for we shall go astray if we fail to note that both exist in the literature, and that we do not have simply the one or simply the other.

The neutralization of Paul in Acts was not done out of any deliberate wish to distort Paul, nor out of any specific animosity towards him, but it is rather the way in which a churchman found that he could have both Paul and also a well organized church. Respecting Paul and Peter in Acts we deal with not some primitive Petrine tradition going back to early times, but with Paul and him neutralized.

From the time of Paul to the time of Acts there is an interval of perhaps three quarters of a century or even a full century. In

---

that they might eat food sacrificed to idols and practice immorality"; the latter (2.20) denounces a woman, a Jezebel, who beguiled people "to practice immorality and to eat food sacrificed to idols." But neither of the passages in Revelation directly refers to the apostolic Decree.

this regard, some other New Testament writings offer their own testimony, which we ought to see and evaluate. They suggest that Acts is not an abrupt, new view, but a matured view. It was ripened by decades of being confronted by Paul or his followers; it was sharpened and made articulate in the middle of the second century by the emergence in the church of the heritage of Paul in the garb of Marcion. The process of the coming to maturity of the view in Acts not only will help us explain Acts, but will help us understand Paul. Hence we turn to some of the other writings in the New Testament. Ultimately we shall look at the writings in their chronological order.

VI

Paul and Other New Testament Writings

We have seen that scholars have supposed an early Petrine tradition; on the basis of material such as Acts, they assert that in early Christianity there was a Gentile diaspora segment of the church, led by Paul, and a Jewish segment, initially limited to Palestine, led by Peter. They add that these two segments differed with each other. Moreover, it has been presumed that this Petrine tradition can carry the student back to Palestine, back to early beginnings, and back to Jesus himself, for Peter was Jesus' leading follower. I have said, to the contrary, that the Petrine tradition is the body of rather late impediments which the church threw up against Paul.

Let us see first what evidence scholars could muster to prove an early Petrine tradition, initially limited to Palestine. A proper understanding of early Christianity should lead us to see not two segments but three. Now one of these was indeed Palestine Jewish Christianity, but *we know precious little about it.* While Paul's Epistles allude to the Church at Jerusalem, it is not until Acts is written that any direct mention is made of it; yet even in Acts there is no consecutive account of what ultimately happened in that church. We get some direct data only in the fourth century; at that time an historian Eusebius (in his *Ecclesiastical History,* III,v,2-3) related only this much, that when war broke out in Palestine in 66 between the Jews and Rome, the Jewish Christians in Palestine fled to Pella across the Jordan.

We know that ultimately the directing leadership of the church shifted from Jerusalem to Rome but we do not know when or by what process this important shift took place. We have one more piece of information about Palestinian Christianity: some church fathers, Jerome (347-420) among them, relate that the Jewish Christians had gospels written *in Hebrew.* Two of these gospels, mentioned in some writings, are known by quotations from them *in Greek.* Those Jewish Christians who possessed one of these gospels are named by the church father Irenaeus (±130-±200) as "Ebionites," and they are listed by him as *heretics,* for they "repudiate the apostle Paul, calling him an apostate from the Law." Jerome claims to have copied the gospel which he saw; he, however, calls its possessors "Nazarenes" and he says that they lived at Beroea in Syria. These gospels, whether of the Ebionites or of the Nazarenes, appear to have been secondary versions of Matthew, but we cannot be completely sure.

Thus two different but possibly similar gospels were apparently in existence, either in Hebrew or in its cousin Aramaic—Greek writers often did not distinguish between these two languages. But the fragmentary nature of the quotations in Greek from them and the vagueness of their mentions tend to put a thick cloud of obscurity on them. Consequently, we have no Christian documents of any kind in Hebrew or Aramaic. The Nazarene and Ebionite gospels, whatever they were, were not accepted into the New Testament. In sum, we do not in our day possess any primitive or even late gospels of Jewish Christians in Hebrew or in Aramaic. Whatever the New Testament discloses about Palestinian Jewish Christianity is revealed in Greek in documents none of which purport to come directly from Jewish Christians—except possibly the earliest of the four gospels found in the New Testament, the Gospel According* to Mark. Thus we have no documents—Greek, Hebrew or Aramaic—which yield direct information regarding an early "Petrine" tradition. The one possible exception, to repeat, is Mark. To its contribution to our quest we now turn. Mark is also our first step in traversing the interval from Paul to Acts.

Eusebius, the fourth century Church historian, whom we mentioned above, quotes from the writings of Papias, a bishop in Phrygia in the first half of the second century, or perhaps between 140 and 160, to the effect that Mark had been Peter's interpreter. Mark had written down "accurately, though not in order" what he (Mark or Peter?) recollected of what Christ had said or done. Do we encounter in Mark a clear picture of an early Petrine influence? Does Mark, supposedly a close associate of "Peter," reflect the authentic "Petrine" segment of the Church?

Papias is the source of a great problem in the history of the interpretation of Mark. Peter is certainly an important character in Mark; but the alleged Petrine influence on Mark has baffled and misguided scholarship very thoroughly. In contrast to Papias' statement, Pfleiderer, a nineteenth century German, noted correctly that the Gospel According to Mark "exhibits plainly various traces of Pauline influences and reminiscences." We are confronted, then, by the paradoxical circumstance that the Gospel supposedly derived directly from Peter is shot through and through with the viewpoint of his rival and opponent, Paul.†

* Virtually all writers use a small letter in "according"; I use the capital deliberately. In the New Testament the books are known without the word Gospel; that is: According to Mark, According to Matthew, and the like. To retain the intent of the Greek, one must read According, not according.

† Conservative scholars treat this circumstance as though it is of no importance by asserting that there were no real and basic issues between Paul and "Peter."

We need to note first the role and status of Peter in Mark. From such notice we shall be able to assess the so-called Petrine tradition therein. Thereafter, on seeing the Paulinism in Mark, we will begin to understand the development within the church from Paul to Acts.

When Peter was first called by Jesus (Mark 1.16-20), he was known as Simon. Then fishermen, Simon and his brother Andrew, were called by Jesus: " 'Follow me and I will make you become fishers of men.' " The text relates that immediately they left their nets and followed Jesus. The reader knows what is intended by the phrase, "fishers of men"; from the immediateness of their following Jesus, we get an initial impression that Simon and Andrew also understood the import of the phrase.

Next come two minor mentions of Peter: Jesus cured Simon's mother-in-law of a fever (1.30-31); Simon and others with him follow Jesus to a lonely place (1.35-39).

The next mention (3.16) tells us that Jesus surnamed Simon Peter. Here twelve disciples are appointed to be sent out to preach and have authority to cast out demons (3.13-19). Next, Peter was among those disciples allowed to follow Jesus into the home of the ruler of the synagogue and to witness Jesus' miraculous restoration of the latter's daughter to life (5.35ff).

Simon was also among those enumerated when Jesus returned to his "own country," where we are told he was unable to do any mighty work. It was at this point that the twelve, appointed earlier, were sent out (6.1-13).

At Caesarea Philippi Jesus asked the disciples how men identified him. Some told Jesus, "John the Baptist"; others, "Elijah." Peter answered Jesus, "You are the Christ" (8.27-29). So far Peter is in a favorable role. Then Jesus began to teach of his future sufferings, his death and Resurrection. Peter took Jesus and "began to rebuke him. But turning and seeing his disciples, he rebuked Peter, and said 'Get behind me, Satan. For you are not on the side of God but of men' " (8.31-33).

At the Transfiguration, during which the clothes of Jesus became whiter than any launderer on earth could bleach them, it is related that Elijah and Moses appeared, and they talked with Jesus, in the presence of Peter, James and John. It was Peter who said to Jesus, " 'Master, it is well that we are here; let us make three booths, one for you and one for Moses and one for Elijah.' For he did not know what to say . . ." (9.2-8). The passage is sufficiently enigmatic to have yielded a variety of interpretations. However, it seems unmistakable that what Mark is driving at is that Peter and the two with him utterly failed to understand the unique role of Jesus, for Mark understands that Jesus' surpasses that of Moses and Elijah.

Next, when Jesus commented on the difficulty of the rich in entering the kingdom of God, it was Peter who "began to say to him, 'Lo, we have left everything and followed you.' " In reply, Jesus mentioned the rewards to come to those who had left things behind to follow him, and he concluded: "But many that are first will be last, and the last first" (10.23-31). Was not Peter the first whom Jesus called? Can Mark's intent have been other than to suggest that Peter's eminence is destined to wane?

Two succeeding passages (Mark 11.20-25 and 13.3) which mention Peter have no real relevancy to our quest.

The next passages, however, do have relevancy. After the "Last Supper," Jesus predicted that his disciples would all fall away. Thereupon Peter said, "Even though they all fall away, I will not." Jesus then predicted that Peter would deny him three times before the cock would crow twice. Peter said, "If I must die with you, I will not deny you" (14.26-31).

At Gethsemane, while Jesus was praying, Peter (and James and John) fell asleep three times (14.32-42). After the arrest of Jesus, Peter followed the crowd into the courtyard of the high priest; he sat by the fire and warmed himself (14.53-54). The maid of the high priest said to him, " 'You also were with the Nazarene, Jesus.' " Peter "denied it, saying 'I neither know nor understand what you mean.' And he went out into the gateway. And the maid saw him, and began again to say to the by-standers,

'This man is one of them.' But again he denied it. And after a little while again the by-standers said to Peter, 'Certainly you are one of them; for you are a Galilean.' But he began to invoke a curse on himself and to swear, 'I do not know this man of whom you speak.' And immediately the cock crowed a second* time" (14.66-72).

And finally, in the last mention, Mary Magdalene, Mary the mother of James, and Salome were told by the young man "dressed in a white robe," whom they encountered at Jesus' strangely empty tomb, to " 'go, tell his disciples and Peter that he [Jesus] is going before you to Galilee' " (16.7). Such, in brief, is a summary of what Mark relates about Peter.

It needs little argument to show that the role of Peter in Mark is scarcely one which reflects credit on the erstwhile fisherman. His triple denial of Jesus, his obtuseness about the real character of Jesus, and his opaqueness about the necessity for the Crucifixion would seem to merit the epithet used on him, "Satan." Now lest it be thought that this interpretation does some modern violence to the role of Peter in Mark, let us note that it is exactly the understanding of Luke 22.31-32: " 'Simon, Simon, behold Satan demanded to have you, that he might sift you like wheat, but I have prayed for you that your faith may not fail; and when you have turned again strengthen your brethren.' " In short, Mark so characterizes Peter that Matthew and Luke and John all find the need of rehabilitating him. This is indeed strange in a Gospel alleged to be Petrine!

Mark's view of Peter can be further discerned by considering his attitude towards the disciples as a group, of whom Peter was the leader. Now Mark suggests that the disciples could not understand parables of Jesus (4.10-13; 7.17-23). Though Jesus was with them in a boat and the sea became calm, they did not know how to obey his injunction to feed the five thousand (6.35ff) and

* A "second" time, since the usual text of Mark omits telling of the first cock crow. Corrective manuscripts insert the first crow after Peter moved to the gateway, verse 68.

they did not understand, we are told, about the loaves used in the feeding (6.52). Again they misunderstood the feeding of the four thousand to the point of requiring rebuke from Jesus (8.1-21). Their four leaders did not comprehend what resurrection meant (9.9-13); a boy with a convulsive spirit the disciples were unable to cure (9.14-29). They did not understand Jesus' prediction of his coming Crucifixion and they were afraid to ask him (9.30-32). They disputed as to who was the greatest among them (9.33-37); they protested to Jesus in vain about someone not of their company who cast out demons in Jesus' name (9.38-40). They did not understand Jesus' words to the Pharisees about marriage and divorce (10.1-12). They would have hindered little children from coming to Jesus (10.13-14); they did not know who gained salvation (10.26). Still another announcement of his impending Crucifixion and Resurrection amazed and frightened them; only James and John requested privileged places with the Risen Christ (10.35-45).

After the account of the Last Supper and the prediction by Jesus that they would all fall away from him (14.27), the disciples as a group are not mentioned again in the Gospel. The women were told after the Resurrection to inform the disciples and Peter that Jesus would go before them to Galilee (16.7).

That Mark derogates the disciples is completely unmistakable. Indeed, it is for this reason, as one who uses a harmony* is sure to see, that Matthew and Luke are put to the task of softening the harsh indictment against the immediate followers of Jesus. The above paragraphs about Peter and the disciples amount to this, that from the standpoint of the author of Mark the immediate followers of Jesus were gifted with the inability to comprehend him. The demons knew Jesus and feared him. The Pharisees and the Sadducees and Jesus' Jewish opponents knew what Jesus was. But according to Mark his immediate followers including Peter

* A harmony, or synopsis, is the printing of the Gospels in parallel columns. Thereby the student can see quickly the similarities and differences in the Gospels.

did not understand him and had absolutely no fidelity to him. Is this what we shall describe as the Petrine tradition?

On the one hand, the Petrine tradition is hardly a dominant motif in Mark. On the other hand, Paulinism is discernible in the Gospel According to Mark. First, Pfleiderer notes this influence in some details (*The Influence of the Apostle Paul on the Development of Christianity,* pp. 139-144). He points to such items as the predestination of salvation for some, and the hardening of the hearts and loss of salvation for others (see Mark 10.40; 4.11-12, and Romans 9.23 and 11.8). Mark "gives special prominence to the dullness and perplexity [of the unbelieving Jews] with regard to the two cardinal articles of the Pauline gospel—the word of the cross and the resurrection of Jesus. . . . Just as Paul placed the imperishable glory of God in the face of Christ in contrast with the transient glory on the face of Moses and inferred thence the inferiority and transient significance of the old covenant . . . as compared with the surpassing and permanent glory of the new covenant . . . ; in like manner [to Paul] the allegorical narrative of the Evangelist [Mark] places the transfigured Jesus side by side with, that is, in contrast to the two representatives of the old covenant, Moses and Elias (Elijah). But what is the relation of the disciples to this allegorical vision? Peter goes so far as to wish to build tabernacles for the common and permanent abode of all three; that is, he desires to see the transient and the permanent associated for all time." Pfleiderer is surely right in his interpretation of the incident and of its purpose in Mark, namely that Peter did not recognize that Jesus' eminence was greater than Moses' and Elijah's, while Mark and Paul understood this perfectly.

So much for Pfleiderer, but there is still more to be said about the Paulinism in Mark. Paulinism is discernible in the very absence in Mark of those things which would characterize any usual Judaism, for Paul significantly broke with normative Judaism, while "Peter" did not. We are not told in Mark of Jesus going to the synagogue or the Temple on the Rosh Hashona (New

Year) or the Yom Kippur (Day of Atonement). We do not have in Mark, as we do in the apocryphal book of Tobit, a reflection of Jewish piety in observing the requirements and exhortations of the Law. We do not see in Mark any defense of Judaism as in Josephus or Philo or other apologists against detraction. Rather, wherever Jesus is confronted by Jews, whether disciples or opponents, it is always a Jesus over and against them. We do not in Mark have a Judaism to which conceptions about Jesus are joined, but rather a Jesus who is more and greater than Judaism. We deal not with Jesus, a Jewish Messiah, but with Jesus Christ, the Son of God (1.1, 11; 3.11)—something unacknowledged by Pharisees, Sadducees, or Jesus' own disciples, but clearly seen by the Roman centurion, a Gentile (15.39). In a word, this is a Jesus distilled by Paulinism and seen through its diaspora-oriented, non-Jewish, Gentile Christian eyes.

Or, approaching it from still another direction, virtually the sole factor in Mark which is out of keeping with Paul is that Mark relates a different aspect of Jesus, and proceeds in a direction which Paul has abandoned: Paul was not interested in the human career of Jesus, but that is exactly what Mark is setting forth for us. A gospel, we must understand, is a tract dealing with the human career of the divine Christ. The very process of dealing with the human career raised a variety of problems for the ancient writer and for his readers. Certain segments in the church objected to the effort as a totality, for, clinging to their view of "docetism," which was denounced as a heresy, they denied any physical reality to the Christ. It may be put in this way, that they believed only in the divinity of Jesus and not in his real humanity, and therefore they objected to a portrayal of the human side of Jesus. Less extremely, others objected not to the endeavor in general, but to particulars in the effort. It is to be recalled that there were many more gospels written than the four which were accepted into the New Testament. Some of these "rejected" gospels represent regional churches and their piety; some of them, however, were efforts to write a gospel more successfully than ones already written and known. When an author like Matthew or Luke used Mark as a source and in effect rewrote Mark, this was not in approval of Mark's gospel, but in some disapproval. This discussion of what Mark stressed will provide a basis for understanding shortly how Matthew and Luke diverge from him.

In writing his gospel, Mark was setting forth an account of the human side of the divine Christ. He used material in existence in his time, though he naturally shaped it by his own style, convictions and bent. It is foreign to my purpose to discuss the materials out of which Mark was composed. I see no reason to differ with the frequent view that Mark is a collection of separate "pericopes" loosely joined together, that these pericopes were utilized in oral teaching and preaching, and that some of the source material may well go back to Jesus himself. Schmiedel, in the *Encyclopaedia Biblica,* II, p. 1881, speaks of foundation pillars, elements of tradition in the Synoptic Gospels, such as the mistaken prediction of the early End, which by virtue of going against the trend of the developing church must be authentic. This may well be. As to the question of written sources, it is my judgment, as I have said, that Mark utilized a written passion narrative as a source.*

Yet, to repeat, the significance of a unified piece of writing is hardly the oral or written sources which went into it, but rather the total effect of the writing. Whatever minor remnants of Palestinian Jewish tradition may be searched out in Mark are completely overlaid with the author's diaspora Gentile Christian interest.

For a purpose of Mark is not to glorify the so-called Petrine tradition, but, on the contrary, to disparage it, even to the point of denying it any virtue whatsoever. The written source of Mark's

* This source, I believe, fixed the date of the Crucifixion as we find it in John, that is *before* the Passover; this, I find, is still adumbrated in Mark 14.2; the transfer of the Crucifixion to the Passover itself I take to be the result of a theological motif developed out of such symbolic utterances as found in I Cor. 5.7: "Cleanse out the old leaven that you may be fresh dough, as you really are unleavened. For Christ, our paschal lamb, has been sacrificed."

passion narrative may well have contained an account of an appearance of the Risen Christ to the disciples; this would put the Palestine, Jewish Christian "Petrine" segment in good light; its absence from our Mark would seem to me to be due not to its having been lost, but either to its suppression or its never having been written. When we recall that Paul's ultimate credential for his apostleship was his claim of having seen the Risen Christ, then we can understand why this Markan effort to disparage the disciples abstains from including such an appearance of the Risen Christ to the disciples. The clues to the significance of Mark are to be found in some striking passages. "A prophet is not without honor, except in his own country, and among his own kin, and in his own house" (6.4). "Whoever does the will of God is my brother, and sister, and mother" (3.35). "To sit at my right hand or at my left is not mine to grant; but it is for those for whom it has been prepared" (10.40); and "Many that are first will be last, and the last first" (10.31). The first passage suggests that it is among the diaspora Gentiles that Christianity is to prosper. In the latter passages, Mark is telling us that a late-comer like Paul is predestined for an eminence above the direct followers of Jesus.

Moreover, the name which is given to the valid succession of Christendom's officials is the "apostolic succession." The Christian literature does not contain a term to describe a similar authority such as a "discipular" succession. "Apostolic succession" would seem to mean then that the chain of Christian authority moved from Jesus to apostles, by-passing the direct disciples, by-passing the so-called "early Petrine" segment. Surely apostolic succession is no accident in nomenclature, but the expression of the accrued conviction of the Church.

A minor digression may perhaps be worth a paragraph. The German title of the celebrated Albert Schweitzer's *The Quest of the Historical Jesus* was *Von Reimarus to Wrede.* Wilhelm Wrede published in 1901 a book which sought to explain the recurrent motif in Mark that the Messiahship of Jesus was a "secret."

Wrede believed that in Jesus' own lifetime he neither claimed to be a Messiah, nor was the claim made for him, but that the Messianic identification came as a matter of history after the belief in his Resurrection arose.

That explanation seems to me as improbable as it is involved. The motif is present in some passages, but Wrede's explanation ascribes to Mark a motive which I believe is totally foreign and even outside Mark's ken. What Mark is saying is not primarily that Jesus' Messiahship was a secret, but that Jesus' closest Palestinian associates could not see what even the opposing demons and antagonistic Jews could see. It is not the secrecy of the Messiahship which is central in Mark, but the opaqueness of the disciples.*

Wrede inadvertently misread Mark; and Mark has been easy to misread, especially after it entered the canon and thereby deprived most students of the ability to look at Mark objectively. As a canonical work, it came to be the object of adulation; it seemed to the pious to be giving accurate history, rather than presenting a polemic against Jewish Christianity.

As to the reliability of Mark's suggestion that the disciples did not know or understand what Jesus was, a short article, "Twixt the Dusk and the Daylight" in *Journal of Biblical Literature,* 1956 (LXXV), pp. 19-26, is masterly. The author, Morton S. Enslin, writes: "This fundamental thesis . . . of the author of our earliest gospel appears to me quite mistaken and in no small part . . . responsible for the popular but . . . wrong-headed notion . . . that no one in his own day really understood Jesus."

Mark is largely a polemical tract of the Church; the aspersion in Mark of Peter and the disciples is polemics, not history. For were it history, the combative Paul of the Epistles, who rebuked Cephas before the church at Antioch, would scarcely have failed

* The abundant arguments by scholars since Wrede's time over whether or not Jesus proclaimed himself the Messiah are quite gratuitous. So too is a spate of derivative literature, especially both the technical and the amateur "psychiatric" studies of Jesus, and the excursions into the psychological.

in his own works to dredge up whatever disparagement of his opponent was known in the available tradition. How differently Galatians would read if the polemics of the Gospel According to Mark had existed before Paul's time!

Mark is later than Paul, and the derogation of Peter and the disciples is later than Paul. Paul never once disparages the disciples of Jesus. He only contends that his credentials are as good, or better, but he neither denies theirs nor belittles them.

Reverting now to our main concern, the acceptance and neutralization of Paul, the Gospel According to Mark has a maximum of acceptance and a minimum of neutralization. It is a Gospel thoroughly in keeping with the essential doctrines of Paul. It is not as sharp and as vivid as Paul, but this may well be due to its preoccupation with what Jesus did, rather than, as in Paul, what Jesus was. I do not know of any striking point in Mark at which Paul is contradicted.

Mark is the end result of a process: the Church felt the need for an ultimate authority, with the result that anecdotes about what Jesus said and did clustered around the figure of Jesus, providing guidance for the future. Ofttimes the authority of Jesus is artificially invoked for things which Paul taught, as for example the dissolution of the food laws (7.14-23). The Gospel According to Mark is Pauline in tone and partisanship. It is not a Gospel which Paul inspired directly; it is, however, a Gospel which grows out of what Paul taught.

Moreover, it is a Gospel rising from the second of the three segments of Christendom, the Pauline segment. That Paul a century after his time was enshrined by a Marcion suggests that there was in all likelihood some kind of continuity from Paul to Marcion. The Gospel According to Mark comes from this possible line of continuity. It is a tract written in the second segment of the Church, the Paulinian, Gentile, diaspora segment, against the first segment, the Palestinian, Jewish Christian segment. Mark is one of our first steps in traversing the interval from Paul to Acts, whereby the former is accepted and neutralized.

We now turn briefly to the Epistle of James which provides us with a further step in this acceptance and neutralization of Paul. But here, as in Mark, much is accepted. James does, however, make some further assumptions and additions. The Epistle of James is an essay, not an epistle. For our purposes, we need advert to only one passage in the essay, 2.14-26. It declares in essence that "faith, by itself, if it has no works, is dead." The author proves his point by a proof-text, that Abraham was justified by works, when he offered Isaac on the altar. In this connection, he applies the verse, Gen. 15.6, that Abraham believed in God and it was reckoned unto him as righteousness, to a purpose exactly antithetical to Paul's application of it in Gal. 3.6.

From this one, single antithesis in the use of the verse, a good many scholars have inferred a full and thorough antithesis in the points of view of "James" and Paul. Moreover, the infrequency with which Jesus is mentioned or alluded to in the essay (only 1.1 and 2.1) has led to a theory that we have here a Jewish writing which has been made Christian only by some minor interpolations. From still another standpoint, Enslin views the passage (*Christian Beginnings,* p. 331) as an "attempt to stir from their smugness indolent Christians who are inclined to apologize for their disinclination to active works by citing their perfect faith." Now all this may well be. But in its final and complete form the essay is not anti-Pauline nor even non-Pauline, at least in this sense, that it does not repudiate Paul's repudiation of the Law of Moses. Later neutralizations of Paul do repudiate his denial of the Law and his clean break from Judaism. As we shall see, they term Jesus a new Moses and the giver of a better law. James is but one of the Church's earlier efforts to gain some conformity in the overt actions of its members. "James" does not deny the primacy of "faith"; it does not quarrel about that aspect of Paul's doctrine. But it says that works are needed also. Thus, he adds to but does not deny Paul.

Turning for a moment to the essay as a whole, it is a series of injunctions to good conduct. This conduct is specified respecting anger, wickedness, slander, teaching, jealousy, ambition, peace, speaking evil, and the like. That is to say, there is no reliance as in Paul on the "fruits of the Spirit," but the counsel is now direct and specific.

But there is in James no re-establishment of the Law of Moses. The essay does not bring us back into the framework of either Judaism or Jewish Christianity.

We have here no rejection of Paul or his doctrine; rather, the essay in its theology consistently implies an acceptance of much that is in Paul, but with the vividness blunted. It is as though the essay said, "Paul is right in everything but one; he should have added to his assertion of the centrality of faith that works are necessary too."

This neutralization of Paul is here in the interest of an incipient regulatory tendency without which the Church could never have survived. Now this is still only a tendency in James. In James we deal not yet with full-blown regulation for right conduct, but with exhortation towards it.

"James" is not out of accord with Paul. Rather, it adds that which it seems to conceive of as something which Paul inadvertently overlooked. The free inspiration of Paul was quite well for the individual; but if a growing church were to become stable, it needed norms of conduct. "James" is a way station towards the institution of these norms. Indeed James is another step in the acceptance of, but also neutralization of Paul. We are moving from Paul to Acts, but we have not yet arrived there.

Our next step is the Gospel According to Matthew. What in James was only exhortation was transformed in Matthew into incipient regulation. Matthew's Gospel begins with the Virgin Birth and then with a number of events strikingly parallel to the childhood of Moses: the "slaughter of the innocents," and the calling of Jesus out of Egypt; moreover, it is on a mount that Jesus sets forth his "teaching"—reminiscent of Moses on Sinai.

Five bodies of teaching material constitute the bulk of Matthew, recalling the divisions of the books traditionally ascribed to Moses.

Some would-be obstacles to a clear understanding of the Gospel According to Matthew must be considered now. Papias, whom we have mentioned, is the source of a tradition about Matthew which, like his statement about Mark, has troubled scholars. According to him, "Matthew composed the Logia ["teachings"] in the Hebrew language, and everyone interpreted them as he was able." Since there was apparently a disciple of Jesus named Matthew in the Gospel According to Matthew, the tradition was strong from the second century into the nineteenth that the author of the Gospel was this disciple. He was therefore an eyewitness of many of the events which are described.

But on the other hand, modern scholarship has in general seen little evidence that Matthew is a translated work; and moreover, as will be recalled, it is virtually axiomatic in modern study that Matthew used Mark as a source. Accordingly, modern scholarship is almost unanimous in asserting that what we have today as the Gospel According to Matthew cannot be the book to which Papias referred, and cannot be the product of an eyewitness.

There is, though, an attempt of the scholars to place Matthew in the period of the first segment, early Palestine Jewish Christianity. Paradoxically, while such scholars deny Matthew was written in Hebrew, they endeavor to see in the frequency with which Old Testament proof texts abound in it a mark of "Jewish" authorship and consequently to make Matthew a Jewish Christian. It is as if to imply that a Gentile Christian some four or five decades after the Crucifixion would be unable to use and quote the Bible. (It is a compliment to us Jews to credit us solely with such facility, but we need gracefully to decline it.) Paul, who insisted that Jesus died *in accordance with the Scripture* and rose *in accordance with the Scripture,* made it inevitable by this line of argument that other Christians would "prove" their arguments from Scripture. It is therefore not surprising that Matthew, too, adopts this approach. For reasons stated above and for reasons to be presented shortly, to make a Jewish Christian out of Matthew on the basis of Scripture quotations is absurd.

But there has been an even greater obstacle to a clear recognition of the function of the Gospel According to Matthew; it merits a somewhat protracted explanation.

The weight of nineteenth century Protestant scholarship was directed towards recovering the "historical" Jesus and putting him into his Jewish setting. The tacit motivation for the search was the conviction that Jesus, if once stripped of the theological trappings unhappily introduced by Paul and others, would abide as an example for modern man to follow. Since the temper of the nineteenth century was largely naturalistic, the scholarship sought to make the achievement of Jesus something which would seem equally natural. When these scholars stopped believing that Jesus was divine, they had to search out some unique human achievement with which they could credit him. They conceived of Jesus as though he were a nineteenth century rationalist who needed no elaborate church organization, ritual, or priestly intermediaries, as the scholars themselves felt they had no need. The human achievement they hit upon was to declare either that Jesus was a social reformer, or that Jesus restored to Judaism something which had been lost through the encroachment into it of its choking legalism; or, if you wished, the two could be blended. A succession of scholars arose who were mostly distinguished both by inability to handle the Jewish legal texts in the original and also by the persistent notion that no religious system was quite as bad as legalism. Blinded by these pre-possessions, these scholars noted almost everything about the Gospel According to Matthew except its fundamental content, that it is the charter of the Christian legalism which flowered into the Canon Law of the Church. Contrary to these scholars, Matthew advocated a very rigid legalism; again contrary to them, Matthew was writing long after the period of Jewish Christianity.

The Pauline view that God has turned from Israel to the Gentiles is basic in Matthew; the injunction at the beginning of Jesus' career, "Go nowhere among the Gentiles and enter no town of the Samaritans, but go rather to the lost sheep of the house of Israel," is balanced, or perhaps superseded, by the words of the Risen Christ, "Go therefore and make disciples of all nations" (10.5 and 28.19). That Israel has been supplanted is expressed in the narrative of the Roman centurion: "Truly, I say to you, not even in Israel have I found such faith. I tell you, many will come from east and west and sit at table with Abraham, Isaac, and Jacob in the kingdom of heaven, while the sons of the kingdom will be thrown into the outer darkness . . ." (8.5-12). Similarly, "God is able from these stones to raise up children to Abraham" (3.9).

The true purpose and import of Matthew is that it is a manual for church organization and regulation. It is not a Jewish manual but a Christian manual. Matthew attempts to introduce order and uniformity into the individualistic and chaotic church of its author's time. It is for that reason that Jesus is portrayed in Matthew as the new lawgiver, offering a law which is more severe and rigorous than the outmoded Mosaic law. "Think not that I have come to abolish the law and the prophets; I have come not to abolish them but to fill them in" (Matthew 5.17); "Go therefore and make disciples of all nations . . . teaching them to observe all that I have commanded you . . ." (28.19-20).

We must notice that from Matthew's standpoint Jesus is not validating the Law of Moses. Rather, he is depicted as instituting a new law which completes the incomplete old one. We can discern therefore that we do not deal with a Jew struggling to rehabilitate Moses; rather, we have the spectacle of an earnest churchman confronted with the implications left by Paul. By ancestry the author could have been either a Gentile or a Jew; it makes no difference, for in thought the author is a Christian concerned with Christian problems and determined to find a solution for Christians.

Matthew does not represent a Jewish Christianity parallel in time with Paul; Matthew, rather, represents a post-Pauline Gentile dispersion Christianity. Indeed, the anti-Jewish tone of Matthew, especially chapter 23, could hardly be more severe.

Now a significant facet of Matthew is the role which Peter plays in the Gospel. The chief passage is Matthew's version of the incident at Caesarea Philippi (16.17) where Jesus is depicted as saying to Peter: "Blessed are you Simon bar-Jona! For flesh and blood has not revealed this to you, but my Father who is in heaven. And I tell you, you are Peter, and on this rock I will build my church." The passage continues: "I will give you the keys of the kingdom of heaven, and whatever you bind on earth shall be bound in heaven, and whatever you loose on earth shall be loosed in heaven." "Bind" and "loose" are known from rabbinic literature to be terms for prohibit and permit; the passage says that a divine sanction existed for the regulations which Peter would provide for the Church.

It will be recalled that the Catholic Church asserts that it was founded by Peter and that through Peter it and it alone is the true legitimate heir of Christ.

Now since Matthew used Mark as a source, he therefore repeated most of the uncomplimentary things which Mark says about Peter. However, he tried to soften them by omitting some passages and recasting others. The romantics (and the novelists) therefore need to portray Peter as a man of some instability and impulsiveness, whose redeeming traits are his recurrent fidelity to Jesus and his appointment by him.

In its dependency on Mark, Matthew is inevitably a product of an atmosphere in which the Marcan Gospel was at least congenial enough to be known. The principal quarrel which Matthew had with Mark is over the role of Peter. Mark had reduced Peter to Satan; Matthew raises him to the prime role as the chief of the disciples. Matthew's inclusion of the enfranchising words to Peter, and his account of the resurrection appearance to Peter in Galilee, bring it about that the Marcan portrait of a fickle and faithless Peter is turned into an assertion that to this very Peter the developed Church owed its fidelity.

In my judgment, "Peter" in Matthew is no more than a device through whom the author neutralizes Paul. On the one hand, Matthew is himself Pauline in the sense that the Law of Moses is no longer binding for him. On the other hand, for Matthew the Law is not, as in Paul, a wrong principle that needs supplanting by the Spirit; rather, the Law is superseded by the newer and better law of Jesus and transmitted to and by Peter.

Why Peter? Because the quarrel recorded in Galatians 1-2 between Paul and Cephas supplies Matthew with the latter figure about whom he can weave the authority for the legalism he wishes to introduce, this against the sturdy disciples of Paul who opposed any laws.

The intentions and manipulations of Matthew and those against whom he was reacting will be even clearer if we consider the question of the identity of Peter-Simon-Cephas. In Gal. 2.8-9 Paul cites the names of three leaders of the Jerusalem church who agreed that Paul should go to Gentiles and that Peter should go to Jews, and one of these three is Cephas. It is not inconceivable that Peter and Cephas may have been one and the same person, as tradition has it; however, it has seemed remarkable to some that Peter, the recipient of the authority to be an apostle to the Jews, should be identical with Cephas, one of the givers of that authority. Eusebius, a fourth century historian, quotes the second century father, Clement of Alexandria, as "believing that Cephas is intended to be different from Peter." Kirsopp Lake, whom I am here paraphrasing (*Harvard Theological Review,* XIV, 1921, pp. 95-98), mentions that in the *Epistola Apostolorum,* a second century work, and in a third century Egyptian work commonly alluded to as *Kirchen-Ordnung,* a list of the apostles includes both Peter and Cephas as two separate individuals. Lake goes on to say that if we had only the *Epistles* alone (that is, if the Gospels did not orient us differently), Cephas would not be regarded as "identical with Peter." An explanation is offered by Lake: "The Gospel of Mark when it breaks off seems to be leading up to an appearance of Jesus to Peter, and that Paul says that the first appearance . . . was to Cephas; and ergo, Peter is Cephas. This is no doubt a reasonable proposition, but it is just as well to understand that it does not rest on the strongest possible authority, for Paul nowhere says that Peter is Cephas." The identification of the two as one is, curiously enough, made specific in John 1.43; "so long as it was believed that the Fourth Gospel was written by one of the Twelve, . . . it was reasonable to accept this as final."

Some twenty years after Lake's article, Donald W. Riddle returned to the problem of Peter and Cephas (*Journal of Biblical Literature,* LIX, 1940, 169-180). Riddle had some illuminating things to say about the manner in which the elevation of Peter grew in New Testament and later tradition: "There was among early Christian leaders one whose name was Cephas. There was another whose name was Simon. A primitive tradition cites Cephas as the person to whom Jesus first 'appeared' after his death. The transition of the early Christian movement to gentile environments involved the change in the language medium from Aramaic to Greek. Since the name Cephas in Aramaic and the name Petros in Greek means 'stone' or 'rock,' the gospel materials in gentile environments came to include references to 'Peter.' In this process the name 'Peter' became allocated with the name 'Simon'; in a number of cases, although 'Simon' was the primary name, 'Peter' the secondary name attached to it, 'Simon' became known as 'Simon Peter' and 'Peter.' Basically this seems to have been because 'Peter' (or 'Simon Peter') became an available figure for the ascription of a heroic role in early Christian legend . . ." Though there is, as I say, illumination in Riddle's study, it seems to me that he does not consider that the identification and the various attendant changes are the result of deliberate alteration.

My own proposal would suppose that there are three stages in the growth of the Peter, Simon, Cephas matter. I begin with an assumption that Cephas, having an Aramaic name, was a Palestinian Jew and a disciple of Jesus. I assume that Peter, the apostle to the Jews of Gal. 2.8, was not a disciple but an apostle like Paul. I would conjecture that this Peter was a Hellenistic Jew, and that his mission to the circumcised was in the diaspora—it is hard to see the need of appointing a special apostle to the Jews, as distinct from non-Jews, within Palestine; for the Gentile population was negligible, so that an apostle to Palestinians would quite automatically have been an apostle to Jews. I would take it, then, that Peter and Cephas became identified as one and the same, perhaps, as Riddle suggests, because the names meant the same thing.

Thereafter, Mark, writing a Gospel in Greek with the motivation of aspersing the immediate followers of Jesus, alluded to that follower in the Greek form of Peter. Matthew, who began the process of "rehabilitating" the immediate followers, set in motion a growing favorable disposition to "Peter." Luke continued what Matthew began. In Galatians the readings vary in the manuscripts; where some say "Peter," others say "Cephas." Some of this interchange is no doubt due to the circumstance that the late copyists, understanding the two to be one and the same, were not punctilious in copying the name. But it is significant for our discussion that some of the variation is deliberate, the product of the later Church's desire to protect "Peter" from aspersion; that is, they would replace "Peter" by "Cephas." *

At all events, there would seem to be discernible in many manuscripts of Galatians this tendency to protect Peter from aspersions; and such protection would come at a stage when

* I would restore the relevant passages in Galatians as follows: 1.18. Then after three years I went up to Jerusalem to visit Cephas. 2.11. But when Peter came to Antioch I opposed him to his face because he stood condemned. 2.14. But when I saw that they were not straightforward about the truth of the Gospel, I said to Peter before them all. . . . I would similarly restore Peter for Cephas in I Cor. 1.12, 3.22, and 9.5. I would, of course, retain Cephas in I Cor. 15.5.

partisans of Peter utilized him as the figure in the Church to be cited as an authority against their opponents who cited Paul. That this conflict is not merely idle speculation should occur to anyone who has examined, on the one hand, the implications of the Marcionite movement, which is an extension of Paulinism, and who considered, on the other hand, the pro-Peter attitude of the Pseudo-Clementine literature.*

What the procedure in Matthew amounted to, then, was to reverse the direction of Mark. Peter was transformed from the villain in Mark into the protagonist second only to Jesus in Matthew. Just as Peter served the Paulinians as the model of villainy in their anti-Palestinian, anti-discipular tendency, so he served the opponents of the Paulinians as an authority for denying Paul's extreme implications. Matthew emerged as a reaction against extreme Pauline practice in the dispersion church. The segment which the Gospel According to Matthew represented is to be regarded as the third segment of the early church.

The first segment, we saw, was that of Palestinian Jewish Christianity. In the Greek Gentile dispersion, the second segment arose under the leadership of Paul and was directly loyal to him. We must ascribe to it a rather continuous history from Paul's time to Marcion's. The third segment broke away from the second. It was also Gentile, also Greek. It broke away not primarily in doctrine but on the practical level of church organization. The Pauline segment contended that one needed only the Spirit; the "Petrine" or third segment contended that Christian Law and Regulations were required. Like James, Matthew does not oppose Paul's doctrine, but only adds the demand that the church be regulated. But James went further than Paul went and pleaded for works; Matthew went further than James and made Jesus a legislator. When Matthew's circle encountered opposition to its wish to have regulations, this opposition came in Paul's

* Concerning the anti-Paulinism of the Pseudo-Clementines, the evidence is unsparingly stated in the *Encyclopedia Biblica,* "Simon Magus," in Vol. IV, 4540-4560. I commented on these writings above, p. 147.

name. This opposition came from those whom we shall term "extreme Paulinists"; Matthew's followers replied by contending that the true line in the church to their day went through Peter, not Paul. It was to give this contention of Matthew even greater weight that scholars later asserted that this Petrine tradition was not a fabrication, but an authentic Jewish Christian tradition. We have indicated the implausibility of this suggestion.

We have seen the Marcan "Peter" and the disciples to whom little integrity has been left. In contrast, we observed Matthew's "Peter" through whom a new law was transmitted. We turn now to Luke and to his confronting of the Gospels of Mark and Matthew which were available in his time for him to read, criticize, and use.

I believe Mark and Matthew both served as sources for Luke, and that Luke's skilfully written Gospel is an effort to correct some of the implications which could be drawn from the earlier two. Luke's objection to Mark is that Mark aspersed the disciples, excessively humanized Jesus, and was guilty of sloppy writing.* His objection to Matthew, however, was even more far-reaching. Through portraying Jesus as a new Moses, Matthew was implying that Christianity was a break with Judaism. Luke asserted the opposite: Christianity was the direct heir of Judaism. Whatever rupture had taken place, was between the ancient Jewish heritage and contemporary Judaism; in Luke's view, Jesus, Stephen, Peter and Paul were all undeviatingly faithful Jews. Thus, Luke has Jesus brought before the Jewish king Herod who, while treating Jesus with contempt, significantly *abstains from condemning him.* So too the Sanhedrin questions Jesus, but does not try him; it too *abstains from condemning Jesus* and merely brings him to Pilate. Pilate finds Jesus innocent but succumbs, however, to the animosity of the "Jews." According to Luke, responsible Jewish officialdom finds nothing un-Jewish about Jesus. It is the Jewish

* In the incident of the Syro-Phoenician woman, as Mark tells it, Jesus seems to say a narrow thing, and the woman the broad humanitarian thing (Mark 7.27-29).

mobs, says Luke, which were opaque to the true Jewish tradition. This is furthermore indicated because the sentence about the Jewish leaders in Mark 14.64 and in Matthew 26.66 is deliberately omitted in Luke; Mark 14.64 says: "They all condemned him as deserving death." Matthew 26.65-66 reads that the high priest said: 'Do we still need witnesses?' They answered 'He deserves death.' Luke, in deferring to Acts his account of the fate of the betrayer Judas, thereby omits the statement in Mt. 27.3 that Judas saw that Jesus was condemned. In Luke Jesus was not condemned. Mark and Matthew had described an unfair trial; Luke tells rather of limited and inconclusive questioning, and then of Pilate's acquiescence in what gives a total effect of a lynching. Through the medium of Pilate's three times proclaiming Jesus' innocence, the blame for the Crucifixion in Luke is laid increasingly at the hands of the masses of "Jews," this more than in the earlier two Gospels. As has long been recognized, Luke was suggesting that Christianity presented no danger to the Romans, and that it was never the initiator but only the victim of difficulties which arose with the Jews. These identical motifs carry over into Acts.

Next, we return to our thread of investigation into "Peter." Luke, on the one hand, omits Matthew's account of Peter's failure to walk on the water; he also lacks the rebuke and epithet of Satan to Peter; these would unduly derogate him; on the other hand, Luke lacks what Matthew had added to Mark, that Peter was the rock on whom the church was to be built, for this would, from Luke's standpoint, unduly aggrandize Peter. Whereas Mark and Matthew portrayed Jesus as sending "disciples" to prepare the "Upper Room," in Luke it was Peter and John who were sent by name. Luke, as we have noticed, preceded the account of Peter's denial of Jesus with Jesus' clear knowledge that Peter would later turn and "strengthen your brethren"; in this scene, as it is found in Luke, Peter is much less vehement in his protestations of loyalty than he is in Mark and Matthew. In the Gethsemane scene, Mark places direct blame on Peter, James, and John for faithlessness in falling asleep; Matthew 26.45 softens the rebuke into a mere question: "Are you sleeping and taking your rest?" Luke walks a middle course by ascribing the act not to infidelity but to their sorrow. After the Resurrection a verse* in Luke relates that Peter went to the tomb, looked in, saw the linen clothes by themselves, and went home wondering what had happened (24.12). Thus Luke does not directly ascribe a Resurrection appearance to Peter alone, or to Peter first; it comes rather to the eleven disciples and those who were with them.† In Luke the Resurrection appearances are in Jerusalem, the center of Jewish life, rather than in the peripheral Galilee where Matthew allocates it.

Matthew's "Peter," the vehicle through whom a new law is transmitted, is absent from Luke; but so too is absent the Marcan "Peter" to whom scarcely a shred of integrity had been left. In short, Peter is not raised to any pinnacle in Luke, nor is he lowered to any marked position of disgrace. Luke walks a middle course; he is tending towards harmonization of dissident factors, towards a neutralization. We know that Matthew emphasized the status of the disciples, this against Mark who disparaged them obliquely and emphasized the apostles. For the sake of Church unity, Luke harmonizes the two. For our understanding of this, the most significant addition in Luke is an account of the appointment, in addition to the twelve, of a group of men numbering seventy, or, as other manuscripts read, the "Seventy-two." Luke has omitted the inability of the disciples to cure the "epileptic" boy, for Luke is jealous of the reputation of the disciples. The seventy appointed, however, are initially commanded to go to those places where Jesus is to come (10.1). Luke portrays the seventy as sent out, and as returning in satisfaction at having in Jesus' name subjected demons to themselves (10.12).

* Found in only some of the manuscripts.

† Luke 24.34 is inconsistent with other Lucan materials; it "recollects" something not narrated in Luke, and intelligible rather from Mark. It is either Luke's afterthought, or a harmonizing addition.

Now in Mark the title for the Twelve is only once "Apostles" (6.30), and this in a context in which earlier in the chapter Jesus has "sent them out," and they now return. The net effect in Mark is that Jesus had twelve "followers." The usual term in Matthew is Disciples, or on one occasion simply the Twelve. Matthew seems to use the two words (in 10.1-2) as though they were in his eyes interchangeable. On several occasions Luke similarly uses the bare term "The Apostles" for the "disciples" (9.10; 17.5; 22.14; 24.10). But elsewhere in Luke a distinction is made on occasion between disciples and *apostles,* for the "disciples" in Luke number a very large group, out of whom Jesus initially selects Twelve to be apostles. In the passage in which Jesus selects Twelve, out of a large number, it is Jesus who selects them and it is Jesus who assigns to them the very name "Apostles." That is to say, the followers of Jesus are sufficiently numerous in Luke (as one can see in 8.3) that Jesus initially appoints Twelve out of the plurality of possibilities (9.1-2), and thereafter Seventy (10.1-16). The difference between Matthew and Mark on the one hand, and Luke on the other, is that the former conceived of Jesus as having a following of Twelve "followers" or "disciples"; but Luke, on the other hand, holds that there was a large following virtually right at the start, and of this large group special appointment of a limited number of *apostles* took place. In Luke's view, for one simply to have been an original follower of Jesus was in itself insufficient for a special eminence; moreover, in his view this special eminence was not limited to only twelve but extended to eighty-four (or eighty-two). Accordingly, when we come to Acts, the continuation of Luke, we are not surprised to read that after the Ascension the "company of persons was in all about a hundred and twenty." When the successor of the unfortunate Judas needed to be named, there were in Luke's view many available; of these two were nominated; of the two, one was named.

It should be clear from all this that "discipleship" is comparatively meaningless to Luke, as "apostleship" is most meaningful. A disciple in Luke, we might say, was a layman; an apostle was an official. It follows, too, that important as the apostle is to Luke, he is not a rarity because apostles have been numerous. In Acts, Luke gives attention to Peter, Philip, James and Paul—along with such companions as Barnabas, John Mark, and Timothy; yet while he gives attention to them, he gives no single apostle any special primacy in church work.

The Tübingen school was right in its view that an irenic* interest about the past is fundamental in Luke-Acts. Its error was in assuming that Luke-Acts was limited to seeking harmony between Peter (the Palestinian church) and Paul (the Hellenistic church); it was much broader than that, for factions were more numerous than only two.

Luke-Acts suggests that the "apostles" were all of the same rank and that they only differed with each other in the areas in which they worked, for Luke-Acts is not only interested in harmonizing Paul's disciples with the post-Pauline opponents of Paul's influence (as for example Matthew), but he wants to effect as wide as possible a harmony within the whole Church. In I Corinthians 1.12, Apollos seems to be the head of a clique or a sect; in Acts we are told that at Ephesus two of Paul's followers, Priscilla and Aquila, straightened out a compliant Apollos on the proper baptism and then sent him off with letters of commendation to Achaia, and, indeed, to Corinth; again, at Ephesus Paul found compliant disciples of Apollos whom he straightens out on the proper baptism. It is all of these various factions which Luke-Acts wants to unify.

The special hegemony of Peter which Matthew had tried to foster was reduced by Luke to a restricted "strengthening of the brethren." Matthew had attempted to create unity in the Church through regulation and by elevating one particular branch—that of "Peter"—at the expense of another. Mark gave no guidance which could lead to Church unity. Luke is

* Tending to promote peace, especially with reference to ecclesiastical differences.

attempting to minimize the differences in the Church and thereby to forge a unity. At only one place does Luke feel constrained to deny that all the early leaders were either of intuitive or moldable accord: this is in the incident of Simon Magus (Acts 8.9-24). The text reveals that Simon Magus had become a Christian (at the hands of Philip), but it also notes that Simon had been converted only "in the name of Jesus," and had not received the Holy Spirit, the mark of *true* apostleship. The text denies not only that Simon had received the Holy Spirit, but it seems to take pains to deny that Simon had the power to confer the Spirit.

We do not know whom Luke means by Simon Magus. There may have really been a man by that name; or the name may be no more than a disparaging disguise, as it is in the frequent allusions in the extra-canonical literature. From Luke's standpoint, especially in his wish for peace and unity in the Church, it seems clear that Luke has drawn a circle which leaves Simon out; or to change the figure, he leaves the door open for Simon's return, for Luke portrays Peter as saying (8.21-23): "You have neither part nor lot in this matter, for your heart is not right before God. Repent therefore of this wickedness of yours, and pray to the Lord that, if possible, the intent of your heart may be forgiven you . . ." Simon answers, "Pray for me to the Lord that nothing of what you have said may come upon me." In general then, and even including the Simon Magus incident, Luke forges a unity.

In no other writings in the New Testament is the equilibrium between the acceptance of Paul and the neutralization of him as complete and as thorough-going as it is in Luke-Acts. Not alone has Paul's individuality disappeared, but the individuality of each of the apostles has also vanished. There is no longer a Peter who is the apostle to the circumcised, nor a Paul with a Gospel from God, not man, for the Gentiles. Except Simon Magus, who was baptized, but never received the Holy Spirit, all preach and teach the same thing.

Luke comes from the same segment of the church as Matthew.

Both, against Paul's followers, wanted order and discipline. Matthew proposed to get it through Church law; Luke proposed to get it through authorized and authoritative persons.

What one notices first in turning from the first three Gospels to the Gospel According to John is the change in style, for John lacks the many narratives and parables of the Synoptics. In manner, John is to the Synoptics as Philo is to the rabbis; the rabbis told anecdotes about biblical personages and dealt in illustrative stories, but Philo, avoiding anecdotes and stories, dealt in symbols and double levels of meaning. The difference can be classified as that between the edifying legends of the rabbis and the Synoptics on the one hand and abstract theosophy on the other. The Synoptics chose an interest in the human career of Jesus which Paul discarded; John, as it were, is saying: If you must have some exposition of the human career of Jesus, my way of exposition is a better way than that of the Synoptics.

John does not really give us the career of Jesus in any of its striking milestones; yet his lack of such things as the baptism of Jesus, the temptation, the confession at Caesarea Philippi, the Transfiguration, and especially the birth story is scarcely to be explained as the result of ignorance, for these items were in the common oral and written tradition. It is more likely to have been a deliberate turning away from them than ignorance of them. The paucity of details about Jesus in John, plus the conception of a pre-existent Christ who becomes Incarnate, reminds one of Paul's view. Now the Synoptics are almost universally believed to have been written in the interval between Paul and John. Interpreters have rushed to a conclusion that John's Gospel *reverts* to a high Christology along Pauline lines, after a theologically lower concept as found in the Synoptics.

In my judgment this is an improper estimate, for we do not have in the Synoptic Gospels a relatively lower Christology, but only the inevitable result of portraying in human categories of expression the impact of a being conceived of in the very highest of metaphysical categories. All three Synoptic evangelists end up their Gospels with assertions that Jesus is the Son of God; that is, they all conclude with a high Christology; the interpreter is bogged down by details when he fails to notice that it is the concluding summary of each evangelist which is the index of the evangelists's evaluation.

There is not in John a Christology which is in itself higher than the Synoptics; and there is no return to Paul, for since there was no real abandonment of Paul's doctrine there was no need of return to it. The Fourth Gospel is not presenting a higher Christology than the Synoptics, but is choosing a better manner of depicting a comparably high Christology. To belabor the point, all four evangelists conceive that Jesus was the "Son of God"; but Mark, to Matthew's horror, depicts Jesus as having been baptized, so that Matthew is impelled to add in his account a denial of the implication of sinfulness on the part of Jesus. Also troubled by the implication, Luke glosses over the incident; and John, to repeat, lacks it. John lacks an account of Jesus' baptism because John is convinced that it is inconsistent with the Christology; that conviction of inconsistency is absent entirely from Mark, and only partially present in Luke and Matthew.

But higher and lower Christologies as such are not at stake here; rather, they dispute the inferences which should or could be made from a rather common conviction. It is as though John's approach to the Synoptics is this: "The important thing about the Christ is his divine nature, his death, and his resurrection; if you insist on portraying his human career, then your way of doing so by anecdotes, aphorisms, and parables is wrong. Your parables and your anecdotes are too trivial for the exalted theme. My tools will be long discourses, monologues as it were. I will not be able to avoid anecdotes entirely. But I shall reduce them to a minimum, and when I do use an anecdote, it will be merely to introduce a monologue by Jesus."

It is quite conceivable that Paul would have scorned the manner of the Synoptic Gospels quite as much as I believe that John did;

and that Paul, if he were perforce to have to approve some Gospel, would have found John the least objectionable. The Church fathers, who called the Fourth Gospel the "spiritual" gospel in contradistinction to the Synoptics, saw quite clearly that the Synoptics were giving an account of the human career of Jesus, while John was giving a distillation of the spiritual significance of that career, and not the career itself.

I am not suggesting that marks of development or change from Paul through the Synoptics to John are totally absent. Indeed, in the attitude expressed towards the Jews, one moves from Paul's bewilderment about them into John's unrelieved antipathy to them. Of other developments, I believe that the "adoptionism" of Mark and the "virgin birth" narrative of Matthew and Luke would have annoyed Paul as much as I believe they annoyed John.

These motifs are scarcely direct products of a low or high Christology, but are only tentative answers to the secondary questions. If you assume that Jesus was the Christ, you might be prompted to ask, How did the Christ get to be in Jesus? That is, they are answers to secondary questions, for they assume the primary conviction. It is secondary to ask, When and how did the Incarnation take place?—or, What is the nature of the divine essence which has become incarnate? Such questions are asked only after a primary basis is already accepted. The primary is common in the New Testament, that Jesus was the Christ. The secondary questions and answers are various, discordant, and even contradictory. Paul and John have great agreement on primary matters. It might be commented, however, that there seems this difference in the view of the Incarnation in Paul and in John: Paul views it that the Son of God became incarnate *in* Jesus, while John holds that the Son of God became incarnate *as* Jesus.

Accordingly, though Mark is a partisanly Pauline Gospel in substance, its manner or approach—a description of Jesus' human career—is distinctly at variance with Paul; John, however, reflects the nearest possible return to Paul's lack of concern with the human career of Jesus, and his emphasis on the spiritual significance of that career. John was perhaps trying to offset the extreme Paulinists of his day. In so doing, he effected a relative return to Paul. But we shall soon see that the developing Church could not embrace this relative return, so it saw fit to make an addition. Before turning to this addition, however, we will look quickly at the Epistle to the Hebrews in which emerges, paradoxically, a Church officialdom in the name of Paul.* John, Hebrews, and later the added last chapter of John and the Pastoral Epistles are all way stations in the eventual neutralization of Paul.

The Epistle to the Hebrews, which is not an Epistle, is an effort to do, in a literary form quite different from the four Gospels, that which the Gospels attempted to do. Hebrews has a persistent theme: the contrast between the imperfection of Judaism and the perfection of Christianity. Hebrews sets this forth in its interpretation of the Crucifixion and the Resurrection of Jesus. From the opening verses unto the very end, the theme is consistent. "In many and various ways God spoke of old to our fathers by the prophets; but in these last days he has spoken to us by a Son. . . ." (1.1-2). ". . . But we see Jesus, who for a little while was made lower than the angels, crowned with glory and honor because of the suffering of death, so that by the grace of God he might taste death for every one . . ." (2.9). "Therefore, holy brethren . . . consider Jesus, the apostle and high priest of our confession. He was faithful to him who appointed him . . ." (3.12). ". . . We have a high priest who has passed through the heavens, Jesus, the Son of God . . ." (4.14). "Christ did not exalt himself to be made a high priest, but was appointed by him who said to him 'Thou art my Son . . ." (5.5). ". . . It was fitting that we should have such a high priest, holy, blameless, unstained, separated from sinners, exalted above the heavens . . ." (7.26). "When Christ appeared as a high priest of the good things that

* Church tradition ascribed Hebrews to Paul's authorship.

have come . . . he entered once and for all into the Holy Place, taking not the blood of goats and calves but his own blood . . ." (9.11-12). "Every priest stands daily at his services, offering repeatedly the same sacrifices, which can never take away sins. But when Christ had offered for all time a single sacrifice for sins, he sat down at the right hand of God . . ." (10.11-12). "Jesus Christ is the same yesterday and today and forever" (13.8). "Now may the God of peace who brought again from the dead our Lord Jesus . . . equip you with everything good that you may do his will . . ." (13.20-21).

Notice that Hebrews invites the reader (6.1) to "leave the elementary doctrines of Christ and go on to maturity . . ." What are these elementary doctrines of Christ? A traditional explanation draws the contrast between the immature apprehension of Christianity fraught with the danger of apostasy, and sound and ripe understanding (Mouton, in Ellicott's *Commentary,* viii, 302). Such an explanation explains nothing, for it fails to identify the elementary and the mature. Were these not, at least in the author's mind, quite specific? In my opinion it is likely that Hebrews is protesting against the kind of material which came into the Gospels, and it is this material which he is denominating, to use his figure of speech, "milk and not strong meat." I believe that Hebrews and John are not alone in aspersing the anecdotes and parables of the Gospels. A passage from one of the Pastoral Epistles, I Timothy, seems to be of the genre of the passage in Hebrews: ". . . You may charge certain persons not to teach any different doctrine, nor to occupy themselves with myths and endless genealogies which promote speculations rather than the divine order" (1.3-4). The usual explanation offered for this I Timothy passage is that the myths and fables which are derogated "were no doubt purely Rabbinical"; and the second part, genealogies, which are also looked on askance, are usually explained as those "genealogies in their proper form, as found in the Book of the Pentateuch, and to which wild allegorical explanations had been assigned." * Further support for this explanation might be Titus 1.14 which alludes to "Jewish" myths, but the fact is that the context in I Timothy deals not with rabbinic matters, but with questions of the proper Christian doctrine. Thus, to offer the irrelevant explanation of rabbinic myths is a bit of special pleading and also a direct unwillingness to face up to the implications of John's failure to use such genealogies as Matthew and Luke provide. Unmistakably I Timothy's objections is to things within Christian lore, and not Jewish lore; besides, the epistle comes from well into the second century when Christianity had become diversified in doctrine and in other ways; what to some Christians was the fullest kind of piety was to others rank heresy. What to the Synoptics was an appropriate expression of piety was abhorrent to John—and to Hebrews also.

Hebrews, then, is to be viewed as a means of describing the human career of Jesus in a manner different from the Synoptics, just as John is an effort to find a manner or device different from the Synoptics. Naturally, each writing responds to multiple needs and situations, and of these our present quest is that of a relationship to Paul. That Hebrews is quite Pauline in basic matters is demonstrated by the fact that tradition incorrectly attributed it to Paul.

Hebrews sets forth that there are in Christendom leaders who are like Jesus. "Consider the outcome of their life and imitate their faith . . . Obey your leaders and submit to them . . ." Now neither Hebrews nor any other New Testament writing applies the Greek word priest to any Christian minister or functionary, yet the conformity of Hebrews to developments in early Christianity is born out in that a functioning priesthood inevitably came into being in Christendom. Just when, we do not know. Protestants regard the priesthood, which they do not accept, as a rather late

* See my "Myths, Genealogies, and Jewish Myths and the Writing of Gospels," in *HUCA,* XXVII, 201-211. I give there the source of the far-fetched explanations here cited.

development, not present in primitive Christianity, and emerging fully only after Christendom had become highly institutionalized after 360. Roman Catholics believe that the Christian priesthood can be traced to Jesus. My own feeling is that priesthood is scarcely traceable back to Jesus, but it was unquestionably present in a pre-institutionalized form in early times. Indeed, I do not believe that Hebrews was attempting to create a priesthood, but rather to justify a priesthood the beginnings of which had already emerged.

It needs to be understood that the terms that describe the various Christian ministers—elder, deacon, bishop, and priest—present the modern scholar with unclarities and confusions. It seems likely that in the widespread and scattered Church, organization varied from place to place; the title used for a certain office in one part of the Church could well have described a different office in some other part. Hebrews and the Pastoral Epistles (Titus and I and II Timothy) have it in common that they deride "elementary" doctrine, and envisage a hierarchical form of the Church in a way different from earlier writings. It is a far development from the Jewish synagogue, through Matthew's prohibition (23.8) against Christians using the title "rabbi," to a church with elders, bishops, and deacons. However unclear the origin is to us of the Church offices, this much is unmistakable, that ultimately they did develop. The Church could not have gotten along without them. The more diverse the Church was in practice and doctrine the more it needed the stabilizing influence of responsible officials.

A church with specified officials in a monarchical form is hardly consistent with Paul's views. Yet Paul gave the impetus for the emergence of just such a church which, for its protection, growth, and integration, came to need a hierarchy. The Pastoral Epistles were written in Paul's name; in the same vein, someone appended some salutations to the end of Hebrews so that it ends as if it too is by Paul—and, as we have said, tradition so ascribed it.

Indeed, the authority of Paul was paradoxically invoked in his neutralization.

We get, then, an officialdom, whether in practice or in theory, attributed to Paul. Now this attribution comes from that same period in which the tradition, though historically flimsy, ascribes hegemony to Peter.

This latter we can see as we revert to the Gospel According to John. It is a standard conclusion among scholars that the last chapter of the Gospel According to John is an addition from a later hand; within it there is clearly discernible still one more effort to rehabilitate Peter. In the Gospel proper Peter is, as elsewhere, a leading disciple of Jesus; but he is neither the opaque follower that he is depicted as being in Mark, nor is he the protagonist which Matthew would make him.

The last chapter of the Gospel seeks to set forth that the whole Gospel is the product of an eye-witness who is Jesus' "beloved disciple." The disciple is mentioned three times in the body of the Gospel (13.23-25; 19.26-27; and 20.2-9). The mentions of the beloved disciple are each in a context in which it is clear that he surpasses Peter. The first passage portrays Peter as asking this beloved disciple, who is leaning on the breast of Jesus, to ask Jesus who his betrayer is to be.

In the second mention, at the Crucifixion, the beloved disciple is present with the mother of Jesus and the two Marys; Peter is not mentioned, for previously he had opaquely offered resistance to those who wanted to arrest Jesus who deliberately was not resisting arrest; and at the "trial" he had three times denied Jesus.

In the third mention, Mary Magdalen has reported to the beloved disciple and to Peter that "They have taken the Lord out of the tomb." Peter and the disciple run, but the disciple outruns Peter and "stopping to look in, he saw the linen cloths lying there, but he did not go in. Then Simon Peter came, following him, and he went into the tomb; he saw the linen cloths lying, and the napkin, which had been on his head, not lying with the linen cloths, but rolled up in a place by itself. Then the other disciple, who reached the tomb first, also went in, and he saw and believed; for as yet they did not know the scripture, that he must rise from the dead." The plain inference here is that the disciple has already believed and that Peter has not.

Thus, for twenty chapters Peter is plainly subordinate to the unnamed "beloved disciple."

Indeed, a resurrection appearance to, and belief in Jesus by Peter is strangely the chief item of the added twenty-first chapter of John's Gospel. Before this chapter Peter had no special eminence, and he had some Mark-like deficiencies. When we remember that according to Paul it was Cephas who first saw the risen Christ, then we see that in the Gospel proper the motif of the beloved disciple overshadows and reduces the sole eminence of Peter. But the added chapter does the opposite; it reduces the role of the beloved disciple to merely that of the supposed eyewitness author, and makes the deficient Peter the chief of the disciples.

We have, then, a Gospel which subordinates Peter to an unnamed disciple, and an appendix which rehabilitates Peter and restores him to a primacy such as he receives in Matthew. Church tradition identifies this unknown disciple as John the son of Zebedee, one of the disciples of Jesus. Modern scholarship has long ago given up the identification, but it has not been able to suggest someone else instead.

In spite of our inability to identify this shadowy disciple, the respective relevancy of the Gospel and its appendix, as these relate to Peter (and thereby to Paul), is quite clear. In respect to Peter, the Gospel proper is suggesting that the authentic leadership of the Church is not that which has emerged in "Petrinism"; the appendix is a deliberate addition to refute this implication of the Gospel proper and to endeavor to restore the hegemony of Peter. With regard to Paul, the Gospel proper constitutes a relative return to Pauline doctrine which maintains that individualism and free religious inspiration are primary while discipleship is secondary. At the same time and tempering Paul, the use of the beloved disciple in the Gospel proper guarantees that its Paul-like message stems from Jesus himself and proceeds in a valid chain of authority through the beloved disciple. Again relating John to Paul, the appendix paradoxically links what amounts to Pauline doctrine to the authority of Peter.

To know the specific times and places where and when these clashing and conflicting motifs were composed can be done only with the sheerest of speculation. Tradition associates the Gospel with Ephesus, in Asia Minor. Perhaps we can infer that at Ephesus the "Petrine" leadership of the Church, probably stemming from Rome, was rejected in favor of some other leadership—though just what or whose is very much uncertain. The testimony is clear in Revelation 2.2-7 that partisan divisions, at least on doctrinal issues, if not personal ones, had produced great divisions in the Church. The Johannine Epistles seem to allude to such division, and even to have rather clear knowledge of the doctrinal issue. We read of a group which is being denounced (I John 2.19 and 22): ". . . They went out from us, but they were not of us, for if they had been of us, they would have continued with us; but they went out, that it might be plain that they all are not of us . . . Who is the liar but he who denies that Jesus is the Christ? This is the antichrist, he who denies the Father and the Son . . ." The issue at stake in this divisiveness, to state it simply, appears to have been that some denied that the heavenly Christ really came into Jesus. It seems that extreme Paulinists transformed Paul's disinterest in the details of Jesus' career into the docetic denial of the historical Jesus.

Perhaps, then, the latter history of the Church at Ephesus was of this kind, that these extreme Paulinists or quasi-Marcionites split off from the Church, and, among other things, embraced this docetism. The Gospel According to John tried to counter this docetism through the incident of doubting Thomas, whose finger needed to touch the physical Jesus before he would believe. In effect, John proper counters the docetic, extreme Paulinists by returning to Paul's original doctrine, but lumping it with a reminder, through the Thomas incident, that the heavenly Christ really entered into Jesus. Also, through the suggestion that there was in its own special tradition a "beloved disciple," the Gospel proper seems to be setting forth that it has an authoritative doctrine continuous with Jesus, and a valid denial of the claims of the dissidents. Here what amounts to Pauline doctrine is linked to a valid chain.

Thereafter, when the Gospel had begun to circulate, the "Petrine" part of the Church rendered the Gospel congenial to itself by adding the appendix to subordinate the beloved disciple to Peter.

I trust that I have clearly enough labelled the latter paragraphs as speculative. The view advanced is plausible, but admittedly it is without substantiation. It is only a belief, not a proved matter, that Paul's disinterest in the historical Jesus was altered in his extremist followers into the docetic denial of the historical Jesus. The total effect of the Gospel and its appendix and the First Epistle of John is to refute such extreme Paulinists in the name of both the beloved disciple and Peter. The advocates of the beloved disciple were, I believe, only a regional local church; the advocates of the Petrine tradition represented no less than a main segment of the Church which added the appendix in order to neutralize Paul and reinstate the hegemony of Peter whereby the officialdom as urged in Hebrews and the Pastoral Epistles could be effected.

But in this neutralization, the influence of the "Petrine" tradition is even surpassed (paradoxically) by the rise of the authority of Paul himself for denying the contentions of the schismatics and the holders of heretical views. It is precisely this purpose which is served by the pseudo-Pauline Pastoral Epistles, First and Second Timothy and Titus. In all three of these falsely titled Epistles there are warnings against those who do not submit to the proper authorities, and there are attacks on those who teach false doctrines which tend to sow strife and to pervert morals (see especially II Tim. 3.13-16 and 4.3-4; Titus 2.1 and 1.10; I Tim. 1.6; 4.1-3; 6.3-5).

Yet the crowning achievement of the Pastoral Epistles is that their major purpose too is to formulate the means for a stable and permanent organization of the Church. Both heresies and schismatics are at most subsidiary interests in these writings; good organization is the primary concern. Therefore they contain the precise instructions for the appointment of bishops and deacons and deaconesses and elders.

It is the paradox of the Pastoral Epistles that the authority of Paul is claimed for a church structure which is the exact antithesis of what Pauline freedom in its simple explanation would mean. It was natural for Paulinism to develop into the individualism, libertinism, and extremism of Marcionites, for that is innate in Paul's implication of the illumination by the Spirit. It was artificial, and in that sense unnatural, and difficult for the Church, long after Paul, to seek to curb the license and unrestricted freedom and to institute an orderly officialdom in the name of Paul.

It is, therefore, no accident that the Pastoral Epistles paradoxically bear Paul's pseudonym. It was quite deliberate, for who else in the early church could have served as well to hold in check the dissidents but the person whom the dissidents themselves accepted as the proper authority? The Pastoral Epistles by the device of claiming to be by Paul sought Paul's authority to curb those who thought they were his direct legatees. In the Pastoral Epistles we have one of the culminating steps in neutralizing Paul's doctrine. After the Pastorals were written, only one more step remained to the process. It was to include Paul's genuine Epistles in a specially arranged collection in a "New" Bible. Just as the prefacing of the Pentateuch to the prophets made their message bearable, so the Church made Paul bearable by prefacing the Gospels and Acts to Paul, and by having James and the Pastorals ensue after him. The New Testament literature as separate writings is a series of way stations towards the Church as a self-contained, permanent entity. The New Testament as a collected end is the result of the Church having become that entity. Along with the New Testament it developed a creed, an officialdom, an organization, and a liturgy.

A tentative schematization of this development is as follows. First there was Palestinian Jewish Christianity. Paul's entry into Christendom is a mark of its extension into the Judaism of the Greek dispersion. Through Paul Christendom admitted into membership Gentiles of the Greek world. Paulinism, whether through Paul himself or the influence of his letters,* provided the Hellenistic, Gentile part of the Church with a justification for both doctrines and procedures which were different from those of the Palestinian Jewish Church.

The basic elements of Pauline doctrine became progressively more and more the norm in the diaspora Church. Conflicts with Palestinian Christians, and with their emissaries and their diaspora supporters, continued for some time. Mark is a product of this period of conflict. It attempted to cut the ground from under the Palestinian Church, and to effect the more complete domination of the Church by Paulinism. Since I believe that Mark 13 reflects the destruction of the Temple at Jerusalem in 70, I would date the Gospel around 72-75.

* Of Paul's Epistles, all but Romans were written as specific answers to real situations. Romans, however, is known to have circulated in the form of the first present fourteen chapters and without carrying the mention of Rome in 1.7 and 1.15 (for the latter omissions there is manuscript evidence). Romans may well have been a kind of circular letter designed for those significant places which Paul had no hope or likelihood of visiting. This Epistle is not designed to make converts out of pagans, but to bring those already converted into the framework of the kind of Gentile churches which he had himself founded. He was ready to concede that there were other versions of the Gospel; in the heat of his anger in Galatians, he denounces those "turning to a different gospel—not that there is another gospel, but there are some who trouble you and want to pervert the gospel." In the circular form of Romans, sent to more than one church, Paul was both commending and also giving an exposition of the uniqueness of his own approach. His attention to Jews and Judaism was great, for in Paul's own day the severance between Judaism and Christianity was only in its beginning stages.

Matthew and James, I would suggest, both come from about the period 95-105. Paulinism has by now so thoroughly gained the ascendancy in the dispersion that the Church was threatened by chaos and anarchy. The two writings were efforts to effect orderliness and law in the thoroughly Gentile Church. They were produced in a period of some tension between extreme Paulinists and their Pauline opponents; these writings come from opponents of the Pauline extremists, but constitute a tempering of Pauline individualism, as well.

Colossians and Ephesians are from approximately this same period. Among other matters they carry the reassurance to Gentile Christians that their Gentile origin is no disqualification to them. They each stress exhortations to proper conduct; they each set forth encouragement, rather than legislation, towards unity and serenity in the Church (Ephesians 5.21-6.9; Colossians 3.18-4.1). These writings reflect a tension similar to that reflected in Matthew and James.

The Johannine Epistles (which do not seem to me to be all from the same hand, or from the same hand which wrote the Gospel and Revelation) come from shortly after the turn of the century, 105-115. They reflect some growing schismatic trends in the Church; they are a repudiation of extreme Paulinism but this by those who accept the basic doctrines of Paulinism.

Luke-Acts is an effort to harmonize the dissidence which has come into the Church. Up to a point it is tolerant of diversity. Luke-Acts credits the early followers of Jesus with worthy leadership, but attributes to no single one any special pre-eminence. It takes a middle position between the extreme Paulinists and their opponents, in that it dissolves the attribution of sole hegemony to Peter but at the same time provides for a succession of many authorized individuals. It enfranchises not a law as such, but accredited persons to administer whatever decisions need to be made. Its date in its present form is likely to be 105-120.

The Gospel According to John, without the last chapter, comes from a time shortly after the Johannine Epistles. It is not directly dependent on the Synoptic Gospels, but uses a selection of the same kind of material which was in oral circulation. It reflects a knowledge of Jewish Christians who have left the Church and returned to Judaism (8.31 ff.); it is confronted with the "docetic" heresy. Relatively Pauline in tone, it too needs to wage the battle against the extreme Paulinists. Its date may well be 110-125.

Hebrews is in its approach thoroughly Pauline. It is not in the form of a Gospel, but it is a Gospel in intent. It commends proper conduct and obedience to leaders (13.1-18). By conceiving of Jesus as a High Priest, it made it later possible to find New Testament support for a functioning priesthood. It is not at variance with Paul; it extends Paul's doctrine; it urges fidelity to the "proper" belief.

From the same circle, probably at Rome, which added the last chapter to the Fourth Gospel, an essay or address to new proselytes on the occasion of their baptism was provided with a superscription and an ending to become the First Epistle of Peter. Thoroughly Pauline in tone, First Peter served to fill the lack of any reliable or credible literature from that personality who had come to be regarded as the single proper vehicle of apostolic succession. Other literature, such as the Gospel According to Peter, the Apocalypse of Peter, and the Kerygma of Peter, were deemed by the developing Church unsuitable; and Eusebius in the fourth century clearly relates the second century rejection of the Gospel According to Peter as spurious. The accepted Epistle served to put into circulation a doctrinally satisfactory writing which at the same time could seem credibly to bear the name of the supposedly foremost among the apostles. It is post-Pauline; its date of composition can only be guessed at.

The Epistle of Jude is a blunt denunciation of certain "errorists" in the Church. They are denounced, not refuted, and it is therefore difficult to the point of impossibility of identifying them except by such a vague term as "gnostics." Similarly, Second Peter attacks certain holders of wrong opinions, particularly those who, after the long delay, have taken to denying the Second

Coming. Second Peter reproduces almost all of Jude. It is Second Peter 3.15-16 which mentions the difficulties raised in the Epistles of Paul, and also refers to them as being twisted by the ignorant and the unstable "as they do to other scriptures." It is not altogether certain that the author of Second Peter actually regards Paul's letters as Scripture, but it is at the minimum an associative idea. Jude is apt to have been written about 125-160, and Second Peter, 140-175. The latter composition increases from one to two the letters ascribed to Paul's rival.

To summarize, let us see how we have moved from Paul, through his neutralization, to Church institutions seeming to stem from him, and coming in his name. Paul's advocacy of individualism, "faith," and free religious expression seems to have been carried beyond his original intention by certain extreme Paulinists; these latter embraced certain docetic views which the developing Church considered heretical and partaking of anarchy. The developing Church seems to answer the extreme Paulinists by saying: "You tried to get at the heart of Pauline doctrine, but look what resulted: docetic denials of the historical Jesus, and license for division and dissension within the Church. This, obviously, will never do if we are to develop an 'effective' Church. What is needed is a check or control by means of institutionalization of some sort." This, then, gives rise to the progressive neutralization of Paul by the creation of the so-called "Petrine" tradition, by Luke-Acts' middle ground, and by exhortation and then legislation for right conduct and an officialdom in Paul's name.

We have seen, then, that Paul, or his doctrine, or his influence impinged upon virtually every book in the New Testament except Revelation.* The original questions which we asked were these: Why was so much of the New Testament by Paul, or attributed to him? Did so few of Paul's contemporaries write? Was it accident that so many letters of Paul survived?

* And in Revelation the prefatory letters have some minor veiled attacks on Paulinists, though I see no anti-Paulinism in the body of the writing.

The answer which we have given has amounted to this: Except for Revelation, every writing in the New Testament is by Paul, or attributed to Paul, or deals with issues and problems created for the Church by reason of Paul's tremendous contribution.

If we have so far suggested what his stature was, now we need to evaluate and assess the man. Or, to put it in another way, so far we have described him. Now let us turn and pass judgment on him.

VII

Paul's Stature

To orient ourselves, we need to recall that Christianity was born within Palestinian Judaism at some time early in the Christian era. If the uncertain date of the Crucifixion of Jesus was 29 or 30, and the latter books of the New Testament come from 150-175, then the New Testament literature spans a period of a century or a little more. The earliest literature, the Epistles of Paul, reflects a schism developing between Jewish Christianity and Gentile; our latest literature reflects a developed, self-sufficient Gentile church, sufficiently large and widespread to require measures to preserve some unity and to regulate its doctrine, practice, and officialdom. There was some reflection in Paul of a Judaism loyal to the Torah and observant of dietary laws, a calendar of festivals such as Tabernacles, Passover, and Pentecost, High Holidays such as the New Year and the Day of Atonement, and the Sabbath on Saturday. From here we have moved into a developed Church which has substituted Sunday (the Lord's Day) for the Sabbath, created its own justification for its Pentecost and Passover, and sloughed off the other holy days of the ordinary Jewish calendar. Moreover, it has added its own uniquely Christian ceremonies in baptism and the Eucharist. Such in brief is the distance which Christianity had traveled by the end of the second century.

Our question now is this, what was Paul's connection with this road? Conceivably all this development might have taken place even if there had never been a Paul. We need to recall that by Paul's own testimony he was not the only Christian missionary, and that others, not Paul, founded the significant churches at Rome, Alexandria and Antioch. Respecting the development by which Jewish Christianity became a religion of salvation, it would be saying too much to attribute to Paul the full measure of the transformation. Certainly minds and hearts other than Paul helped to adapt Christianity to the Greek world. Philo, shortly before Paul's time, reflects also a congruent adaptation of Judaism to the Greek world, so that we should realize that Paul's action was in the air at that time. Hellenistic Jewish Christians apart from Paul may have preceded Paul in introducing into their religion of salvation Jesus as the Christ and the Savior. That almost half of the New Testament literature is, correctly or incorrectly, attributed to Paul may induce us to put too much weight on the immediate personal achievement of Paul himself. The influence may have been only that of his letters.

It is not to be ruled out that Paul's personal influence in his own lifetime was considerably less than the influence of his Epistles after his lifetime. It is possible that his travels, compared to those of others, were relatively restricted and relatively unimportant, and that the true leverage which he exercised came from his pen and his disciples. This question cannot be answered; it needs to be left open.

The difficulty is that we know nothing of any real substance about Paul's contemporaries. To conjecture about them and their contribution is to replace with an unknown that which is known.

In the absence of other records, it is Paul who needs to be conceived of as the turning point.

On the basis of the surviving documents this much seems quite certain: Next to Jesus, Paul was the most significant person in early Christianity.

Various attempts have been made to assess the real significance of Paul. By considering the advantages and shortcomings of these view-points, we can better evaluate Paul's connection with early Church developments. In the middle of the nineteenth century the phrase was coined that "Paul substituted a religion about Jesus for the religion of Jesus." This epigram is usually attributed to the Frenchman Ernest Renan.

It is an epigram whose difficulty is its partial truth. But there are also some facets of falseness in this facile summary. First of all, we need to remember the enthusiasm which greeted statements of this kind. In the background there was an accrued anti-Paulinism which had been born in the Age of Enlightenment, at the end of the eighteenth century. It held, as intimated above, that if the theological trappings could be removed from Jesus, then there would emerge an understandable human being who could serve modern rationalistic men as an exemplar of right living and as a supreme teacher. By theological trappings, one meant Paul, for the other side of the coin of recovering the historical Jesus was to get rid of Paul. The metaphysics of Paul was too involved for modern men, his helplessness was out of keeping with the sense of assurance attained in the new rationalistic learning, and his teachings about marriage were scandalous. To say that Paul substituted a religion about Jesus for the religion of Jesus was not a sober effort to describe Paul's accomplishment, but only a subtle disparagement of him.

The relevance of my insistence that there were missionaries other than Paul can now be established. If it was true that there was substituted for the religion of Jesus a religion about him, then it was not Paul alone who made that substitution; while Cephas and Apollos may not have shared Paul's Christology, they nevertheless were teaching something distinctive about Jesus which was scarcely some usual version of Judaism. That is, they too were transmitting a message about Jesus rather than of or by Jesus. Consequently, the epigram needs this modification at the minimum, that Paul was the foremost among others who made the substitution.

But even more important, the epigram is untrue in this sense, that Jesus as Jesus meant nothing to Paul. It was God revealed in Christ Jesus who meant something to Paul. Many of the nineteenth century commentators read into Paul their own all-consuming interest in Jesus—and Paul simply had no such preoccupation. Such is Paul's message in the now oft quoted statement from II Cor. 5.16.

Not only does the epigram falsely imply that Paul was interested in the man Jesus, but it inaccurately sets Jesus and Paul into sharp contrast with each other (almost as sharp as that of hero and villain). Such a contrast implies that we have knowledge of Jesus uncolored by his biographers. So certain were the scholars in the nineteenth century that they had recovered the historical Jesus that from the time of Strauss (1835), no German professor who held a chair in New Testament could abstain from following Strauss' example and writing a "Life of Jesus." As Albert Schweitzer and C. C. McCown have shown, almost every one of these books was an effort to refute some earlier scholar's book! Indeed, as often as a scholar strongly suggested that Jesus and Paul were in no way affirmatively related to each other, there was usually a response from a conservative scholar to demonstrate that there was virtually no difference at all between the teachings of Jesus and Paul.

The contrast between Jesus and Paul is both false and impossible to construct. If nineteenth century scholarship has taught us anything, it has been that Schweitzer's conclusion is correct: The "historical" Jesus is beyond recovery. We can see him only through the eyes of the writers of the Gospels. Such a Jesus is not a historical character. He is an expression of piety and adulation.

It is impossible to compare the relatively unknown Jesus with the known Paul.

This statement may perhaps need clarification. About 1855 Bruno Bauer denied that a Jesus ever existed, and in the twentieth century Drews, Robertson, and W. B. Smith issued similar denials. Bauer deserved to be taken seriously before being dismissed, but these others can be laughed out of court. The best refutation of them was by F. C. Conybeare, a man who was both an independent scholar and also a satirist of smug traditional piety. Two different things should not be confused; to deny that Jesus existed is quite far removed from stating that Jesus was an historical person about whom little accurate information can be assembled. The former part of the sentence is untrue; the latter is true.

Therefore we cannot compare Jesus and Paul, neither with the intent to show them on the same side of the fence, nor on opposing sides.

We can compare, however, what Paul taught and what the authors of the Gospels taught. We can compare Paul and Mark, Paul and Luke, or Paul and Matthew. If, however, we get confused and fail to remember that it is one of the evangelists we are comparing with Paul, then we inadvertently find ourselves comparing Jesus and Paul. A comparison of Paul and Jesus would predispose us to exalt Jesus above Paul. But Mark is not Jesus, nor is Luke; and surely Paul's eminence is such that in these comparisons we need not begin defensively with Paul. Indeed, were I a Christian, and faced with the need to choose between Paul and one of the evangelists, I would tend on most matters to prefer Paul.

The evangelists, in any impartial consideration, faced an uphill struggle in their effort to depict the human career of Jesus. They were impelled to describe him doing things and saying things, with the tacit assumption that the things done and said were unique and without parallel in exaltation. But from the seventeenth century on, scholarship has assembled the things done and said by certain Greeks and by certain rabbis; as a result, fairminded persons must conclude that little of Jesus' teaching can be called unique. The partisan, of course, finds such uniqueness, but he finds it where it does not exist. The Golden Rule, for example, is much older than Jesus, and is, indeed, a common and widespread saying. The pithy statements attributed to Jesus are amply paralleled in the rabbinic literature, and so are a good many of the parables.

The circular argument exists in some Christian circles that the teachings of Jesus in the Gospels are superior teachings, and therefore Jesus was a superior person, and therefore his teachings were superior. It is the apperceptive background of Christians which thereby attributes to the evangelists' accounts a merit which they scarcely have. The parable of the sower in Mark (and in Matthew and Luke) is so presented in the Gospels as to have us believe that, clear as it was, the disciples did not understand it and they require explanation in private. The Gospel would have us suppose that there was more in the parable than meets the eye. Unhappily, there is not. The same is true in page after page of the Gospels.

The evangelists tell us, for example, about Jesus and his exorcism of demons; but according to rabbinic literature there were rabbis who had similar power (assuming that we believe in the existence of demons!). Apollonius of Tyanna (born about 4 B.C.) was the subject of a third century "biography," possibly also derived from Christian sources, in which wonder-working akin to that of Jesus was alleged. It is as legitimate to suggest that Apollonius was indulging in Freudian techniques as to declare, as some have in recent years, that the exorcism stories in the Gospels show us the psychiatric side of Jesus' accomplishments.

To put matters in another way, it was quite impossible for the evangelists to depict the human side of Jesus and at the same time to portray him lastingly as super-human. It has been the paradoxical fate of the Gospels in the last two centuries that these documents, written to elicit Christian faith, have managed to destroy it among countless individuals. The timeless truths in them, about the heart and the human quest, are accompanied by other matters; these latter confront an inquiring mind of our day with problems and doubts, rather than with solutions. It is not that the Gospels alone in the religious literature create such difficulties; the Old Testament does so too. But the religious pre-eminence of the Gospels in literature makes them pre-eminently difficult for the modern mind. The wish to recover the historical Jesus which dominated Protestant scholarship for about a century and a quarter is testimony to the desire among modern men to separate the human Jesus from the evangelists' blending of the human and divine aspects of Christ Jesus. The deficiency in the Gospels is not that great teachings are absent from them, but that these teachings, though they are often great, are not the greatest; they are not in themselves *greater* than other teachings. They are equalled in many literatures.

But the inherent difficulty is even deeper. If for a moment we were to assume that the Gospels present incidents, parables and teachings which are truly unique, then their pages would present us with the portrait of some supremely gifted man, but still no more than a man. The qualities might include the personal elevation and martyrdom of a Socrates, the parabolic skill of an Aesop and the humanitarianism of a Lincoln—but it would still be a man. However much the human gifts attributed to Jesus might be apotheosized, they remain only human gifts. The point is this: the Gospels seek to describe a divine being in human terms of parables and incidents. The inevitable result is that once they depict his human career, abundant glorification still cannot transcend his humanity. Now the evangelists and the Church in New Testament times were talking about a divine being, though in human terms. In telling of the human career of Jesus, the Gospels invite a serious misunderstanding, one which was in its acme in the nineteenth century. At that time, scholars, especially Unitarians, were interested in reducing the Christ Jesus into simply Jesus. But the basic New Testament contention, it seems to me, was accurately reflected by a Roman Catholic priest I once heard. This priest denied that "Christ" was a social reformer, or a teacher, or a prophet; rather, he said, Christ was God.

Thus we can see that the Gospels proceeded in a direction not only different from Paul's way, but almost in direct defiance of his own example. The shortcoming of the evangelists' approach was shown above. Paul, we know, had proceeded in a different direction. Now it seems to me that Paul's choice was a conscious one, made for basic reasons and yielding significant results. Why do I say that Paul's was a deliberate choice? That Paul quoted the words of the Lord on divorce in I Cor. 7.10 ("To the married I give charge, not I but the Lord, that the wife should not separate from her husband.") demonstrates that in Paul's ken there were available circulating oral recollections of things which Jesus had taught. Paul's determination not to speak of the human career of Jesus rests unmistakably on a choice in which the alternatives of using it or not using it lay before him. Had the details of the career of Jesus been a useful tool to Paul, or a satisfying one, he would have chosen to use them. But it is almost impossible for anyone to stress the real humanity of Jesus without overstressing it; for Paul and for his successors, it was the divinity of the Christ Jesus which was paramount. The death of *Jesus* meant nothing to Paul; the death of the *Christ Jesus* meant a cosmic incident. The Pauline way led naturally to the view of the Christ expressed in Colossians 1.15-16: "He is the image of the invisible God, the first-born of all creation, for in him all things were created, in heaven and on earth, visible and invisible . . . all things were created through him and for him."

Christ, as the creator of the world, is a conception on a level far removed from that of an exorcizer of demons, a speaker in parables, or a wonder-working healer. It is the former which Paul chose for his manner; it is the latter which he rejected and the Gospels embraced. The way of Paul presents to the fairminded student a formidable and challenging set of conceptions about a supposed divine plan in the universe; the way of the Synoptic Gospels is not as much an intellectual challenge as it is diversion, pleasant and edifying (like rabbinic moralistic tales), but scarcely profound metaphysics.

That the Church needed to neutralize Paul, and did so, must not be understood as mere caprice on its part. Beyond whatever partisan impulse may have promoted the neutralization, it was an urgent necessity. As we have seen, it is the paradox of Pauline teaching that Paul himself knew that he was on the threshold of founding something new, and his missionary activity was in that behalf, but that which is fundamental in Paul is fatal to any emerging, stable institution. A settled church needs inner regulation, procedures, some established way of doing things. While Paul spoke of the Church as the body of Christ with all its members serving each his proper function, Paul is himself the great example of the rupture of procedure, orderliness, and inner regulation.

Protestantism frequently reproaches Roman Catholicism for not taking Paul seriously. The fact is that the Catholic Church took Paul so seriously that it was under the urgent constraint of holding his doctrines in check. Had the Catholic Church not tempered its heritage of Paulinism with its Petrine tradition, there would have scarcely lasted some institution which could preserve Paul into the sixteenth century, to serve then as the exemplar par excellence of Protestants in breaking with Catholicism.

Without Paul, the Church would scarcely have swept the Hellenistic world; without neutralizing Paul, it would in all likelihood have had the same fate as the cult of Isis or of Mithraism. The latter cult, especially, was a real rival of Christianity, but it died out. So too would have been the probable fate of Christianity, had it tried to survive in some purely Pauline form.

The Church had the choice of totally repudiating Paul as it had repudiated Jewish Christianity (I refer to the Church's action in condemning the Jewish Ebionites* and their Gospel; it is almost the equivalent of Canada, South Africa and Australia excommunicating England from the British Empire). Or, it might have totally

* The Ebionites, whose Gospel we spoke of above, p. 164, were the Jewish Christians who observed the law of Moses. They are referred to in many of the Church fathers. Still in existence in 175, they were by then regarded as a heretical sect. A good summary about them is in the *Catholic Encyclopedia,* V, pp. 242-244.

accepted Paul, thereby remaining in such ferment that it would never have grown to become the official religion of the Roman Empire. Or it could accept him—with implicit reservations.

The issue, indeed, resolves itself into the question of whether any one man, however eminent, is greater than a collective church. In limiting Paulinism, the Church embraced the more practical way out of its dilemma; Protestants seem to me to be somewhat opaquely severe on the Catholic Church in not recognizing the dilemma.

Indeed, in evaluating Paul the danger exists that perspective can be totally lost. A limited perspective would conceive of Paul as a partisan party in the squabble of an evolving Church. A broader perspective, which understands Paul's background, comprehends a much more universal message in Paul's attitude. In order to obtain this wider view, we need to recall that when Paul discusses who is the person religiously on the right track, he asks, not who is the true Christian, but who is the true Jew? In his strictures against Judaism, Paul in large measure felt that he was dealing partly with an internal Jewish affair. It was Paul the Jew criticizing his inherited Judaism. He was no more fair-minded to Judaism than was Martin Luther to Catholicism, or than the American sect, The Church of Christ, is in its criticism of Protestants. The allegations which Paul makes about the Law are subjective and one-sided; thus, the picture of Judaism evolved from the New Testament is a grotesque caricature. Paul's is the characteristic criticism which emanates in an established religion from the individual who makes the claim of immediate divine revelation. An understanding, then, of the "limits" of Paul's background paradoxically yields an "unlimited" or broader view of him, for Paul's strictures, in this light, are universal in their application. What he says about the alleged deficiency of Judaism is quite as applicable to any historic communion within Christendom. Paul represents not so much a protest against Judaism (though of course he makes the protest), as a protest against all institutionalized religion. The parable of the mote and the beam (whether one reads it in the

New Testament or in the rabbis, for it is found in both) is quite applicable here. Unless Paul is regarded as saying something of continuing relevance, his strictures about Judaism in particular are of mere antiquarian interest. And if they are of abiding relevance, then their application is universal to all historic churches, Catholic and Protestant.

It is an ungrudging conclusion that Paul taught some lasting things, but he also taught some which were transient. As for the latter, his view on marriage was abandoned by the Church (all too often the modern school of psychiatrists confuse Paul's unfortunate attitude toward marriage with the total Christian attitude). His expectation of the immediate End was wrong. He carried to an extreme his sense of man's helplessness (though Augustine and Calvin went even beyond Paul). It is likely that in his mind evil was a personified force.

Yet one needs only a glimpse at the history of Europe and America since the veritable rediscovery of Paul by Martin Luther to discern the permanent and imperishable. It was out of a renewed emphasis upon Paul that there developed, albeit in secularized form, those attitudes toward the individual, toward freedom of the conscience, and toward the inviolability of the conscience which made the transition from the middle ages to modern times. There is a sense in which Galatians and Romans are the spiritual charter of modern men who believe in personal liberty and personal freedom. Now these ideals cannot be traced directly as a legacy from Paul, but those who believe in them can find in Paul eloquent affirmations of them.

Indeed, they are so characteristically Pauline, that these modern doctrines raise in the political sphere of our age exactly the same problem which existed for the early church. How can one promote the individual's freedom without having it develop into license? How can one harmonize the right of the individual with the impulses and needs of society at large?

Do we not have democracy in its highest form when we are restrained in the minimum by local and national laws? And does not democracy tend to fade as our freedoms become reduced through prohibitions and curtailments? But in the complexities of economic, social, and political problems of our times can we rely exclusively on "the spirit"? Or, on the other hand, can we assume that lawmakers can legislate our way to security and peace, without having first enlisted the hearts of men?

Perhaps the most lasting contribution in the legacy of Paul is not his doctrine, but his example. He rebelled, not for the sake of mere rebellion, but, in his own wish, to be nearer to God. The religious partisan and the theologian care whether Paul was in their judgment right or wrong. The historian does not care; he seeks to understand Paul, not to confirm or refute him. The historian sees in Paul one of history's paramount religious geniuses. A modern Jew can certainly not follow Paul. But he can try to assess him more justly than Paul assessed Judaism.

Paul cut a road from Palestinian Jewish Christianity that went almost all the way to the Dispersion Gentile church. There was little more to cut in later times. It was a narrow road that wound its way around hills and through valleys. But the path could be traveled. The later Church widened the road, paved it, repaired it, re-surfaced it, planted trees along the improvements, and extended it a little. But it was the genius of Paul which cut the road.

To the New Testament Scholar

The origin of this essay on Paul is threefold. First of all, it is derivative from my studies with Dr. Erwin R. Goodenough of Yale University. He opened up to me the vistas of Greek religion in general and of Hellenistic Judaism in particular.

Second, my Ph.D. dissertation was a study of the traditions about Abraham in the various strands of Hebrew, Aramaic and Greek literature. When years later I rewrote the dissertation, now published as a book, *Philo's Place in Judaism: A Study of Conceptions of Abraham*, Cincinnati, 1956, I was struck by the freedom with which writers and thinkers in the New Testament age wove around Abraham the conceptions and interest of their own time. It paralleled what I had been taught about the Gospels, for I had been trained to regard them as reflecting more the church which produced them than the age of Jesus. It seemed to me, as I later wrote in an article, "Myths, Genealogies, and Jewish Myths and the

Writing of Gospels," in the *Hebrew Union College Annual,* XXVII (1956), pp. 201-211, that a similar freedom and subjectivity might mark the authors of Gospels. A series of articles in *Journal of Biblical Literature* by Mary Andrews on Baur led ultimately to Baur himself, particularly to *Die christliche Gnosis,*and the conviction that I needed to re-examine the Gospels as totalities to determine for myself whether or not *Tendenz* was present, and, if so, if Baur had accurately identified the Tendenz.

Third, my cherished colleague at Vanderbilt University, Robert M. Hawkins, had presented me with his provocative volume, *The Recovery of the Historical Paul.* Scholarship had wrestled for a long time with the problems of alleged inconsistencies in Paul. Professor Hawkins turned back to a theory of interpolation to explain the inconsistencies. Such theories, one learned from Schweitzer and Moffatt, were set forth by Weisse in 1855-62 and Völter, 1882-1890; there are on record other such efforts such as supposing that there were two Pauls, one of Tarsus and one of Rome—and the like. Professor Hawkins' theory was that Paul's letters were interpolated by the Roman Catholic Church. His procedure in his effort to isolate and remove these interpolations rested primarily on a minute, ruthlessly logical analysis of the Epistles and a renewed comparison of Acts and Galatians. I worked through Dr. Hawkins' book with the double conviction that there was truly in the New Testament literature the problem of isolating the historical Paul, and that all the affection and admiration which I had, and still have, for Dr. Hawkins could not move me from the feeling that his logical analysis involved both a high measure of subjectivity and also an absence of some more or less fixed measuring rod. My essay, then, is derived in its basic quest from Dr. Hawkins; and that my proposal is far-removed from him does not wipe out that debt. His continuing devotion to what I have often heard him speak of as the quest for truth is so strong that I have no doubt that he will endorse the purpose of my effort, even if he should not agree with my conclusions. One important truth that he taught me is this: It is wrong to begin with theology and then approach the man; first isolate the man, and then you can begin to grasp his theology.

At about the same time when I was in close touch with Dr. Hawkins, two works of significance came to my attention and I studied them both very carefully. One was Hans Joachim Schoeps, *Theologie und Geschichte des Judenchristentums;* the other was W. D. Davies, *Paul and Rabbinic Judaism: Some Rabbinic Elements in Pauline Theology.* The former book seemed to me, despite its erudition, to deal in impossible combinations of materials; and the approach to the Pseudo-Clementines wrong headed. The more I puzzled over the book the more I tended in a direction the reverse of the author's, for he succeeded with me in pushing from my mind some conceptions that had been there previously about Jewish Christianity. After my study of Schoeps, I felt that I knew really nothing about Jewish Christianity—and that almost nothing was, on the basis of the records, knowable. Recourse to Hort, Sorley, and the recent monograph by Elliott-Binns has not modified this opinion. I reread Lohmeyer, *Galiläa und Jerusalem,* and Cullman, *The Early Church* and *Peter: Disciple-Apostle-Martyr,* and still feel that I know virtually nothing about Palestinian Jewish Christianity.

Davies' book is an admirable book, indeed, a great one—and one with which I disagree almost one hundred per cent. What seemed to me initially to be faulty in Davies was his procedure in setting up Montefiore, *Judaism and St. Paul,* as a straw man and attempting to demolish it, and a progression thereafter to an assumption of a similarity in Diaspora and Palestinian Judaism that my work in Philo persuaded me was wrong. On its affirmative side, Davies' case seemed to me to be this at a maximum, that affinities between Paul and the Rabbis were limited to some minor and elusive strands, and that Davies, rather than proving his case, had disproved it.

At this juncture I was awarded the President's Fellowship by Brown University and I prepared *A Jewish Understanding of the New Testament,* which was not published until 1956. From some standpoints the book amounts to an "introduction" to the New Testament. That I was writing for readers who I assumed knew nothing about the New Testament created many problems of omission and inclusion, especially the need to select for presentation a single view where often there were many available; for I wanted Jewish readers to have some rather good reflection of Protestant New Testament scholarship. The task that fell upon me quite naturally was to revert to the materials and notes which I had gone through and prepared for my qualifying examinations for the Ph.D. at Yale. Now, though, I believed that I had begun to gain some personal viewpoint and to feel the capacity, and necessity, of giving an independent judgment. The chapter in my book on Acts, which some reviewers have regarded as over-skeptical, emerged not only from my reading and study but from my notes taken in a fascinating seminar in Luke-Acts under the late Clarence Tucker Craig at Yale.

In the volume alluded to, it seemed best for me to refrain as much as possible from cluttering up the reader with too many theories, and the determination to keep these at a minimum meant to withhold some of my own also. I spent there about fifty pages on Paul; though the theory found in this essay was then in my mind, I did not include it.

I confess that in my research and re-reading for that volume I concentrated much more heavily on Paul and on the Gospels than on the other New Testament writings. For the Gospels I used the standard commentaries (*ICC,* with its conservative bent), the various volumes in the Lietzmann series, *Handbuch zum Neuen Testament;* and I read K. L. Schmidt, *Der Rahmen der Geschichte Jesu* and the materials on form criticism in Bultmann and Kundsin. I utilized the standard encyclopedia, *Hastings' Dictionary of the Bible, Encyclopaedia Biblica, Jewish Encyclopedia, Catholic Encyclopedia,* the *RGG,* and the like. I went through Loisy, Goguel, and Guignebert. I used Montefiore and Israel Abrahams and Billerbeck. Donald W. Riddle I found to be very enlightening. Easton's unjustly ignored book *The Gospel before the Gospels* was most illuminating. Perhaps I should single out Bultmann's commentary on John and Creed's on Luke for special mention and appreciation.

On Acts of the Apostles I utilized not only the standard works, including the recent one by Dibelius, but in addition I made as diligent a search as I could through the periodical literature: *Harvard Theological Review, Jewish Quarterly Review, Journal of Theological Studies, ZNW, Crozer Quarterly,* and the like. I studied the "apostolic age" in the books by McGiffert, McKinnon, Ropes, Weiszäcker, Harnack—and even Neander. Of great influence upon me was Walter Bauer, *Rechtgläubigkeit und Ketzerei im ältesten Christentum.* Though not relating directly to the subject, I received great illumination from Marcel Simon, *Verus Israel.* Barnett, *Paul Becomes a Literary Influence,* I found valuable. Goodspeed, *New Solutions of New Testament Problems* and *The Meaning of Ephesians,* stimulated me—but I cannot accept the validity of Goodspeed's major arguments and conclusions. I studied the Foakes-Jackson-Kirsopp Lake *The Beginnings of Christianity* and also, less admiringly, Burkitt's criticism and retort. As to Paul, I used, of course, Schweitzer's two books. My remarks in the essay about "Christ-mysticism" are directed at Schweitzer. My admiration for him as a man is not accompanied by an admiration of his special theories in New Testament. I found two essays by C. C. McCown—one of my favorite New Testament scholars—most beneficial as an antidote. One was his paper on "eschatology"; the other was an essay in *Munera Studiosa,* "The Sources of Paul's Mysticism." Of books on Paul or on his theology, I have used Pfleiderer, Ramsay, Weinel, Nock, Kirsopp Lake, Foakes-Jackson, Dibelius-Kummel, Carré, Prat, Klausner's incredibly bad *From Jesus to Paul* (I used it in the Hebrew); Hayes, Wilfred Knox—*St. Paul and the Church at Jerusalem* and *St. Paul and the Church of the Gentiles* are as fine as his *Acts of the Apostles* is poor; Enslin's excellent *The Ethics of Paul,* Riddle's brief but suggestive *Paul Man of Conflict,* Knox, *Some Chapters in the Life of Paul* (the first half of which I found fine, and the second half disappointing). I should mention using Lightfoot's commentaries, and also Conybeare and Howson. I must pay tribute to Machen's book, *The Origin of Paul's Religion;* I could scarcely be separated more fully in presupposition from any author than from Machen, and I read him with both continual disagreement and also continual admiration. Of special studies, I take the space to mention that I have studied Reitzenstein and Deissmann and Fascher; and that I have gone through as carefully as possible the works by Angus and Kennedy and Machiachoro—and Boendermaker's *Paulus en het Orfisme,* though Dutch is incredibly difficult for me. Christians who may not be aware of its existence can read a brilliant (though wrong!) interpretation of Paul in Graetz' *History of the Jews,* (Eng. trans. II, 219-232; Graetz' theory on p. 225 reappears in *The Journal of Jewish Studies,* III, 1952, pages 105-107, in an article by my esteemed and justly revered colleague, the late Leo Baeck, "The Faith of Paul"; the article runs from 93-110.

I cannot accept Teicher's identification of the Teacher of Righteousness and the Prophet of Untruth of the Dead Sea Scrolls with Jesus and Paul (*Journal of Jewish Studies,* II, 97-98). Dr. Teicher's proposal is made with a becoming lack of dogmatism, and he is a fine scholar. His proposal is no more extreme than are those of many others who have emerged from the Dead Sea Scrolls with shouts of Eureka. While I do not share Dr. Zeitlin's unrelenting and total skepticism about the Dead Sea Scrolls being a hoax, I have enjoyed most of the acrid style with which he has punctured the pretentiousness of his literary opponents; I have occasionally felt that his remarks would be stronger if they were gentler. My attitude towards the Scrolls can be summarized briefly. Even if all they contain is truly authentic and credible, the contents are so vastly vague that the vagueness has prompted a spate of scholarly theories which contradict each other. It is not the deficiency of the scholars, but their wish to penetrate the vagueness of the material that leads to the bewildering array of theories —of which Edmund Wilson appears to have known primarily

Dupont Sommer. Material as vague as the Dead Sea Scrolls does not lend itself to being attached to fixed points in history; the identifications have ranged from about 325 B.C. to the Karaitic period of medieval history—a span of at least 1,000 years.

In my *The First Christian Century in Judaism and Christianity: Certainties and Uncertainties,* I have tried to give a tolerably relaxed assessment of the Scrolls, now that they are no longer novelties. I gave a tabulation of the pages contained in the sectarian documents, to show that, in the matter of quantity, the Scrolls represent only a very small body of literature, compared with the abundance of pages of intertestamental, hellenistic Jewish and Rabbinic literatures. Next, as to quality, I stress the absence from the Scrolls of the precise pegs on which to hang historical events, with the consequence that historical vagueness is not very well dissolved. I alluded, moreover, to my essay, "Parallelomania" (*Journal of Biblical Literature* LXXXI, 1962, pp. 1-13) and to my discussion of what have seemed to me to be excesses in the discovery of alleged parallels, and unrealistic and untenable theories of source and derivation. The upshot is not to scorn the Scrolls as unimportant, but to contend for an only limited importance to them for New Testament studies in general, and for Paul in particular.

Acknowledgments

I am indebted to Professors Lindsay Pherigo of Scarritt College, Jim Sanders of Colgate-Rochester and T. C. Smith of Southern Baptist Seminary, who participated in seminars of mine at Hebrew Union College and helped me greatly to focus some issues more sharply than I believe I could have without them. Professor James Harrell Cobb of Yankton Seminary read the manuscript and graciously sent me extended notes on many passages; he invited my attention to a variety and abundance of places where error was patent or latent. I owe him a great debt. Rabbi Abraham Shinedling has given the manuscript the close and solicitous scrutiny for which he is justly esteemed in rabbinic circles. Miss Judy Rauh of Cincinnati, a Wellesley student, helped me greatly by reading a typescript and annotating it in such a way that I have been able with her help to handle those passages which could conceivably be unclear for the general reader. Dr. Nelson Glueck, President of the Hebrew Union College-Jewish Institute of Religion, made available to me, as he does to my colleagues, the resources of our school and its library.

My student Charles Kroloff helped me immeasurably in editing the manuscript and I am grateful to him for innumerable suggestions. Mrs. Helen Lederer has demonstrated that a fine typist can read both an illegible scrawl and a typed page replete with scratchings, arrows and annotations between lines.

To another student, Mr. Joseph Levine, I am indebted for checking the biblical citations and references, and for his welcome help on the Index.

Permission to quote from the Revised Standard Version has graciously been given by the owners of the copyright, the National Council of the Churches of Christ in the United States.

i

Index to Subjects and Names

Abraham, 26, 46, 52
Acts of the Apostles, The, 6, 128-161; resume of contents, 129ff.; and Galatians, 144ff.; scholarly judgments on, 149ff.; Paul in, 141ff.
Adoption, 92
Adoptionism, 81, 194
Agrippa, 143
Allegory, 11, 52f.
Amos, 76-78, 155
"Antinomianism," 40
Apocalyptic, 17-19, 24; *see also* Eschatology, Second Coming
Apollonius of Tyana, 214
Apollos, 6, 107, 136, 211
Apostle, 98-119, 129; meaning of the term, 98-101; Paul *The* A., 106ff.; in Luke-Acts, 189-190
Apostolic Council, 134, 143f.
Apostolic Decree, 134, 160-161
Apostolic Succession, 173, 189
Aramaic, 6, 164ff.
Aretas, 5
Ascension, The, 96f.
Atoning Death, 87-88; *see also* Transformation
Authority, 117, 160-161; sought from Jesus, 175; officialdom, 197ff.; *see also* Apostolic Succession

Baptism, 81, 85, 96, 210
Bauer, Bruno, 213
Baur, F. C., 149, 222
Beloved Disciple, 200f.

Cephas, 37ff.; 103, 120, 142, 147ff., 200ff., 211; Peter in Mark, 165ff.; in Matthew, 181ff.; in

Luke, 188ff.; in John, 199ff.; not identical with Cephas, 182-185
Christ, The, 67-75; and Holy Spirit, 80f.; as Creator, 217; *see also* Jesus, Risen Christ, Incarnation
Christianity, term unknown to Paul, 21; second beginning of, 112ff.
Christology, 74, 192-193
Church law, *see* Legalism
Circumcision of Timothy, not of Titus, 142
Colossians, The Epistle to the, 4, 68, 205
Communion with God, *see* Mystic, Paul a
Conversion, meaning of the term 63f.; Paul's, 24, 28, 61ff.
Corinthians, The Epistles to the, 6-7, 107
Covenant, Old and New, 106-107
Cults, *see* Mystery Religions

Damascus, 13, 122; Road to, 143, 156
Davies, W. D., 223
Day of Atonement, 58-59
Dead Sea Scrolls, xii, 226-227
"Death," 87ff.
Diaspora, *see* Hellenistic Judaism
Dispersion, *see* Hellenistic Judaism
Disciples, The, 169, 189-190; *see also* Apostle
Docetism, 201, 207
Divorce, 107-108, 216
Dodd, C. H., 158
"Dying" to the body, *see* "Death"

Ebionites, 164, 217
End, The, *see* Eschatology, Second Coming
Enslin, Morton S., 174
Ephesians, The Epistle to the, 4, 205
Epilepsy alleged, 34
Epistles of Paul, 4, 7, 25-26, 62
Escape, *see* Salvation
Eschatology, 93ff., 219; *see also* Second Coming
Ethics, Paul's, 116-117
"Eucharist," 85-87, 96, 108-109, 126, 210
Eusebius, 49, 164-165

Faith, 91f.
Fellowship, 83-84
Foakes-Jackson, 149
Fourth Gospel, *see* John, According to
Fruits of the spirit, 116

Galatians, The Epistle to the, 7, 26, 37ff., 149ff.; and Acts, 144ff.
Galilee, alleged birthplace, 5
Gamaliel, 13, 130, 138, 156
Genesis and Law of Nature, 50f.
Gentiles, 100, 112ff., 142; Paul destined for, 101f.; segments of the Church, 175, 181, 185; conversion of, 38ff.
God, remoteness of, 66ff.; *see also* Lord
"God-man," 66
Goodenough, Erwin R., 221
Gospels, character of, 121ff.; in Greek, not Hebrew, 164; not history, 125-128, 213ff.; a problem to modern reader, 214-215; and Paul, 107ff.
Grace, 116

Haggai, 76
Harnack, 152
Hawkins, Robert M., 222-223
Hebrews, The Epistle to the, 195ff.; not by Paul, 4, 195; a Gospel, 195ff.; Pauline basis of, 197, 206
Hegel, 146ff.
Hellenistic Judaism, 9ff.; and Law of Moses, 30ff.

Holy Spirit, 80-81, 83-84, 159-160
Human Predicament, 21ff.

Immortality, 90-91, 95
Incarnation, 68f.; The I., 68f., 81ff., 194
Inge, Dean, 159
Interpretation of Scripture, 11ff.; "prefiguration," 114; *see also* Allegory
Irenaeus, 164
Isaiah, 76-77, 155

James, 38, 103, 120, 142
James, The Epistle of, 155, 176-177, 205
Jeremiah, 76-77, 155
Jerome, 164
Jerusalem Church, 8, 44, 103, 111f., 122, 155, 163, 223; *see also* Petrine Tradition
Jesus, date of Crucifixion, 6; as the Christ, 18, 66ff., 192, 194; and "clean food," 38-39; of history, 179ff.; Paul's disinterest in, 107ff.; alleged to be merely a prophet, 104-105
Johannine Epistles, 205
John, According to, 192ff., 198ff., 205; Chapter 21 an appendix to, 199-200
Judaism, Paul's loyalty to, 62, 218; P.'s unfairness to, 29-30; *see also* Hellenistic Judaism, Rabbinic Judaism
Judaizing, 112ff.
Judas, 109, 129, 189
Jude, The Epistle of, 206-207
Justification, 91f.

Kenosis, 67ff.
Knox, John, 152ff.

Lake, Kirsopp, 149, 182
Law incarnate, 50-51
Law of Moses, 27; Paul and, 37ff.; 55ff., 106ff.; Hellenistic Jews and, 48ff.; and Law of Nature, 49ff.; and Gentile law, 49ff.; effect of P.'s abolition of, 117ff.
Law of Nature, 50-53
Legalism, 48; Christian legalism, 179ff.
License, 118, 203
Logos, 68ff.
Lord, 68; Christ as L., 68ff.; and God, 71ff.; received from the L., 85, 108-109
Lord's Supper, *see* "Eucharist"
Luke, According to, 126ff., 157, 186ff., 205
Luther, 117, 219

Marcion, 152ff., 162, 175, 201
Mark, According to, 126ff., 155; alleged Petrine writing, 165ff.; Paul's influence on, 165, 170ff.
Marriage, 94-95, 216
Matthias, 129, 189
Matthew, According to, 126ff., 177ff., 205; Peter in, 181ff.
McCown, C. C., 212
Mediator, 72-73
Messianic thought, Jewish, 17-19, 40-41
Missionary, Paul as a, 77
Moore, George Foot, 40
Moses, 36, 60; Paul contrasted with, 106; *see also* Law of Moses
Mystic, Paul a, 63, 71-72, 75-79
Mystery religions, 22f., 75

Nazarenes, 164
Neo-Orthodoxy, 34
Neutralization of Paul, 154ff., 177ff., 202ff., 217
New Testament, xii, 123ff., 155f., 165
Nomos, 46ff.
Nicodemus, 79

Palestinian Christianity, *see* Jerusalem Church
Papias, 158, 165, 178
Parousia, *see* Second Coming
Passover, 84-85
Pastoral Epistles, 4, 118, 195-197, 203-204
Paul, apocalypticism of, 17, 18, 24; a Hellenistic Jew, 8ff., 12ff.; disturbed state, 33-35; epilepsy alleged to, 34; honesty of, 25-32; hypocrisy alleged to, 26-27, 216ff.; personality of, 6-7, 25ff.; not a theologian, 64f.; legend versus history about, 4, 12-13, 141ff.; opponents of, 107-111; a tentmaker, 135; alleged martyrdom, 157; Roman citizenship of, 156; unique preachment by, 143; persecutes Church, 8, 156; a Pharisee, meaning, 13ff.; modified universalism of, 20f.; and rabbinic Judaism, 57-60; shares apostate's scorn, 29-30, 218; compared with Gospel writers, 213; P. and Jesus not comparable, 211ff.; Jewish education of, 17, 45
Pentecost, 83-84
Peter, *see* Cephas
Peter, First Epistle of, 206; Second Epistle of, 206-207
Petrine tradition, 146-147, 157ff., 163ff., 200ff.
Pfleiderer, 165, 170f.
Pharisaism and Pharisees, 13ff., 44f.
Philemon, The Epistle to, 6
Philo, 17-23, 46, 192, 210; and Paul, 32, 53-55, 68, 115
Plato, 12
Predestination, 101ff.
Priesthood, 194ff.
Phophet, Phophecy, 75-78, 118-119
Pseudo-Clementines, 147f., 185

Q, Quelle, 127

Rabbi, role of, 43-44; title forbidden Christians, 198
Rabbinic Judaism, 57ff.
Rebirth, *see* Transformation
Reconciliation, 92
Redemption, 92f.
Regeneration, *see* Transformation
Regulation, *see* Authority
Renan, Ernest, 151, 211
Repentance, 58f.
Resurrection, meaning of, 88; and immortality, 88ff.; of Jesus, 96ff.; *see also* Risen Christ
Resurrection body, 89-90
Revelation, 60; of Law of Moses, 60; of God in Christ, 74, 106
Revelation of John, The, 207-208
Riddle, Donald W., 183
Risen Christ, Vision of the, 70f., 102ff., 120; absent from Mark, 172-173
Romans, The Epistle to the, 26; a circular letter, 204
Rome, 123, 164

Sabbath, 209f.
Sadducees, 14ff.
Salvation, 24, 53-55, 87ff.
"Saul," 4, 156
Schoeps, H. J., 223
Schmiedel, 172
Schweitzer, Albert, 93, 173, 212, 225
Second Coming, 45, 88f., 93ff.
Septuagint, 10
Simon Peter, *see* Cephas
Simon Magus, 191
Sin, 58f.
Son of God, 68, 70, 72, 81f., 193f.
Spirit, meaning of the term, 78-79; *see also* Holy Spirit
Stephen, 13, 130f., 141
Stoics, 11, 73f.

Strauss, D. F., 212
Synagogue, 43-45

Table Fellowship, 38ff.
Tarsus, 5, 132, 138
Temple in Jerusalem, 42-45
Tendentiousness, 148
Tertullian, 152-153
Testament, *see* Covenant
Thomas, "Doubting," 201
Timothy, Epistles to, *see* Pastoral Epistles
Titus, The Epistle to, *see* Pastoral Epistles
Torah, 46; equated with *nomos,* 47ff.
Transformation, 56ff., 79-84, 89ff.
Travels, Paul's, xi, 5-6, 77
Troki, Isaac, 118
Tübingen School, 146ff., 191
"Twelve," The, *see* Disciples and Apostles

Universalism, 20f.

Virgin birth, 94

"We-sections," 135
Whitehead, Alfred N., 61
Wilson, Edmund, xii, 226
"Written" law, 31f., 49ff.

Zechariah, 76

Index to Scriptural Passages

The numbers under the heading Scriptural Passages refer to chapters of Scripture, and, when preceded by a decimal point, to verses within a chapter. Thus Genesis 15.6 refers to the fifteenth chapter of Genesis, sixth verse.

SCRIPTURAL PASSAGES	BOOK PAGE NUMBER
Genesis	
14	54
15.6	51, 176
18	70
20	11
22	46
Exodus	
cc. 1-11	47-48
3.4	73
Exodus	
12	47
cc. 19-24	106
22.28	139
23.17	42
24.7	106
34.23	42
Deuteronomy	
16.6	42
Isaiah	
6.1	76, 105

Jeremiah

1.4-10 76
7.21-22 78

Amos

5.21-22 78
9.1 76

Matthew

3.9 180
5.17 180
8.5-12 180
10.1-2 189
10.5 180
13.57 105
15.11 38-39
16.13-17 105
16.17 181
21.11, 46 105
22.20-33 89
23 181
23.8 198
26.26-29 86
26.45 188
26.65-66 187
27.3 187
27.3-10 129
28.19-20 180

Mark

1.1 171
1.11 171
1.16-20 166
1.30-31 166
1.35-39 166
3.11 171
3.13-19 166
3.16 166
3.35 173
4.10-13 168
4.11-12 170
5.35ff. 166
6.1-13 166
6.4 105, 173
6.30 189
6.35ff. 168
6.52 169
7.1-19 38-39
7.14-23 175
7.17-23 168
7.27-29 186
8.1-21 168
8.27-29 166
8.27-30 105
8.31-33 166
9.2-8 167
9.9-13 169
9.14-29 169
9.30-32 169
9.33-37 169
9.38-40 169
10.1-12 169
10.13-14 169
10.26 169
10.23-31 167
10.31 173
10.35-45 169
10.40 170, 173
11.20-25 167
12.18-27 89
13 204
13.3 167
14.2 172
14.22-25 86
14.26-31 167
14.27 169
14.32-42 167
14.53-54 167
14.64 187
14.66-72 167-168
15.39 171
16.7 168-169

Luke

7.16-27 105
8.3 189

Luke

9.1-2 189
9.10 189
9.18-20 105
10.1 188
10.1-16 189
10.12 188
11.39-41 38-39
13.33 105
17.5 189
20.27-38 89
22.14 189
22.14-33 86
22.31-32 168
22.45 188
24.10 189
24.12 187
.19 105
24.34 188

John

1.43 183
3.1-4 79
6.14 105
7.40-41 105
8.31ff. 206
13.23-25 199
19.26-27 199
20.2-9 199
21 201

Acts of the Apostles

1.15 189
2.1ff. 85
7.53 55
7.58 13, 142
8.1 142
8.1-3 13
8.9-24 191
8.21-23 191
9.1 13
9.1-27 147
11.30 144

Acts of the Apostles

12.25 132
15 134, 143ff.
21.20 142
21.26 134
22.3 13
23.6 143f.

Romans

1.1 100
1.3-4 82
1.7 204
1.15 204
2 21
2.4 58-59
2.14-15 56
2.17-18 47
2.21-24 30
3.24-25 92-93
5.10 92
6.1-11 96
6.3-4 84
7 27-33, 56
7.15-24 32
8.9 30
8.9 83-84
8.15-23 92
8.29-30 101
9-11 142
9.4 92
9.23 170
10.14-15 101
11.8 170
15.25 5

I Corinthians

1.1 100
1.9 83
1.12 184, 190
1.23 96
3.16 45
3.22 184
5.7 84, 172

I Corinthians

6.1-11 96
6.19 45
7.1-7 94-95
7.15-24 32
9.1 102
9.5 184
9.20-22 26-27
10.1-4 114
10.16 84
10.23 27
11.23 85, 109
12-14 118
12.1-14.40 99-100
13 30, 159
15 88ff.
15.2-5 102-103
15.5 184
15.5-7 120-121
15.8 103ff.
15.45ff. 80
15.51 90-91
16.8 85

II Corinthians

1.1 101
2.10 101
3 106ff.
3.12ff. 55
3.18 83
5.16 82, 107-108, 212
6.16 45
5.17ff. 92
10.8-13 102
10.13
11 102
11.5 104
11.14 143
11.23 104
11.32-33 5
12.1-5 100
12.2-4 102
13.14 84

Galatians

1-2 182
1.1 100, 104
1.6-11 143
1.6-5.1 37-38
1.11-12 104
1.12-15 100
1.14 45
1.15-16 101
1.15-22 13
1.15-24 142
1.18 184
1.22 13
2 144-145
2.2 144
2.3 144
2.7-9 101
2.8 184
2.8-9 182
2.11 184
2.14 184
2.20 83
3.1 96
3.6 176
3.13 92-93
3.19 55
3.19-20 72
3.27 84
4.5 92
5.12 30

Ephesians

5.26-6.9 205

Colossians

1.15-16 216
3.18-4.1 205

Philippians

2.6-11 67
3.2 30
3.4-6 13-14
3.10-12 79

I Thessalonians

4.13-17 89
4.13-18 88

II Thessalonians

2.4 44-45

Hebrews

1.1-2 105-106, 195
2.2 55
2.9 195
2.15 105
3.1 105
3.12 195
4.14 195
5.1-10 105
5.5 195
6.1 196
7.26 195
8.6 72
9.11-12 195-196
9.15 72
10.11-12 196
12.24 72
13 196, 206
13.8 196
13.20-21 196

I Timothy

1.3-4 196
1.6 203
2.5 72
4.1-3 203
6.3-5 203

II Timothy

3.13-16 203
4.3-4 203

Titus

1.10 203
1.14 197
2.1 203

James

1.1 176
2.1 176
2.14-26 176

II Peter

3.15-16 207
3.16 159

I John

2.19, 22 201

Revelation

2.2-7 201
2.14 134
2.20 134